Microsoft Security Operations Analyst Exam Ref SC-200 Certification Guide

Manage, monitor, and respond to threats using Microsoft Security Stack for securing IT systems

Trevor Stuart

Joe Anich

BIRMINGHAM—MUMBAI

Microsoft Security Operations Analyst Exam Ref SC-200 Certification Guide

Group Product Manager: Vijin Boricha

Publishing Product Manager: Mohd Riyan Khan

Senior Editor: Shazeen Iqbal

Content Development Editor: Rafiaa Khan

Technical Editor: Shruthi Shetty

Copy Editor: Safis Editing

Project Coordinator: Ajesh Devavaram

Proofreader: Safis Editing

Indexer: Subalakshmi Govindhan

Production Designer: Alishon Mendonca

Marketing Coordinator: Hemangi Lotlikar

First published: April 2022

Production reference: 1140222

Published by Packt Publishing Ltd.

Livery Place

35 Livery Street

Birmingham

B3 2PB, UK.

ISBN 978-1-80323-189-1

www.packt.com

I want to dedicate this book to the love of my life, Iveth. Thank you for always supporting me, encouraging me, and allowing me to live out my dreams. Most of all, thank you for your love!

– Trevor Stuart

I want to dedicate this book to the boys, John, Jeff, Trent, and Bgriz. John, hoping you can read by the time this comes out, it'll be so exciting!

– Joe Anich

Contributors

About the authors

Trevor Stuart has over 15 years of experience in IT. He started with SMS and Active Directory and maintained exposure in the field through various naming changes and technical additions. Trevor has a passion for IT but more so for cybersecurity. Trevor swiftly moved into cybersecurity and focused on securing privileged access, hardening operating systems, implementing tiering within AD, tying identities to modern authentication mechanisms, scaling out identities to the hybrid world, carrying out application migration in a secure manner in Azure, and leveraging built-in security controls in multiple clouds and platforms to secure workloads. Trevor is a technology enthusiast at heart and the world of cybersecurity lights the fire of passion inside of him.

Joe Anich has 13 years of experience in the IT industry ranging from endpoint management with a focus on **Microsoft Endpoint Configuration Manager** (MECM, formerly *SCCM*) and Intune to endpoint security and incident response. As Joe dug deeper into security, he realized where his passion resided, and that was in incident response working with the Microsoft **Detection and Response Team** (**DART**). Working in incident response has given Joe insight into SOC operations and how to help teams around the world improve their security posture within the Microsoft 365 security stack. Outside of IR, he is in constant pursuit of continued education, whether that be SANS courses such as the GCED or GCFA or internal threat hunting training.

About the reviewers

Nitish Anand, CISSP, is a cybersecurity analyst at Microsoft. Nitish has been actively working in the cybersecurity domain for the past 7 years, primarily in a Security Operations Center. His career in cybersecurity began at Wipro Technologies working in the financial domain as a security analyst, and then working with Value Labs LLP for one of the healthcare clients. For the last 3 years, Nitish has been working for Microsoft and has focused primarily on SIEM use case development and tuning and malware and phishing analysis. Nitish received his bachelor's degree in computer science and engineering in 2014 from Cochin University, Kochi. He holds CCNA, ITIL, CEH, and other security certifications. In his free time, he loves photography and traveling.

Rafik Gerges is a highly successful security and compliance professional, with 12 years of experience in cybersecurity and compliance. He holds an information risk management master's degree, in addition to a machine learning diploma and 30+ international certifications.

Rafik has successfully created new IPs, product enhancement, and readiness and go-to-market materials, led consulting teams, and much more.

Besides being an innovative engineer, Rafik spends his free time working out at the gym, practicing boxing, being his own mechanic, and hanging out with friends.

Chris Smith spent 8 years in the United States Marine Corps serving in all disciplines of IT, including system administration, network administration, and defensive cyber operations. Upon discharge from the Marine Corps, Chris joined Microsoft and now supports organizations through their security journey. He has since developed skillsets in Azure, Microsoft 365, security operations, and incident response. Using these skills, Chris assists organizations in the deployment and operation of tools such as Defender for Endpoint, Defender for Identity, and Defender for Cloud.

My greatest thanks to the authors of this book and the Packt team for affording me the opportunity to help develop this content.

Table of Contents

Section 2 – Implementing Microsoft 365 Defender Solutions

3

Implementing Microsoft Defender for Endpoint

4

Implementing Microsoft Defender for Identity

5

Understanding and Implementing Microsoft Defender for Cloud (Microsoft Defender for Cloud Standard Tier)

Section 3 – Familiarizing Yourself with Alerts, Incidents, Evidence, and Dashboards

6

An Overview: Microsoft Defender for Endpoint Alerts, Incidents, Evidence, and Dashboards

7

Microsoft Defender for Identity, What Happened, Alerts, and Incidents

8

Microsoft Defender for Office – Threats to Productivity

9

Microsoft Defender for Cloud Apps and Protecting Your Cloud Apps

Section 4 – Setting Up and Connecting Data Sources to Microsoft Sentinel

10

Setting Up and Configuring Microsoft Sentinel

Section 5 – Hunting Threats within Microsoft 365 Defender and Microsoft Sentinel

11
Advanced Threat Hunting, Microsoft 365 Defender Portal, and Sentinel

12
Knowledge Check

Index
Other Books You May Enjoy

Preface

This book covers in detail all the objectives of the SC-200: Microsoft Security Operations Analyst exam. It offers a blend of theory and practical examples that will help you not only pass this exam but also implement the knowledge in real-world scenarios.

Who this book is for

This SC-series prep book is meant for current or future IT professionals who seek to pass the Microsoft SC-200 exam, but most importantly want to know more about how the Microsoft SC-200 exam and the Microsoft security stack aid in the successful mitigation and threat hunting activities that are required of a security analyst every day!

What this book covers

Chapter 1, Preparing for the Microsoft Exam and SC-200 Objectives, gets you started in your preparation for the exam.

Chapter 2, The Evolution of Security and Security Operations, provides a brief history of the evolution of SOC operations.

Chapter 3, Implementing Microsoft Defender for Endpoint, covers working through **Microsoft Defender for Endpoint (MDE)** deployments.

Chapter 4, Implementing Microsoft Defender for Identity, covers working through **Microsoft Defender for Identity (MDI)** deployments.

Chapter 5, Understanding and Implementing Microsoft Defender for Cloud (Microsoft Defender for Cloud Standard Tier), covers working through the setup and configuration of Defender for Cloud deployments.

Chapter 6, An Overview: Microsoft Defender for Endpoint Alerts, Incidents, Evidence, and Dashboards, provides a walk-through of alerts in the M365D portal.

Chapter 7, Microsoft Defender for Identity: Alerts and Incidents, provides a walk-through of alerts in the M365D portal.

Chapter 8, Microsoft Defender for Office: Threats to Productivity, provides a walk-through of alerts in the M365D portal.

Chapter 9, Microsoft Defender for Cloud Apps and Protecting your Cloud Apps, provides a walk-through of alerts in the M365D portal.

Chapter 10, Setting Up and Configuring Microsoft Sentinel, provides a walk-through of alerts in the Sentinel portal.

Chapter 11, Advanced Threat Hunting, Microsoft 365 Defender Portal, and Sentinel, provides a walk-through of KQL, queries, and basic threat hunting skills.

Chapter 12, Knowledge Check, provides a knowledge check.

To get the most out of this book

To get the most of out this book, come with some prior knowledge of the following:

- MITRE ATT&CK framework
- Security monitoring
- Security engineering
- Log Analytics (Azure)
- Level 50-100 knowledge of Microsoft security technologies, including the following:

  - Microsoft Defender for Endpoint
  - Microsoft Defender for Identity
  - Microsoft Defender for Office 365
  - Microsoft Defender for Cloud Apps
  - Microsoft Defender for Cloud
  - Microsoft Sentinel

You should also currently be, or aspire to be, working in a security analyst role.

It is important to note that in November 21 some Microsoft Security Services have been renamed. These are renamed as follows:

- Microsoft Cloud App Security (MCAS) is now called Microsoft Defender for Cloud Apps

- System Center Configuration Manager (SCCM) is now called Microsoft Endpoint Configuration Manager (MECM)

- Azure Sentinel is now called Microsoft Sentinel

- Azure defender is now Microsoft Defender for Cloud

- Azure Security Center is now called Microsoft Defender for Cloud

- Playbook is now called Workflow automation

Download the color images

We also provide a PDF file that has color images of the screenshots/diagrams used in this book. You can download it here: `https://static.packt-cdn.com/downloads/9781803231891_ColorImages.pdf`.

Conventions used

There are a number of text conventions used throughout this book.

`Code in text`: Indicates code words in text, database table names, folder names, filenames, file extensions, pathnames, dummy URLs, user input, and Twitter handles. Here is an example: "To configure the host side of the network, you need the `tunctl` command from the **User Mode Linux** (**UML**) project."

A block of code is set as follows:

```
#include <stdio.h>
#include <stdlib.h>
int main (int argc, char *argv[])
{
    printf ("Hello, world!\n");
    return 0;
}
```

Any command-line input or output is written as follows:

```
$ sudo tunctl -u $(whoami) -t tap0
```

Bold: Indicates a new term, an important word, or words that you see onscreen. For example, words in menus or dialog boxes appear in the text like this. Here is an example: "Click **Flash** from Etcher to write the image."

> **Tips or Important Notes**
> Appear like this.

Get in touch

Feedback from our readers is always welcome.

General feedback: If you have questions about any aspect of this book, mention the book title in the subject of your message and email us at customercare@packtpub.com.

Errata: Although we have taken every care to ensure the accuracy of our content, mistakes do happen. If you have found a mistake in this book, we would be grateful if you would report this to us. Please visit www.packtpub.com/support/errata, selecting your book, clicking on the Errata Submission Form link, and entering the details.

Piracy: If you come across any illegal copies of our works in any form on the Internet, we would be grateful if you would provide us with the location address or website name. Please contact us at copyright@packt.com with a link to the material.

If you are interested in becoming an author: If there is a topic that you have expertise in and you are interested in either writing or contributing to a book, please visit authors.packtpub.com.

Reviews

Please leave a review. Once you have read and used this book, why not leave a review on the site that you purchased it from? Potential readers can then see and use your unbiased opinion to make purchase decisions, we at Packt can understand what you think about our products, and our authors can see your feedback on their book. Thank you!

For more information about Packt, please visit packt.com.

Share Your Thoughts

Once you've read *Microsoft Security Operations Analyst Exam Ref SC-200 Certification Guide*, we'd love to hear your thoughts! Scan the QR code below to go straight to the Amazon review page for this book and share your feedback.

https://packt.link/r/1-803-23189-0

Your review is important to us and the tech community and will help us make sure we're delivering excellent quality content.

Section 1 – Exam Overview and Evolution of Security Operations

Section 1 will give you an understanding of the exam, as well as providing evolutionary context to how security operations have changed over time.

This part of the book comprises the following chapters:

- *Chapter 1, Preparing for the Microsoft Exam and SC-200 Objectives*
- *Chapter 2, The Evolution of Security and Security Operations*

1
Preparing for Your Microsoft Exam and SC-200 Objectives

Welcome to *Microsoft SC-200 Exam Prep and Beyond* and *Chapter 1*, *Preparing for Your Microsoft Exam and SC-200 Objectives*. This chapter is dedicated to ensuring that you are ready for the **Microsoft SC-200 exam** and that you fully understand the objectives, along with how they apply in the real world. It's one thing to pass an exam but a whole other thing to apply exam topics to your day-to-day job. Let's get into it!

In both traditional and modern enterprises, the **Microsoft security operations analyst** is the key pivot point and collaborator with both individual contributors and enterprise stakeholders. This role in most organizations has one goal in mind – to protect against, secure against, detect, and respond to threats present in an enterprise as expeditiously as possible. They are responsible for reducing organizational risk by rapidly remediating active attacks in the environment, advising on improvements to threat protection practices, and referring violations of organizational policies to appropriate teams and stakeholders. Historically, this level of responsibility came with a lot of tooling, alert fatigue, manual or human interaction in investigations, and so on.

What we hope to make clear is that there has been a massive evolution of **security operations** for most enterprises. Tooling has changed, and the power of the cloud has added great value to tools that **Security Operations Team** (**SOC**) analysts are required to use day to day to successfully deliver in the Microsoft security operations analyst position for enterprises today.

This chapter will cover the following topics to get us started:

- Preparing for a Microsoft exam
- Introducing the resources available and accessing Microsoft Learn
- Creating a Microsoft demo tenant

It is important to note that in November 21 some Microsoft Security Services have been renamed. These are renamed as follows:

- **Microsoft Cloud App Security** (**MCAS**) is now called Microsoft Defender for Cloud Apps
- **System Center Configuration Manager** (**SCCM**) is now called Microsoft Endpoint Configuration Manager (MECM)
- Azure Sentinel is now called Microsoft Sentinel
- Azure defender is now Microsoft Defender for Cloud
- Azure Security Center is now called Microsoft Defender for Cloud
- Playbook is now called Workflow automation

Technical requirements

In order to proceed with this chapter, you need to have the following requirements ready:

- Full understanding of **Defender for Endpoint**, from onboarding and configuring endpoints to investigating alerts.
- Understanding of **Microsoft 365 Defender** with **identity protection, Defender for Office, Defender for Identity, Defender for Cloud Apps to DLP**, and **insider risk**.
- **Microsoft Defender for Cloud**: Be familiar with Azure services that can be protected.
- Configuring **Sentinel**, connecting logs, handling detections, investigations, and threat hunting.
- **Kusto Query Language** (**KQL**).

Preparing for a Microsoft exam

When preparing for a **Microsoft exam**, there are a few things to keep in mind. First, Microsoft always provides the *Skills measured* section on the exam page, which will list everything in play for assessment during the exam. In this *Skills measured* outline, it will also give an estimate of what percentage of the exam will be about that subject. In our experience, those are usually spot on, so it's worth noting that if you're lacking in some of the bigger sections, spend more time studying and practicing in the lab on those subjects.

Another thing worth mentioning is that a lot of the sections mentioned in this *Skills measured* outline will align with the modules for the **SC-200 learning path**, so if you incorporate that into your training, you'll find it easy to ramp up in the section of the outline you're looking for. I'll talk more about the **learning path modules** in the next section. If you're curious about learning more outside of the module links provided on the exam page, go to `https://docs.microsoft.com/en-us/learn/` and search for more topics of interest.

Generally, when I prepare for these exams, I'm looking at all resources available, whether that be the *product documentation*, *learning path modules*, or testing things out in a lab, with the lab being the most important to me, as that seems to stick out more. We'll cover setting up labs for testing in later sections.

Once you're settled on preparation for the exam, it becomes a lot clearer when considering the resources available, which we will cover in the next section. So, for now, let's focus on diving into what's laid out for us!

Introducing the resources available and accessing Microsoft Learn

When looking at training or studying resources, Microsoft does a great job of giving you structure as it pertains to the exams. The following is the list we're focusing on for resources, starting with the learning paths on the exam page:

- The learning path for the SC-200 exam: `https://aka.ms/LearnSC200`.

- Search for the *Docs* page that aligns with *Skills measured*: `Docs.microsoft.com`.

- The Microsoft Defender for Endpoint *Evaluation lab*: `https://aka.ms/MDEEvaluation`.

When looking into everything available to begin your journey toward taking the SC-200 exam, as well as learning the skills needed to be successful in your career as a SOC analyst specializing in the *M365* security stack, it's important to know that it takes time. There is a lot of content for all the features available; therefore, it's beneficial to take your time to pick it all up.

For me, I always start in the order of the bullet list provided at the start of this section, and I'll explain why. I like to go through the learning paths and listen to the content laid out for me. There are some basic knowledge checks to ensure that you're getting the information down. If there are items in the modules that I'm either stuck on or just want additional information on, I start looking for the *Docs* page that aligns. Once I've completed the learning path, I'll start setting up a lab and essentially starting in the order outlined in the exam.

In the next sections, I will summarize some of the larger portions of the learning paths, as they're critical to ensure that you learn, for both the exam and tasks that you may encounter in your career. As for the third bullet point in the list, we'll discuss that in the next topic of this chapter after learning a little more about what the learning path has to offer!

Microsoft Defender for Endpoint

We will start with **Microsoft Defender for Endpoint** (**MDE**), Microsoft's endpoint detection and response platform. Having a basic understanding of this platform will be critical for success, which includes understanding how to create the Defender for Endpoint environment, onboard endpoints to be monitored, and configuring the various settings. So, for example, you will need to be familiar with the rights needed to access the `https://securitycenter.windows.com` portal for the first time and go through the wizard that guides you through your initial configuration.

Beyond setting up the tenant, you will need to know onboarding devices in your environment quite well. You will want to understand the various operating systems in your environment to ensure they are supported, addressing any down-level devices that may no longer be supported. Make notes, as there are numerous configuration differences as you move down-level, whether that be the type of onboarding method or the state of Microsoft Defender Antivirus, especially if you are running any third-party antivirus software. We will cover that in more depth later in the book.

In *Figure 1.1*, you can see an example of the onboarding page for MDE, where you'll select the different operating systems and deployment methods. You'll notice that as you change the OS or deployment methods, you're presented with different packages or information to help with onboarding the sensor. Along with this, a command you can run in **Command Prompt** to throw a test alert is available. This is really just an easy test to see that the sensor is reporting back properly:

Figure 1.1 – Endpoint onboarding

As you onboard your devices, you will want to start defining who can access what device pages and take what actions on those devices. At this point, understanding **Role-Based Access Control (RBAC)** will be important, as that will help ensure the various roles in your SOC have the right access to perform their job. Creating your device groups will also be extremely critical to ensure that you have the proper remediation settings for your subsets of devices, as you will be applying different auto-remediation settings to different device groups.

The last topic to familiarize yourself with during that initial tenant setup and device onboarding will be configuring the **advanced features**. Here, you will switch settings on and off depending on what you want to light up in the environment. These include features such as integration with Microsoft Defender for Identity, Cloud App Security, Azure Information Protection, Secure Score, and Intune.

Being able to detect, investigate, and respond to threats in your environment will be at the forefront of your thinking.

Microsoft 365 Defender

When focusing on the other aspects of Microsoft 365 Defender, you will need to know about protections such as **Identity Protection** within Azure AD. This means understanding how to configure Azure AD Identity Protection policies such as **sign-in risk** and **user risk**, as well as investigating and remediating risks detected by the policies you have put into place.

Another aspect of the Microsoft 365 Defender umbrella is **Microsoft Defender for Office (MDO)** 365, the set of protections that help safeguard your organization against malware and viruses as they come in through email or malicious links. With MDO, you will need to understand how to configure various policies such as **Safe Links** or **Safe Attachments**, as well as policies such as anti-malware, anti-phishing, and anti-spam.

Continuing down the list of capabilities within Microsoft 365 Defender, **Microsoft Defender for Identity (MDI)** will be especially important to know; I would say more so for real-world skills, as the exam will not go very deep into it. We will cover MDI in much more depth later in the book, as we feel it is one of the, if not the, most important security tools in the suite. For the exam though, have a good understanding of configuring the sensors on your servers, reviewing alerts in the portal, and how MDI integrates into other tools such as Microsoft Defender for Cloud Apps.

Next up is **Microsoft Defender for Cloud Apps (MDCA)**, which we alluded to earlier in the chapter. With MDCA, you will want to have a good understanding of the cloud app security framework, how to explore apps that are discovered within Cloud Discovery, how to protect your data and apps with Conditional Access with App Control policies, classifying and protecting sensitive information, and detecting threats.

Lastly, we need to know about **Data Loss Prevention (DLP)** and **insider risk**. Being able to understand and describe the different data loss prevention components in Microsoft 365, such as investigating DLP alerts in the compliance center (a dedicated DLP dashboard), as well as within Microsoft Defender for Cloud Apps where you'll see file policy violation alerts if you have file policies created, will be necessary.

When it comes to insider risk, you will need to be able to understand and explain how to use *insider risk management* with the Microsoft 365 framework to prevent, detect, and contain internal risks. This will help with scenario-based questions where you need to choose solutions that meet the need. Most of these things we can do with pre-defined policy templates and insider risk policies. With those, knowing and understanding the types of actions you can take on cases within risk management cases will be good to know.

Microsoft Defender for Cloud

Microsoft Defender will be one of the lengthier sections, primarily because you need to understand a good chunk of the Azure services that can be protected. Starting with **Microsoft Defender for Cloud**, which will be the primary portal for Microsoft Defender for Cloud, you will learn to assess your environment and understand the resources you have that need protection. The integrations available make it quite easy to see the risk and take action to bring that workload into a protected state. Beyond connecting workloads, Azure assets, and non-Azure resources, you will need to understand remediating security alerts within Microsoft Defender for Cloud.

Microsoft Sentinel

Microsoft Sentinel is Microsoft's cloud-native **Security Information and Events Management (SIEM)** and **Security Orchestration, Automation, and Response (SOAR)** solution. While it is new in the SIEM space, it has quickly gained much traction within the cybersecurity space due to its scalability, cost benefits as compared to traditional on-premises SIEMS (such as **SPLUNK**), and its quick integration capabilities to existing systems.

Microsoft Sentinel topics end up being about 20% of the SC-200 exam from a content perspective, and due to that, be prepared to cover the following topics – we will dive a bit deeper than the requirements to merely pass this section of the exam so that you are prepared to immediately apply the knowledge in your enterprise today.

Topics covered in *KQL and data analysis* are as follows:

- **Begin understanding KQL statement structure**: This will be a critical item to begin to know. The main way a Microsoft security operations analyst will begin threat hunting and creating automation will be backed by KQL.

- **Begin understanding results from KQL**: This will be another high-priority item to begin to know. It is one thing for a Microsoft security operations analyst to create KQL statements, but being able to confidently understand results will make or break automation and dispositions on threats.

- **Begin to understand how to build multi-table statements using KQL**: As we move from basic queries and basic resultant sets of data, we will take it one step further and begin sharing information on how to build multi-table statements using KQL. As a Microsoft security operations analyst, you will find this extremely useful in your day-to-day threat hunting and dashboard building.

- **Begin working with data in Microsoft Sentinel using KQL**: Once we have covered the preceding topics, we will move into data manipulation and management. This will be another highly necessary skill set to possess as a Microsoft security operations analyst. We will begin extracting data from structured and unstructured string fields, integrating external data, and creating parsers with functions. Soon, you will see the true power you have at your fingertips using Microsoft Sentinel as your SIEM and SOAR solution.

Topics covered in *Setup and configuration* are as follows:

- **Create and manage Microsoft Sentinel workspaces**: One of the first things the Microsoft security operations analyst will have to decide will be the overall SIEM architecture with Microsoft Sentinel. Will you use one or many workspaces to fuel the data? How will you manage RBAC? What about your cross-workspace queries? Will logging and alerting be centralized? Decentralized? We will look in depth at the options and best practices accordingly.

- **Query logs in Microsoft Sentinel**: As a Microsoft security operations analyst, you must be able to understand how to query data, tables, and fields that are ingested into your workspace. This will be critical for not only data discovery and investigation but also knowing where data is from a table perspective, which will allow you to granularly apply RBAC as your enterprise team members need.

- **Using watchlists in Microsoft Sentinel**: Learn how to create Microsoft Sentinel watchlists that are a named list of imported data. Once created, you can easily use the named watchlist in KQL queries.

- **Utilize threat intelligence in Microsoft Sentinel**: Learn how the Microsoft Sentinel threat intelligence page enables you to manage threat indicators.

After all this, we're left with the final topic of interest, which is **KQL**. This will be a staple of the threat hunting aspect within Microsoft 365.

KQL

KQL is the read-only query language that was created to work specifically with large datasets within Azure. You will need to know KQL to be successful on the threat-hunting side of things. Whether you are in the Microsoft 365 security portal or Sentinel, KQL will be needed for hunting.

We will cover the skills needed for both the exam as well as the skills needed to start your threat-hunting journey within the context of Microsoft 365. We will be covering topics such as constructing statements, analyzing the results, as well as building custom detections.

I know that's a lot of information to take in, especially if you're new to it all, but if you stay on course, then it will all come together. Getting through these topics as you work through the learning paths, with subsequent documentation article reading, setting up, and working in a demo tenant in this next section, will help write that to memory! The nice thing about it is you can always go back to a section and walk through what's being discussed within the portal. Let's dive into getting a **demo tenant** ready!

Creating a Microsoft demo tenant

The following are two URLs that are mentioned a few times in the section. These will be handy to keep bookmarked so that you can quickly get back to them:

- Trial information for MDE: `https:/aka.ms/MDETrial`
- Evaluation lab documentation: `https://aka.ms/MDEEvaluation`

One of the absolute best things you can do to get hands-on experience is to build a lab! Many will do this first, and that's totally fine – everyone has their own style of learning. My hesitation for doing that first is that I end up bouncing around all over the place because I don't have any context for what to do or where to start. There are many shiny things to distract me.

Having gone through the learning paths, with various knowledge checks and additional documentation articles, I'm ready to tackle the real thing! I have a sense of structure, where to start, where to end, and what is in between.

To get started with setting up your lab, you'll need to satisfy one of the following licensing requirements. The reason for *E5* and *A5* is because those contain everything you'll be learning about in the learning paths in one easy package:

- **Windows 10 Enterprise E5**

- **Windows 10 Education A5**

- **Microsoft 365 E5 (M365 E5)**, which includes Windows 10 Enterprise E5

- **Microsoft 365 A5 (M365 A5)**

- **Microsoft 365 E5 Security**

- **Microsoft 365 A5 Security**

- **MDE**

With these subscriptions, you can more freely test with onboarding your own lab devices too, as well as configuring the other components of the license, such as Microsoft Endpoint Manager, formerly Intune. With that, you can learn to configure a host of security features that are otherwise already enabled in the pre-provisioned devices in the evaluation lab aspect of the license.

Some things to note about the evaluation lab aspect of the trial are as follows:

- Enough device allotment for a month of testing.

- Renewing resources allowed once a month.

- Pre-provisioned machines for testing.

- Full access to the capabilities of MDE.

- Threat simulators.

- To get a wonderful overarching picture of the lab itself and what you can get from it, please watch the video at the following link: `aka.ms/MDEEvaluation`.

The following screenshot shows what the lab section of the portal will look like before you configure it:

Figure 1.2 – The Evaluation Lab setup

Note that when you get to the *provisioning screen*, you'll select the number of devices you want as well as the duration of each. Now, remember, whatever you select, that's all you get for 30 days, so carefully plan out how you want to test these machines. If you're after more specific tests, perhaps to see how MDE handles various attacks, then the shorter durations may be better suited, but for the use case of studying for an exam, the longer-duration machines may be best.

Summary

In summary, there is a lot to know! It may seem overwhelming if you're new to the Microsoft 365 stack, but as you start learning one area, you'll see how well it translates to other areas, so I advise you to go with the flow and stick with it. As you work through understanding MDE, you'll leave with a great understanding of navigating through the security portal, making it easier to pick up knowledge in other areas.

As Microsoft builds out the `Security.Microsoft.com` portal, you'll find it easier to start digging into the other areas, such as Defender for Office and Defender for Identity.

With the knowledge you have picked up in those first few sections, moving into Sentinel will be a familiar one, as you continue to build on the nomenclature. With KQL, you'll be able to apply that in any portal where advanced hunting is available, as well as any Log Analytics workspace.

We're both excited to get started on the next chapter to continue your Microsoft 365 Defender adventure! See you in *Chapter 2, The Evolution of Security Operations*!

2
The Evolution of Security and Security Operations

In order to understand the true importance and impact of the **Microsoft Security Operations Analyst** and their role within an organization, we need to take a quick step back and understand the true evolution of both **security** and **security operations**.

In this chapter, we hope to outline some important topics to give a passionate learner the ability to understand the past a bit. You must understand this because it quickly becomes an important part of your role! The topics we will cover will include the following:

- A quick introduction to the terminology
- Understanding the traditional approach to security
- Introducing the modern approach to security
- Getting to know traditional SOC issues
- Exploring modern ways to resolve traditional SOC issues

Let's dive into each topic throughout this chapter to hopefully give you a better understanding of the *evolution of security and security operations*.

A quick introduction to the terminology

During this chapter, we will be using the terms **feeds** and **alerts** very frequently. We want to ensure that you have a full understanding of the differences and the use cases. What is a feed? What is an alert? Let's get right into this!

Feed

A feed is a constant stream of activity that has been configured for ingestion or analysis. This activity is used for statistical purposes, and sometimes this is referred to as an audit trail or log/logging:

- *Example*: A record of each time a door opens and closes. This would be an audit of how many times and each time the door was opened or shut.

Alert

An alert is a notification generated in response to an event or a sequence of events that is characteristic of suspicious behavior. The alert is intended to bring the event(s) to the attention of an operator or a **Security Operations Center** (**SOC**) analyst:

- *Example*: Whenever that same door is *slammed* opened or *slammed* shut, an alert will be generated. You will then be able to review the audit log/feed of how many times it was opened and closed before it was slammed opened or slammed shut.

Now that we have covered these topics and terminologies, let's dive into a little background on what the traditional approach to security has been, along with the downfalls that allow you to fully understand the importance of modern security operations in your enterprise today!

Understanding the traditional approach to security

Security. It has always been important to enterprises worldwide because without it, the risk factors of compromise, data exfiltration, and overall breach, which may or may not be publicly disclosed, having a massive financial and trust impact on an enterprise increases greatly. Most of us realize the shift that is occurring in the world of security. Historically, if you look back at security, it has been focused on network boundaries, getting feeds and logging from all network appliances and all devices, and very much a *four-wall* approach to any resource access – meaning, an employee must be within a known network boundary, such as a **Virtual Private Network** (**VPN**) connection, if they are not within the office, or of course, within an office subnet or known network segment. While network segmentation and security boundaries do indeed possess their importance in security, it has been an increasingly losing battle, one that comes with many gaps and downfalls. Such downfalls are as follows:

- SOC analysts are completely overwhelmed by alert influx and fatigue.
- SOC analysts are struggling to keep traditional values relevant in a modern "remote work" world.
- SOC analysts are spending too much time investigating, versus proactively protecting or allowing modern technologies to do the anomalous behavior analysis.

Traditionally, SOC analysts spend their day analyzing feed and signal data, collaborating with other teammates to make a disposition on the next steps for alerts that come into their **Security Incident and Event Management** (**SIEM**)/security tools. However, with this ever-growing threat landscape, there must be a mechanism in place that decreases the requirement for human interaction and coordination and increases the ability to have tools in an enterprise that include automatic investigation, triaging, comparison, and even remediation of active threats in an enterprise. The issue here is that traditionally, the tools and operations available did not support these new preferred requirements. These are indeed requirements in the world we live in today – there is a ridiculously small chance that keeping such processes in place will allow your enterprise to maintain a healthy and secure environment.

So, what has changed? Is it just merely tooling? Or is there more to this story? Let's dive into the next section, review the modern approach to security, and move onward to what has changed in the approach and evolution to security operations.

Introducing the modern approach to security

Many of you will have noticed some noticeably substantial changes in the approach to security. In **modern enterprises**, teams can shift their focus from the traditional approach, as discussed previously, and move toward an approach that fits the requirements and landscape of their enterprises. We have all heard of security teams ingesting and analyzing network-level logging details, keeping as much authentication, access, and authorization internal as possible and approaching service publishing with a block-first mentality.

Here is the thing: this approach simply does not fit the mold of how end users and enterprises are required to function anymore. Increasingly, there are online services, such as Office 365, Teams, or Dynamics, that enterprises use that require a shift of security mindset and operations around how enterprise end users can access such online services. Additionally, online services are not the only items that require a shift. Often, there is an increasing number of end users that are working remotely; this can be by design or by situation – either way, remote work has increased tremendously over the past few years, and security needs to provide services to remote workers in a secure manner just like they would if they were in the office.

So, how does a security team shift and meet these newer and more modern requirements? **Zero trust**! Security teams must understand zero trust. There are so many vendors out in the security world that have a zero-trust model defined for enterprises to follow. For us, however, we will be following and referring to the **Microsoft Zero Trust framework**.

In today's world, cloud application usage, such as Office 365 and other online services, mixed with the increasing amount of mobile and remote workforces, has forced the security perimeter to be redefined. End users and employees are more commonly bringing in their own devices to the office and many are even working remotely. Corporate data is being accessed from locations that are outside the standard corporate network; this same data is also being shared and collaborated on with external partners and businesses. Enterprise applications and data are moving from a traditional on-premises location to hybrid and many times cloud-only. The traditional approach of security using physical locations and network devices to define the perimeter now shifts to essentially every single access location and point where corporate data and applications/services are accessed.

Nowadays, whenever an end user or employee goes to access such resources, the traditional on-premises perimeter is bypassed, and security models that are dependent on network firewalls and VPNs are null and void. Any enterprise that relies on those traditional security models will lack the visibility, solutioning, and ability to deliver timely, end-to-end SOC coverage.

So, what is required? What must change? Enterprises need a new security model and approach that adapts to the changes and complexity of the new requirements and new business interactions. This model must embrace and understand the mobile workforce, the remote workforce, and the accessibility of cloud applications that go far beyond the traditional perimeter. This is the absolute core of zero trust.

The following diagram shows that shift, the signals, the processing, then the authorization that exists in this new model:

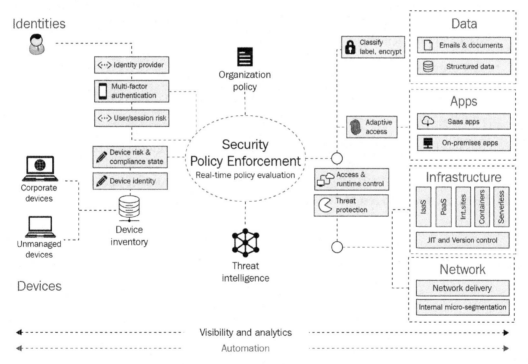

Figure 2.1 – Zero-trust model

So, what is at the core of the zero-trust model? Every single access request by any user (employee, partner, or vendor) must be authenticated, then it must be authorized by an **enterprise policy**, and then inspected for any anomalies before granting access. There are various feeds that will be a part of the inspection process that we will cover in later chapters. Again, every single access request, by any user, will be inspected no matter where that request is coming from; that's the core of zero trust.

In summary, here are the general *guiding principles* of zero trust:

- **Verify explicitly**. Always authenticate and authorize based on all available data points, including user identity, location, device health, service or workload, data classification, and anomalies. This must be done for all requests. Ensure your enterprise policies and discussions fully take this into account.

- **Use least privileged access**. Limit user access with **Just-In-Time and Just-Enough Access (JIT/JEA)**, risk-based adaptive policies, and data protection to protect both data and productivity.

- **Assume breach**. Minimize the blast radius for breaches and prevent lateral movement by segmenting access by network, user, device, and application awareness. Verify all sessions are encrypted end to end. Use analytics to get visibility, drive threat detection, and improve defenses.

With this model in place, security teams can begin supporting modern access and security needs effectively and efficiently. But with such a shift also comes a shift in how the SOC operates with this new model. Let's dive into the traditional issues prevalent within a SOC and the modern ways to resolve the issues accordingly.

Getting to know traditional SOC issues

With the **traditional approach** to security being in place for years, it should not be a surprise that with such an approach, naturally there are SOC issues. There have been numerous studies conducted by Cisco, Exabeam, ESG, and Microsoft that have deeply reviewed how SOC teams work and what the gaps are that bring about issues and security threats. Think about it, with every gap, with every moment wasted on a slow triage process, the security threat increases. We will spend a little bit of time here going over the main issues and sub-issues of traditional operations within a SOC, as follows:

- **Tooling, tooling, and tooling**: One of the first gaps that have been assessed in studies comes down to *what tools do SOC analysts have in their reach to be effective?* What we have come to find out is that there are numerous teams without a proper set of tools to secure operations effectively. There might be an enterprise with a centralized logging infrastructure; in addition to the logging infrastructure, there is a monitoring infrastructure; in addition to logging and monitoring, there is another team that manages performance; in addition to logging and monitoring and performance, there is another team that manages tooling for closing out alerts; in addition to that... *you see where this is going.* There are too many tools, doing completely different aspects of management, managed by different teams, which simply causes problems. Even writing this out was painful; imagine having to operate within it and keep it up to date. It becomes increasingly difficult to know what is important to focus on, who needs to be involved, and what tool is triggering the alert or feed.

- **Alert fatigue**: With improper tooling comes another ridiculously huge issue in traditional SOCs and that is alert fatigue. Alert fatigue can have an adverse impact on your business's cybersecurity. Usually, over 50% of alerts in any organization are false positives. Most businesses deal with this problem by having a particular threshold that reduces the alert. Nevertheless, other businesses choose to ignore specific alert categories. This desensitization due to an overabundance of alerts can weaken your security system. However, with effective cybersecurity services, you can address security alert fatigue, minimizing the chances of a successful cybercrime.

- **Slow triage time**: Often, because of improper tooling, there is a slow triage or response time. This is because there are so many tools present, none of which integrate or talk to each other even from an API perspective, and each tool requires a different team to manage it. This quickly brings up confusing and deep communication requirements that many times do not exist within enterprises. With slow triaging and response comes the increased chance that the security threat will only spread, or at worst be missed altogether.

So, how do we resolve these traditional SOC issues? Let's discuss that in the next section!

Exploring modern ways to resolve traditional SOC issues

Keeping in mind the security shift that is required to be successful in a modern world, one of the first things enterprises must do from a security perspective to resolve traditional SOC issues is to review tooling and coverage. As we covered in the previous section, tooling has such a drastic impact on the SOC.

The overarching solution to common and traditional SOC issues is to begin integrating enterprise internal security systems into automation, coordination, and other threat intelligence backends. This type of data and integration will allow enterprises to have insight into threats that far surpass what is merely in their environments. Whenever you bring in these vast external data sources (primarily through native tooling, such as your EDR or SIEM solution), security teams in enterprises gain way more context into the actual threat that exists in their enterprise and what each alert means, but most importantly, how to act on each alert.

This solution then turns traditional SOC issues into remediated key capabilities:

- **Filter out false positives**: Know which alarms can truly be ignored.
- **Speed up triage**: Prioritize investigations based on the presence in your enterprise and the severity of the impact the threat already possesses.
- **Simplify incident analysis**: Determine quickly what has already been impacted, protect other vulnerable assets, and contain the damage.

The Microsoft 365 Defender stack (Microsoft Defender for Cloud, Microsoft Defender for Endpoint, Microsoft Defender for Identity, Microsoft Defender Antivirus, Microsoft Defender for Cloud Apps, and Microsoft Sentinel) provides an all-around solution that provides proper tooling, insight, and automation to effectively manage a modern enterprise. This solution helps resolve traditional SOC issues greatly! The rest of the chapters will be dedicated to diving into each of these tools within the solution and explaining their importance in the SOC and what you need to know to deploy and manage, and then, of course, to pass the SC-200 exam!

Summary

To conclude our chapter, security and security operations have evolved vastly over the years. Change is *good*! There have been numerous traditional approaches to security, and with that comes traditional ways to manage the enterprise SOC – but with the ever-changing technical world and tools enterprises must operate in and adopt, there needs to be a *shift*; a shift from the traditional to the modern; a shift from the network to the identity; a shift from manual SOC processes with multiple tools and no integration to fewer tools, more efficiency, automation, and less alert fatigue.

We hope this chapter has laid out some additional foundations in your knowledge for your journey! Now that we have this under our belts, we can move on to our chapters on *Microsoft Security Operations Analyst* tools and deep dives. Let's go!

Section 2 – Implementing Microsoft 365 Defender Solutions

This part of the book is dedicated to assisting you in understanding the requirements for implementing and deploying Microsoft 365 Defender solutions. This includes the full stack. This will be immensely beneficial from a practical application as well as exam knowledge requirements perspective.

This part of the book comprises the following chapters:

- *Chapter 3, Implementing Microsoft Defender for Endpoint*

- *Chapter 4, Implementing Microsoft Defender for Identity*

- *Chapter 5, Understanding and Implementing Microsoft Defender for Cloud (Microsoft Defender for Cloud Standard Tier)*

3

Implementing Microsoft Defender for Endpoint

When it comes to things you can do to help protect your enterprise networks by detecting, preventing, and investigating threats on your endpoints, **Microsoft Defender for Endpoint (MDE)** is one of the best things you can implement. This is whether you're using Windows 10, where you can leverage technology built into the operating system, or down-level systems such as *Server 2016* through to *2008 R2*, where you can add in the cloud service aspect to give additional coverage and protection until you get them upgraded.

In this chapter, we're going to dive into the groundwork of getting MDE saturated in your environments. We'll cover everything, from the *prerequisites* needed to begin and deployment options with troubleshooting to verifying that it's installed properly. By the end of this chapter, you'll understand what you need to do to get started on your onboarding journey and be on your way to a better understanding of what's going on in your infrastructure. Let's go!

Before we begin, we'll break everything down into the following bullet points, which will cover the onboarding process from beginning to end.

We're going to cover the following main topics:

- Understanding the prerequisites
- Deployment options – onboarding
- Troubleshooting
- Sensor status and verification

Technical requirements

Before we get going, let's look at a list of core concepts and technologies that we'll want to have some understanding of, as it will only make you more successful:

- Running scripts
- Group Policy
- **Microsoft Endpoint Manager** (MEM, formerly *Intune*)
- **Microsoft Endpoint Configuration Manager** (MECM, formerly *SCCM*)

Understanding the prerequisites

When it comes to planning your MDE deployments, getting a grasp of the requirements needed for each operating system will only add to a successful project. One of the core differences between, let's say, Server 2019 and Server 2016 is the fact that the **Endpoint Detection and Response (EDR)** capabilities in Server 2016 are not built in like they are in Server 2019. So, we need to install the **Microsoft Monitoring Agent (MMA)** in these down-level scenarios so that we can send sensor data to the MDE backend. The same requirements and scenario apply to Windows 10, where Windows 8.1 and older are down-level.

Other prerequisites to look for on down-level operating systems are as follows:

- If you're using **Microsoft Endpoint Configuration Manager (MECM)**, you'll need to configure **System Center Endpoint Protection (SCEP)**. This also has its own patch requirements as well as configurations. That's not too important for the exam but something to know for the real world, as you're likely to see down-level. SCEP can also be deployed with **Group Policy** if that's your preferred method.

- When onboarding down-level servers, you'll need to install the MMA. That comes with a few prerequisites such as certain monthly rollup patches, .NET Framework updates, or diagnostic patches. Just make sure to check the docs when you're ready to deploy, as they may change.

The following screenshot is an example of the patch requirements Microsoft calls out to be installed before rolling out the MMA sensor:

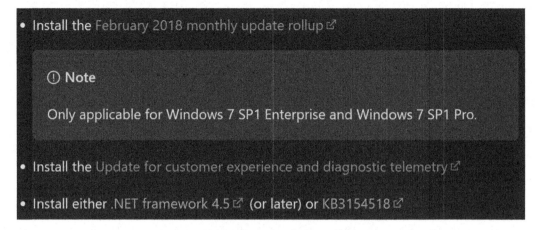

Figure 3.1 – An example of MMA requirements

Check out the following link for further information on these topics as well as to see how prerequisites change at down-level: `https://aka.ms/MDEDownLevel`

Continuing with the prerequisites, let's talk about your **Antivirus (AV)**. Depending on your role, whether that's in-house IT as an administrator or in consulting where you're helping many companies at once, you're going to come across many different AV platforms. At the end of the day, the **AV** a company uses is up to them and whatever they feel works best.

With that said, there are so many reasons to want to stick to native software, and with **Microsoft Defender Antivirus (MDAV)** being cooked into the current Windows operating system releases (that is, Windows Server 2019 and Windows 10), it has many benefits. If we talk about the AV itself for a moment and not in conjunction with **MDE**, it's a legit market contender for one of the best AVs, which most of us probably would not have said years ago.

Let's dive into that a little further before we move on to how our AV can be configured, and touch on some of the highlights (you can find a longer list of benefits to using the OS-native MDAV here: `https://docs.microsoft.com/en-us/microsoft-365/security/defender-endpoint/why-use-microsoft-defender-antivirus?view=o365-worldwide#11-reasons-to-use-microsoft-defender-antivirus-together-with-microsoft-defender-for-endpoint`):

- The native MDAV engine can collect OS data that can be used by the threat analytics portion of the security portal. This gives you the ability to assess how emerging threats can impact you and measure that with a secure score to build your security posture. With that ability, you'll get remediations to take to increase your resilience. One of my absolute favorite parts of this is the analyst reports, which we'll cover more in depth in a later chapter.

- Another point to mention is the performance; MDAV is meant to work with MDE, being the engine for the EDR side of things. Both being native to the OS, they work seamlessly together.

- When using MDAV, you get enhanced auditing information that is otherwise not available with a third-party AV, which gives you more insight on alerts generated.

- There is added protection from *ransomware* when using MDAV. When used with OneDrive for Business, MDAV can help you restore your files from a time prior to the detection of the attack. You can read more about that recovery process here: `https://support.microsoft.com/en-us/office/restore-your-onedrive-fa231298-759d-41cf-bcd0-25ac53eb8a15?ui=en-us&rs=en-us&ad=us`.

Getting back to MDAV from a prerequisite standpoint, what I wanted to discuss was the state of it when you are considering onboarding your devices to MDE. Depending on what OS version you're deploying to, MDAV will either put itself in a specific state or will need to be addressed manually, all of which we'll cover here.

To give you an idea of what we're talking about, *Figure 3.2* is a sample of the different states of MDAV when using Windows 10 with either MDAV or a third party. I highly recommend you read the following article, as it describes this at length: `https://aka.ms/MDAVCompat`:

Windows version	Antivirus/antimalware solution	Onboarded to Defender for Endpoint?	Microsoft Defender Antivirus state
Windows 10	Microsoft Defender Antivirus	Yes	Active mode
Windows 10	Microsoft Defender Antivirus	No	Active mode
Windows 10	A non-Microsoft antivirus/antimalware solution	Yes	Passive mode (automatically)
Windows 10	A non-Microsoft antivirus/antimalware solution	No	Disabled mode (automatically)

Figure 3.2 – A sample of MDAV states

The reason I think this topic is so important is due to the added benefits you get with MDE when MDAV is the *active* AV. Let's highlight a few of those here:

- **Real-time protection** and **cloud-delivered protection**. First, what they are – real-time protection is a series of configurable settings that enables extra behavioral monitoring settings that pertain to **Auto-Start Extensibility Points** (**ASEPs**). These are activities where something malicious makes unusual changes to files on the system, especially creating or modifying startup registry keys or startup locations.

  Cloud-delivered protection is referring to what we used to call **MAPS**, or **Microsoft Active Protection Service**. In fact, when you configure the policies for this or enable them through PowerShell, you'll likely still see the MAPS acronym. Cloud protection is enhancing real-time protection by giving you updates as they're available instead of the traditional approach where you update intelligence updates on an interval.

- **Threat detection and remediation**. MDAV has a list of configurable settings that tells it how to handle threats it detects. You can define when and how often it scans, how long it will keep items in quarantine, as well as the action taken per detected threat level. An example of that would be if something is detected and assigned a high threat level, you can have settings to automatically remove or quarantine the file.

Another big part of preparation is ensuring your network is ready, making sure that your endpoints can talk out over the internet to the MDE services. Now, the simple place to start is to determine which devices require a proxy to access the internet. If you have a proxy or firewall between your endpoints and the internet, refer to the following spreadsheet to identify the URLs that you'll need open:

- Spreadsheet of domain lists for MDE service locations: `https://docs.`
`microsoft.com/en-us/microsoft-365/security/defender-`
`endpoint/production-deployment?view=o365-worldwide#proxy-`
`service-urls`

For information on how to configure proxies on endpoints, see the following section in the MDE docs: `https://docs.microsoft.com/en-us/microsoft-365/`
`security/defender-endpoint/production-deployment?view=o365-`
`worldwide#network-configuration`.

To summarize what we have covered in the prerequisites, let's call out a few high-level items:

- Document the OS versions across the environment.

- Understand the onboarding requirements for each OS version.

- Understand the AV being used and the state it should be in to include features you seek to enable.

- Understand the network configuration needed for endpoints to talk to the MDE backend.

Overall, the more prep work you put in beforehand, the more success you'll have in getting your devices onboarded with minimal troubleshooting to MDE. Have fun with the prep work too; learn the ins and outs. The chances are that the more effort you put in, the more you'll likely learn about your own environment too!

Deployment options – onboarding

Now that we've put in the work going over the prerequisites to prepare the environment for success as we look to onboard our devices to MDE, we'll look at the onboarding steps in more detail. The following is a screenshot from the security portal (**Settings – Endpoints – Onboarding**), where we will select the OS we're onboarding:

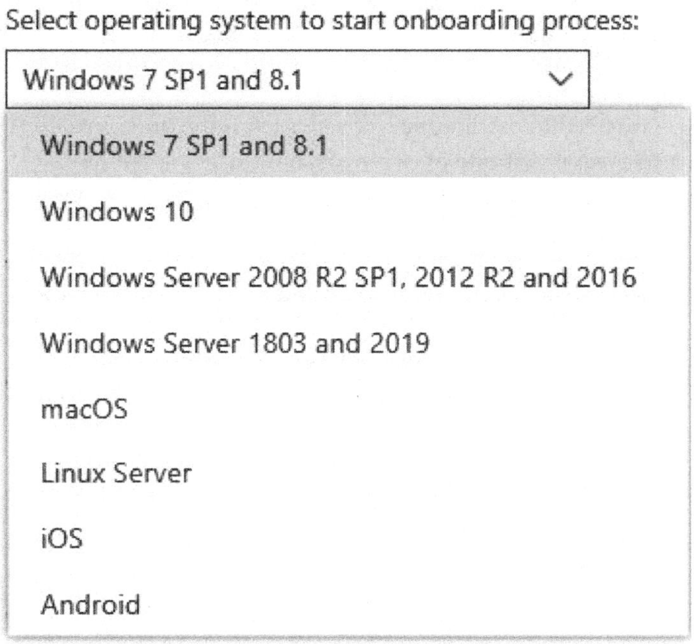

Select operating system to start onboarding process:

Windows 7 SP1 and 8.1 ⌄
Windows 7 SP1 and 8.1
Windows 10
Windows Server 2008 R2 SP1, 2012 R2 and 2016
Windows Server 1803 and 2019
macOS
Linux Server
iOS
Android

Figure 3.3 – The OS selection for onboarding

We'll start with **Windows 7 SP1 and 8.1**, as well as **Windows Server 2008 R2 SP1, 2012 R2 and 2016**, as the onboarding process is very similar. These are the down-level versions that will require the MMA that we alluded to earlier. Again, the MMA is needed, as we need a sensor to report data back to the MDE backend, and it's not built into the OS until Windows 10 or Server 1803.

Since the MMA is an executable, the preferred deployment method would be to use some sort of endpoint management software where we can deploy applications or packages.

With the focus on Microsoft technologies, we're going to use **Configuration Manager** in this example to show how simple the deployment can be. Let's go and get the MMA executable files from the following URLs. Once we have acquired them, we'll begin building a package:

- Windows 64-bit agent: https://go.microsoft.com/ fwlink/?LinkId=828603

- Windows 32-bit agent: https://go.microsoft.com/ fwlink/?LinkId=828604

First things first – we need to extract the .exe files from the downloaded MMASetup-AMD64.exe file. We can run it one of two ways, both listed as follows:

```
MMASetup-AMD64.exe /c
```

```
MMASetup-AMD64.exe /c /t:C:\Temp\MMAgent
```

These are two examples of how to extract the files, one with just the /c, which will cause a prompt (shown in *Figure 3.4*), asking where you want to extract. The second option is with the path:

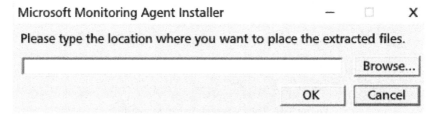

Figure 3.4 – The MMA extraction prompt

Within the extracted files, we're going to see setup.exe, which will be used for the installation. Now, if we were just going to manually install this, we could just run MMASetup-AMD64.exe, and it would bring up the wizard. The goal with the command-line installation, in conjunction with the package, is to automate the two screens we can see in *Figure 3.5* and *Figure 3.6*:

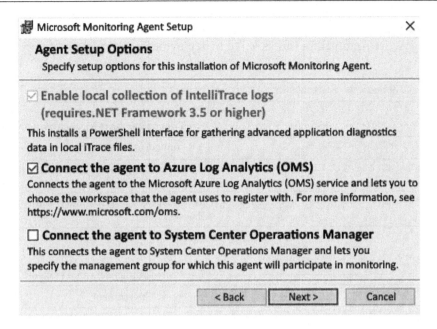

Figure 3.5 – The MMA setup wizard workspace options

This is the second screen:

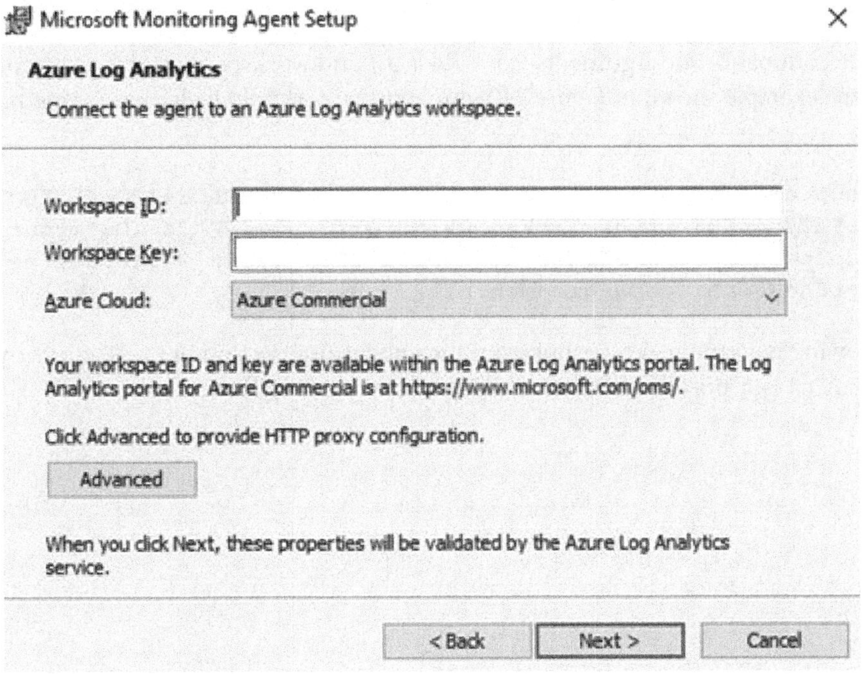

Figure 3.6 – The MMA setup wizard workspace settings

The following table shows us the parameters that are supported by setup for the MMA when using Azure Automation (not covered in deployment methods) and command-line installations:

MMA-specific options	Notes
NOAPM=1	Optional parameter. Installs the agent without .NET application performance monitoring
ADD_OPINSIGHTS_WORKSPACE	1 = configure the agent to report to a workspace
OPINSIGHTS_WORKSPACE_ID	Workspace ID (**Globally Unique Identifier** (**GUID**) for the workspace to add)
OPINSIGHTS_WORKSPACE_KEY	Workspace key used to initially authenticate with the workspace
OPINSIGHTS_WORKSPACE_AZURE_CLOUD_TYPE	Specify the cloud environment where the workspace is located 0 = Azure commercial cloud (default) 1 = Azure Government
OPINSIGHTS_PROXY_URL	URI for the proxy to use
OPINSIGHTS_PROXY_USERNAME	Username to access an authenticated proxy
OPINSIGHTS_PROXY_PASSWORD	Password to access an authenticated proxy

Table 3.1 – Supported parameters for the command line installation

Using the command-line arguments from *Table 3.1* and workspace information from the portal (the example shown in *Figure 3.7*), our command should be looking something like this:

```
setup.exe /qn NOAPM=1 ADD_OPINSIGHTS_WORKSPACE=1 OPINSIGHTS_
WORKSPACE_AZURE_CLOUD_TYPE=0 OPINSIGHTS_WORKSPACE_ID="<your
workspace ID>" OPINSIGHTS_WORKSPACE_KEY="<your workspace key>"
AcceptEndUserLicenseAgreement=1
```

The following is a sample screenshot from the onboarding section of the Security. Microsoft.com portal, where you retrieve the workspace ID and key:

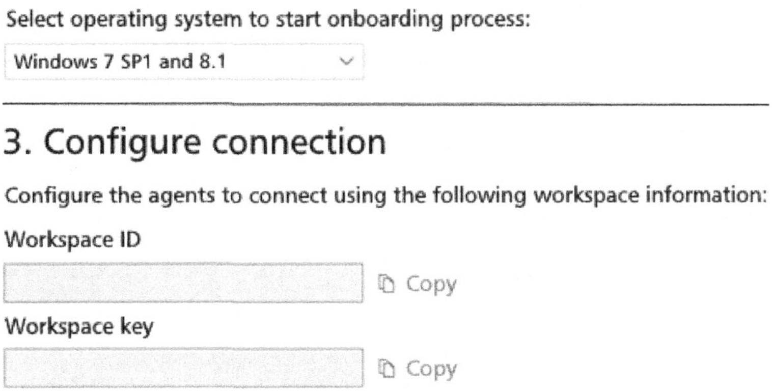

Select operating system to start onboarding process:

Windows 7 SP1 and 8.1

3. Configure connection

Configure the agents to connect using the following workspace information:

Workspace ID

🗋 Copy

Workspace key

🗋 Copy

Figure 3.7 – A workspace information example from the portal

Now, we can kick off the command line and install the MMA with the workspace settings all in place for us. See *Figure 3.8* as an example of what you'll want to see:

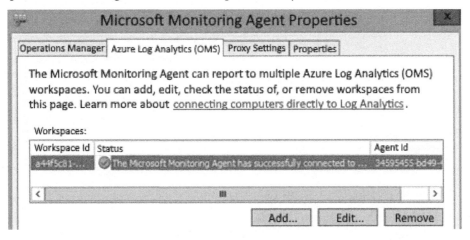

Figure 3.8 – The MMA app in the control panel

Now that we know our command line has worked and was error-free, we can continue putting this into a package for automation! Let's look at what that looks like now using Configuration Manager. There are going to be numerous ways for you to either *command-line* this, *PowerShell-script* this, or even *batch-file* this, so do what works best for you. For me, this is such a simple and perfect task for a batch file. Toss the command we built out previously into a text file and save it as <name>.cmd, as shown in *Figure 3.9*:

Figure 3.9 – A batch file containing onboarding information

Next, you're going to create a package with a standard program and select the extracted files from before as the source file. After that, you'll simply set the command line to mma. cmd (shown in *Figure 3.10*), which we created earlier:

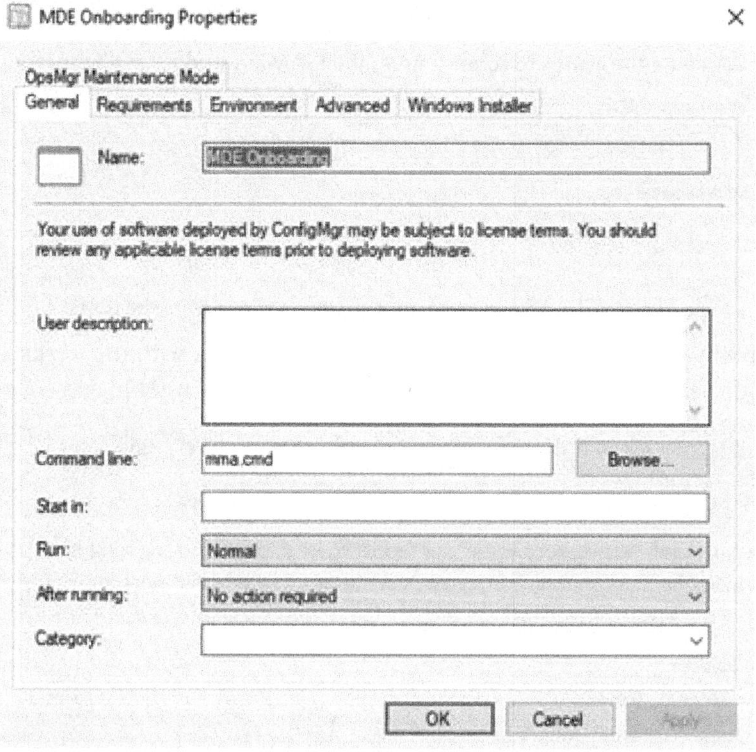

Figure 3.10 – A MECM package with a standard program

That's it! Distribute the content and deploy. I've sent mine to a 2012 R2 box in my lab; let's go and check the portal to see whether it's reporting in yet. There it is, ready to rock:

srv2012r2   ▰▰▰ No known risks ⚠ Low   Windows Server 2012 R2   Active   Onboarded

Figure 3.11 – A 2012 R2 server onboarded to MDE

At this point, the process is to rinse and repeat on all your down-level machines, which again includes Windows 7, Windows 8.1, Server 2008 R2, Server 2012 R2, and Server 2016. Of course, we want to upgrade those devices to *really* address the security aspect, but sometimes in the real world, that's easier said than done. So, the best we can do for now is protect those assets as best as we can. Don't worry – we'll cover some basic troubleshooting in a later section in this chapter, but let's get through our deployments for Server 1803 and above, as well as Windows 10 devices.

In these later versions, the EDR aspect of this is cooked into the OS, so the onboarding process is running a script to flip that light switch on. Again, there are numerous ways we can do this, as we can see in the documentation. For further instructions on all methods, refer to the following URL: `https://docs.microsoft.com/en-us/microsoft-365/security/defender-endpoint/onboarding?view=o365-worldwide#onboarding-tool-options`.

The following screenshot is a sample of the onboarding options for Windows, with the full list in the documentation article listed previously:

Endpoint	Tool options
Windows	Local script (up to 10 devices)
	Group Policy
	Microsoft Endpoint Manager/ Mobile Device Manager
	Microsoft Endpoint Configuration Manager
	VDI scripts
	Integration with Integration with Microsoft Defender for Endpoint

Figure 3.12 – A snippet of the tool options for deploying the onboarding script

For this chapter, we'll focus on the three methods you'll see most often, which would be either using Group Policy, MECM, or MEM.

The Group Policy onboarding method is simple; if you're familiar with even basic Group Policy deployments, this should be very straightforward. First, go and grab the onboarding package from the portal, selecting **Windows 10** as the OS and **Group policy** as the deployment method, and then click **Download**. This will give you a ZIP file with `WindowsDefenderATPOnboardingScript.cmd`.

You or your customer will likely have various **Organizational Units (OUs)** in **Active Directory Users and Computers** that house the endpoints. Those are the OUs where we'll be defining this new Group Policy. From the Group Policy Management Editor, navigate to the policy you're going to use or create a GPO in this domain, and link it here.

Once you have that created, right-click on the policy and choose **Edit**. Then, navigate to **Computer Configuration – Preferences – Control Panel settings**.

Now, right-click on **Scheduled tasks – New – Immediate task (At least Windows 7)**. An example of what you should be seeing is in *Figure 3.13*. Make sure to give it a name, set the account the task will run as **System**, select **Run whether user is logged on or not**, and check **Run with highest privileges**:

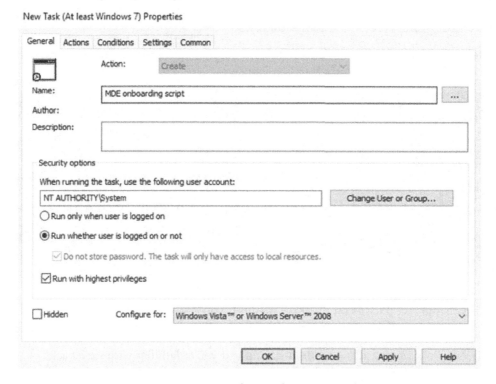

Figure 3.13 – A new task example in Group Policy

Lastly, click the **Actions** tab and click **New**, keep the default action as **Start a program**, and then browse to the location of `WindowsDefenderATPOnboardingScript.cmd`. Click **OK** and close any remaining windows. That's it!

If you would like to control any additional information, such as file sampling for analysis, you can use the additional policies that come with the package you got from the portal. Refer to the following URL for guidance: `https://docs.microsoft.com/en-us/microsoft-365/security/defender-endpoint/configure-endpoints-gp?view=o365-worldwide#additional-defender-for-endpoint-configuration-settings`.

We will be switching gears to another deployment method, **MECM**. Within MECM, navigate to **Assets and Compliance – Endpoint Protection – Microsoft Defender ATP Policies**. This deployment method will cover Windows 10 and Server 1803 and beyond:

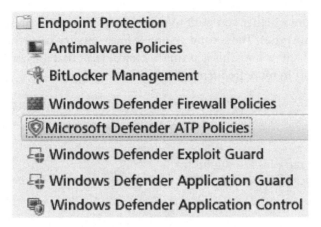

Figure 3.14 – A screenshot from MECM

Again, this should be a very straightforward process, as shown in *Figure 3.15*. Go ahead and create a new Defender policy; give it a name, choose **Onboarding**, and click **Next**:

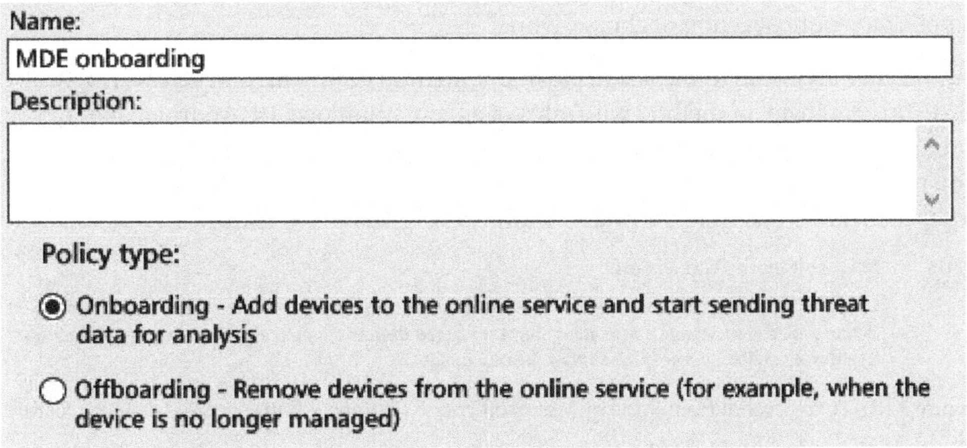

Figure 3.15 – A screenshot from MECM – Defender ATP policy

In the next screen, you're going to select the `onboarding` file that was downloaded from the portal, which will automatically put in your organization ID:

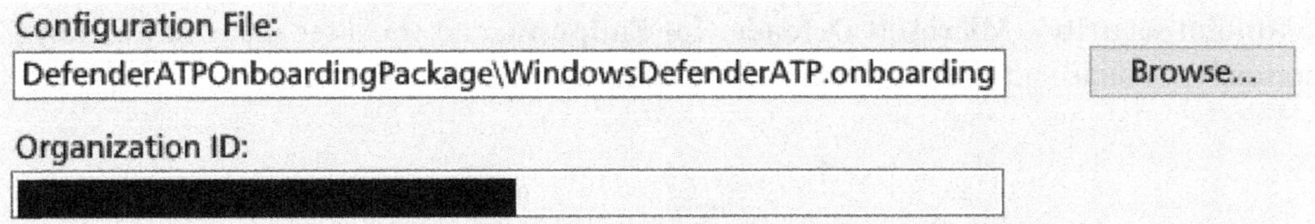

Figure 3.16 – A screenshot from MECM – Defender ATP policy

Lastly, you'll configure whether you want to share sample files for analysis, which can be set to **None** or **All file types**. The second setting is for telemetry reporting and whether you want that expedited or not. This is primarily for devices that are considered high risk; you can have it report in more frequently throughout the day:

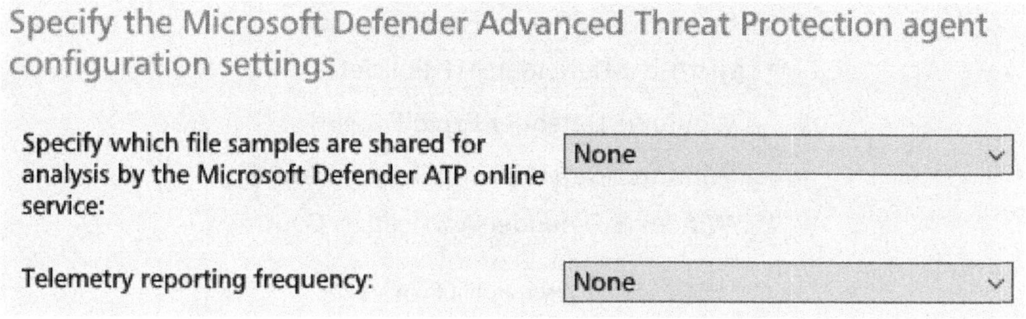

Figure 3.17 – A screenshot from MECM – Defender ATP policy

After you have completed the Defender ATP policy wizard, close the dialog and deploy the policy to your collection of choice. Done!

Now, we are moving on to the last deployment method of the three we're covering – MEM. This deployment method will only cover your Windows 10, Android, and iOS devices. We'll focus on the Windows 10 side of things, however. One thing to note is if you're going to deploy with MEM, then just connect MEM and MDE in the security portal. You can do this from **Settings – Endpoints – Advanced features**:

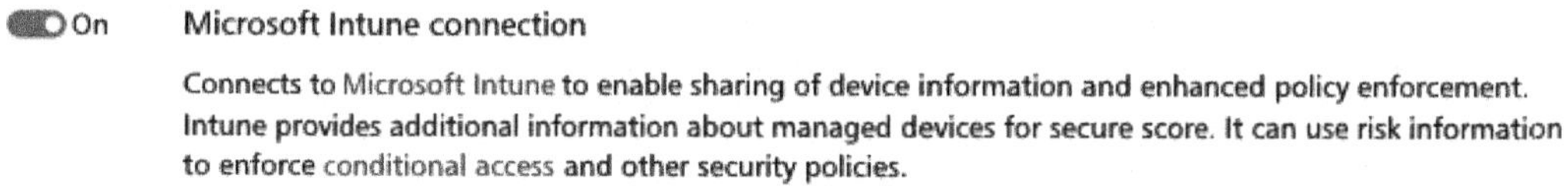

Figure 3.18 – A screenshot from Security.Microsoft.com – Settings – Endpoints – Advanced features

The reason for this is the added device details that MEM will provide to enhance your security posture by collecting data about the machine's risk. This information can then be used for compliance policies and in turn Conditional Access.

Once that is enabled, you can head back to `endpoint.microsoft.com`, then **Endpoint security – Microsoft Defender for Endpoint**, and you'll see that **Connection status** is available and shows **Enabled**. See *Figure 3.19* for an example:

🛡 **Endpoint security** | Microsoft Defender for Endpoint   ⋯

| 🔍 Search (Ctrl+/) | « | ○ Refresh 🖫 Save ✕ Discard 🗑 Delete |

Overview

ⓘ Overview

🔳 All devices

🔲 Security baselines

🛡 Security tasks

Manage

> ℹ The Microsoft Defender for Endpoint connector is active for Windows Defender for Endpoint section.

Connection status   Last synchronized

✅ Enabled   2/2/2022, 6:26:10 PM

Figure 3.19 – A screenshot from MEM – Endpoint security – Microsoft Defender for Endpoint

Once the connection is live, you can go ahead and set **MDM Compliance Policy Settings**, which lets you use threat-level compliance policies, as it can now use data from MDE:

MDM Compliance Policy Settings

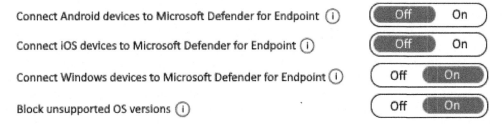

Connect Android devices to Microsoft Defender for Endpoint ⓘ   (**Off**   On)

Connect iOS devices to Microsoft Defender for Endpoint ⓘ   (**Off**   On)

Connect Windows devices to Microsoft Defender for Endpoint ⓘ   (Off   **On**)

Block unsupported OS versions ⓘ   (Off   **On**)

Figure 3.20 – A screenshot from MEM – Endpoint security > Microsoft Defender for Endpoint

---

Important Note

If you enable the connection between MDE and MEM, you will not need to use the onboarding file provided in the onboarding section of the security portal. This is because the profile has it baked in now. If you do not tie the MEM service to MDE, then the configuration profile for MDE will have an option to upload the onboarding package.

Let's move on to *onboarding devices*, now that MEM and MDE are talking to each other. The next steps are to create a device configuration profile to set up the sensor. You can do this from the MEM portal through **Endpoint security – Endpoint Detection and Response**. Since the onboarding information is already included, there are only two things to configure. That is the **Sample sharing** setting, as well as the expedited telemetry reporting, as we saw in MECM.

Now that we've covered the deployment methods and caveats for each, we're ready to move on to the troubleshooting section. We'll cover the different ways to fix endpoints that are not reporting in or reporting in with limited information.

Troubleshooting

Troubleshooting! Oddly, one of my favorite things to do. *I know, I know…*doesn't that imply that we did something wrong, or something isn't working as intended? Maybe, but we're going to dig in and learn what we missed or see what we need to adjust.

One thing I would recommend first is to read the *Troubleshoot issues during onboarding* documentation, as that provides a good basis for what could be wrong and where to start. You can find it at the following link: `https://docs.microsoft.com/en-us/microsoft-365/security/defender-endpoint/troubleshoot-onboarding?view=o365-worldwide`.

This article has a lot of good information in it to help with Windows event logs if you are having issues with the Group Policy deployment, providing a bunch of event IDs to look for and explaining what they mean, as well as a resolution to try out. The other nice chunk of information provided is a handful of *error codes* that you might see from a MEM deployment, including the possible causes and troubleshooting steps.

My personal favorite troubleshooting MDE client step is the **BetaMDEAnalyzer script**. This provides so much insight into what's going on. When the script is run, it outputs the results into a nice `.htm` file that opens automatically and tells us things, such as whether the device can talk out to the MDE backend URLs needed for service, whether the right services are running, and what state MDAV is in. Some of the connectivity tests include checks to the EDR cloud service, the EDR **Automated Investigation and Response** (**AIR**) service, sample uploads, MDAV, and certificate revocation services.

Other helpful pieces of information are things such as the *device name*, *OS*, *device ID*, and *organization ID*. All these things can be useful for troubleshooting. You can find this nifty utility directly at the following URL: `https://aka.ms/Betamdeanalyzer` (this is also listed in the previous URL).

Let's dive into this tool a little further, as it has much more to offer. First, it can be run on any MDE-supported OS, which means machines running the MMA. When the script runs, it creates a `Results` folder with the following structure and substructure (current at the time of writing this book):

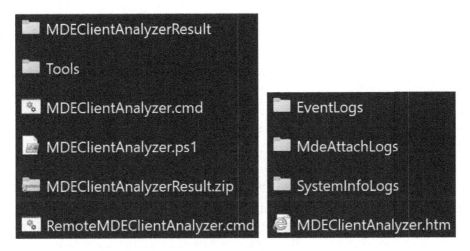

Figure 3.21 – An example of a script output folder structure

> **Important Note**
> This script is constantly updated, so get used to pulling down a new version each time to get the latest changes.

In the `MDEClientAnalyzerResult` folder shown on the left in *Figure 3.21*, you'll see the structure on the right in *Figure 3.21*. In the `SystemInfoLogs` folder, there is an `MDEClientAnalyzer` text file, which is where all the juicy details live, so let's look at that!

Right away, we have the full device information summary, which includes relevant information on the OS, the **sense version**, and the configuration, which will indicate whether it's using an MMA or not; then, depending on the OS, it will give the MDAV information and status. If it's a down-level machine, you'll see the **OMS validation details** in the next section, with the relevant checks for that client type following. Otherwise, you'll see the built-in checks for current OS versions that use the more well-known sense service.

The following is an example of the difference in results when run on a device with the built-in sensor that we enabled and the MMA – Windows 11 (that OS version was not in the detection yet at the time of writing) on the left and a down-level Server 2012 R2 on the right:

```
######################## device Info summary ##########################
Device name: <DeviceName>
Device Operating System: Windows 10 Enterprise
OS build number: Microsoft Windows NT 10.0.22000.0.100
OS Edition: Client
OS Architecture: AMD64
Device ID: <DeviceID>
Orgnization Id: <OrgID>
Sense version: 10.7910.22000.1
Sense Configuration version: 10.7910.6310690.6285570.6209732.6301756.6181664
Sense GUID is: <SenseID>
Last Sense Seen TimeStamp is: Tuesday, August 3, 2021 1:41:29 AM
Sense service Status: Running
DiagTrack (UTC) Service Status: Running
Defender AV Service Status: Running
Windows Security Center Service Status: Running
Windows Security Health Service Status: Running
Microsoft Account Sign-in Assistant Start Type: Manual
Defender AV mode: Active
Defender AV Platform Version: 4.18.2107.4-0
Defender AV Security Intelligence Version: 1.343.2145.0
Defender AV engine Version: 1.1.18400.4
Last SevilleDiagTrack LastNormalUploadTime TimeStamp: Tuesday, August 3, 2021 1:41:51 AM
Last SevilleDiagTrack LastRealTimeUploadTime TimeStamp: Tuesday, August 3, 2021 1:40:57 AM
Last SevilleDiagTrack LastInvalidHttpCode: 0
```

```
####################### device Info summary ##########################
Device name: <DeviceName>
Device Operating System: Windows Server 2012 R2 Standard
OS build number: Microsoft Windows NT 6.3.9600.0.20045
OS Edition: Server
OS Architecture: AMD64
Device ID: <DeviceID>
Orgnization Id: <OrgID>
Sense Configuration version: 10.3720.6277166
Sense GUID is: <SenseID>
Last Sense Seen TimeStamp is: Monday, August 2, 2021 1:09:07 PM
OS Environment is  supported: Microsoft Windows NT 6.3.9600.0
Command and Control channel as System Account: Passed validation
Command and Control channel as User Account: Passed validation

#################### OMS validation details ########################
OMS channel: Passed validation
Service Microsoft Monitoring Agent is Running
Health Service DLL version is: 10.20.18053.0

#################### OS validation details ##########################
The version 6.3.9600.17958 of tdh.dll is supported
The version 6.3.9600.19940 of wintrust.dll is supported
####################################################################
```

Figure 3.22 – An example of script output

Further down these files, you'll see the full extent of the information provided, which is all very helpful for troubleshooting, especially networking issues. You'll see whether the machine is failing to talk to any of the service endpoints, as well as any detected proxies in place that you can verify. See *Figure 3.23* for a sample of the connectivity tests:

```
Important notes:
1. If at least one of the connectivity options returns status (200), then Defender for Endpoint
sensor can properly communicate with the tested URL using this connectivity method.
2. For *.blob.core.*.net URLs, return status (400) is expected. However, the current connectivity
test on Azure blob URLs cannot detect SSL inspection scenarios as it is performed without
certificate pinning.
For more information on certificate pinning, please refer to: https://docs.microsoft.com/en-
us/windows/security/identity-protection/enterprise-certificate-pinning

Connectivity output, using psexec -s:
Proxy config: Method=Direct, address=
****************************************************************
****************************************************************
Testing URL : https://winatp-gw-cus.microsoft.com/commands/test
1 - Default proxy: Succeeded (200)
2 - Proxy auto discovery (WPAD): Succeeded (200)
3 - Proxy disabled: Succeeded (200)
4 - Named proxy: Doesn't exist
5 - Command line proxy: Doesn't exist
****************************************************************
****************************************************************
```

Figure 3.23 – An example of script output

With everything discussed, you should now be in good shape in order to have your troublesome devices reporting in properly. Of course, there are many more things we could go into about the rare cases of troubleshooting, but since the core priority of the book is the exam, deep troubleshooting isn't necessary. Do keep a lookout for posts by the authors on social media for deeper topics!

Moving on from troubleshooting, we're going to now cover sensor status and verification to ensure that our endpoints are in the proper state. These will be things we'll use post-troubleshooting, as well as general health checks, or even simply checks to just see what's going on.

Sensor status and verification

Now we're moving on to viewing the fruits of our labor, verifying, and working with our newly onboarded devices! Before we look at the portal, I do want to point out that the BetaMDEAnalyzer script that we ran in the preview section is also a super-great way to verify that the machine is running as expected, especially the fields listed in the following bullet points. We can see when the sensor last reported in, its status and supplementary services, as well as the AV status. If we think about it, that sums it up; we know that the machine should be in the portal and healthy because at this point, it should have passed our troubleshooting measures:

- The last time the sense service was seen was Tuesday, August 3, 2021, 1:41:29 AM.
- **Sense service status**: Running.
- **DiagTrack (UTC) service status**: Running.
- **Defender AV service status**: Running.
- **Windows Security Center service status**: Running.
- **Windows Security Health service status**: Running.
- **Microsoft Account Sign-in Assistant start type**: Manual.
- **Defender AV mode**: Active.

Okay, okay – we can view the portal now. *I'll quit rambling!* Navigating through `Security.Microsoft.com` – **Endpoints** – **Device inventory**, we should see our devices reporting in. You may see limited information on them until more telemetry comes in, but eventually, you'll start seeing all the fields fill in:

Device name	Risk level ⓘ	Exposure level ⓘ ↓	OS platform	Health state	Onboarding status	Last device update ⓘ
srv2012r2	▦▦▦ No known risks	⚠ High	Windows Server 2012 R2	Active	Onboarded	8/1/2021, 9:39 AM
desktop	▦▦▦ Medium	⚠ Medium	Windows 10	Active	Onboarded	8/3/2021, 8:42 AM
laptop	▦▦▦ No known risks	⚠ Medium	Windows 10	Active	Onboarded	8/3/2021, 9:09 PM
cm1	▦▦▦ No known risks	⚠ Medium	Windows Server 2019	Active	Onboarded	8/3/2021, 7:43 PM
dc1	▦▦▦ No known risks	⚠ Low	Windows Server 2019	Active	Onboarded	8/3/2021, 9:25 AM
lab-win11	▦▦▦ No known risks	⚠ Low	Windows 10	Active	Onboarded	8/3/2021, 7:38 PM

Figure 3.24 – An example of onboarded devices

Now, of course, the fun part of verification is to make sure it's working, like *working working*. If we go back to the onboarding portion of the security portal, we'll see a line of PowerShell that we can run to trigger an alert that looks like what we can see in *Figure 3.25*. As you can see, once run successfully, it should read **First device detection test: Completed**. That is the cue that the device is functioning as expected!

2. Run a detection test

First device detection test: Completed ✅

To verify that the device is properly onboarded and reporting to the service, run the detection script on the newly onboarded device:

    a. Open a Command Prompt window

    b. At the prompt, copy and run the command below. The Command Prompt window will close automatically.

```
powershell.exe -NoExit -ExecutionPolicy Bypass -WindowStyle Hidden $ErrorActionPreference= 'silentlycontinue';(New-Object
System.Net.WebClient).DownloadFile('http://127.0.0.1/1.exe', 'C:\\test-WDATP-test\\invoice.exe');Start-Process 'C:\\test-
WDATP-test\\invoice.exe'
```

Figure 3.25 – A detection test example

That's really it – you've verified that your devices are onboarded, communicating, and reporting as expected! The next step from here is furthering your testing, which you can do with the simulations and tutorials provided at the following link. We will cover some of these in *Chapter 6, An Overview: Microsoft Defender for Endpoint Alerts, Incidents, Evidence, and Dashboards* where we will work through alerts and incidents and the evidence coming in. See you there.

MDE simulations: `https://Security.Microsoft.com/tutorials/ simulations`

Summary

Now that we've completed our MDE onboarding, learned how to troubleshoot installations and deployments, and verified that the endpoints are reporting in, it's time to move on to the next chapter.

With the skills we've learned, we can start to focus more on the alerts coming in from these endpoints and how to deal with them, working more from a **Security Operations Center (SOC)** analyst role. Before we get totally immersed into triaging alerts though, let's get a few more tools rolled out.

In the next chapter, we'll cover *onboarding Microsoft Defender for Identity*. **Defender for Identity** is potentially my favorite tool in the M365 security stack, and I'm excited to get into it!

4
Implementing Microsoft Defender for Identity

Now that we've covered the deployment process of **Microsoft Defender for Endpoint (MDE)**, it's time to move on to **Microsoft Defender for Identity (MDI)**. This tool, in my opinion, is perhaps one of the best, if not the best, tools in the Microsoft 365 security stack. We can talk all day long about how the cloud is everything right now, but the reality is that most businesses have an on-premises presence, and that almost always means Active Directory. With Active Directory being at the core of operations as the hierarchal structure of your computer and user accounts within an environment, it's critical we keep it protected by monitoring its signals.

Firstly, its previous name is **Azure Advanced Threat Protection (AATP)**, and no – it's not the same as **Advanced Threat Analytics (ATA)**. I'll explain why. I always hear confusion about ATA, AATP, and MDI, with people asking whether MDI is an improvement over ATA or just a rebrand. First, ATA is still ATA, which is an on-premises-only product. It used a network parsing engine to digest the network traffic that it gathered. Since it was on-premises only, it was collected by either a port-mirroring method or from an ATA gateway installed on the domain controllers that sends data to the ATA center, which is where the behavioral machine learning happened to detect threats. ATA has since been deprecated, with mainstream support ending on January 12, 2021, and extended support continuing until January 2026.

Let's spend a little time talking about MDI and all the wonderful things it can do. For clarification, AATP became MDI, and that was to align with the Defender nomenclature. I generally get annoyed with rebrands, but this one made sense. MDI is a cloud-based solution that takes signals from Active Directory and analyzes them to help detect and identify threats, compromised accounts, or even insider activities. Let's look at a few things to highlight that:

- **Monitor user behavior and activities**: MDI monitors user activity and information as it traverses the network, things such as permission and group changes, and tries to create *what's normal for this user?*, and this acts as a baseline to compare future anomalies when determining malicious behavior.

- **Protect your user identities' attack surface**: With information being analyzed by MDI, it can give you insights into your posture and where improvements can be made. One such area where you can see these suggestions is the Identity Security Posture page within the Cloud App Security portal. An example of this can be seen in *Figure 4.1*.

- **Identify activities and attacks across the kill chain**: MDI will help identify attacks launched against any monitored entity such as low-privileged users, where an attacker then moves to more sensitive assets such as domain admin or sensitive data repositories. When it comes to the kill chain, we're looking at areas such as the following:

  a. **Reconnaissance**: Being able to identify rogue users or threat actors trying to acquire information by searching around for details on user accounts, group memberships, and IP addresses

  b. **Compromised credentials**: Picking up on brute-force attacks, failed authentications, or odd group membership changes.

c. **Lateral movement**: Detecting pass the ticket, pass the hash, or overpass the hash attacks so that threat actors can move laterally to gain more sensitive access

d. **Domain dominance**: Observing behaviors that highlight that a domain has been compromised; such activities include DCSync attacks, Golden Ticket usage, or remote code execution attempts.

Identity Security Posture ⓘ

Improvement action	Related entities	Security assessment report	Urgency	Resolution
Stop clear text credentials exposure	0	Entities exposing credentials in clear text	—	COMPLETED
Stop legacy protocols communication	0	Legacy protocols usage	—	COMPLETED
Stop weak cipher usage	0	Weak cipher usage	—	COMPLETED
Modify unsecure Kerberos delegations	0	Unsecure Kerberos delegation	—	COMPLETED
Disable Print spooler service on domain controllers	0	Domain controllers with Print Spooler service available	—	COMPLETED
Remove dormant entities from sensitive groups	0	Dormant entities in sensitive groups	—	COMPLETED
Install Microsoft Defender for Identity sensors on all Domain Controllers	0	Unmonitored domain controllers	—	COMPLETED
Deploy Microsoft LAPS on every windows device	1	Microsoft LAPS usage	▮▮▮ High	OPEN
Reduce lateral movement path risk to sensitive entities	0	Risky lateral movement paths	—	COMPLETED
Remove unsecure SID history attributes from entities	0	Unsecure SID history attributes	—	COMPLETED
Resolve unsecure account attributes	1	Unsecure account attributes	▮▮▮ High	OPEN

Figure 4.1 – An example of the Identity Security Posture report

To add to its capabilities, you can integrate MDI with MDE to provide another layer of detection details to give a complete picture of a potential threat.

Now that we've talked a little bit about what MDI is, let's dive into the chapter. Following a similar structure to *Chapter 3, Implementing Microsoft Defender for Endpoint*, we're going to cover the following main topics:

- Understanding the prerequisites
- Deployment options
- A troubleshooting guide
- Service status and verification

Technical requirements

Just like the last chapter, we'll talk about a few technical requirements that will make some of this easier, as well as allow you to explore further if you wish to:

- Basic executable installations

- Command Prompt

- A basic networking knowledge

- Microsoft Endpoint Configuration Manager (optional – you'll see why later)

Understanding the prerequisites

While the prerequisites for MDI are a lot less complex than MDE, there are still some newer concepts that can be tricky for some, but don't worry – we'll cover most of them. However, before we get into that, I wanted to go over the architecture of the MDI sensor and service so that you can conceptually understand the data flow.

Next, in *Figure 4.2*, we have a nice diagram that's provided to us by Microsoft, which can be found on the MDI architecture docs page (`https://docs.microsoft.com/en-us/defender-for-identity/architecture`). It shows how sensors installed on the domain controllers or **Active Directory Federation Services** (**AD FS**) servers send the captured data, which has been nicely parsed, to the MDI backend. From there, the activities and alerts are presented in the **Microsoft Defender for Cloud Apps** (**MDCA**) portal. Alerts pertaining to MDI are now also in the `security.microsoft.com` portal. Time will tell whether the sole resting place for alerts will be there; it certainly seems like a single pane of glass is the goal.

Microsoft Defender for Identity Architecture

Activities
Alerts
Identity metadata

Microsoft
365
Defender

Microsoft
Defender for Identity

Microsoft
Cloud App
Security

Integration points (configuration required)
- SIEM integration
- Mail notification
- Azure Sentinel
- Microsoft Security Graph

Active Directory entities
Parsed network traffic
Windows Events and traces

MDI
Sensor

MDI
Sensor

AD FS

Domain Controller

Console experience:
Cloud App Security portal

Figure 4.2 – Microsoft Defender for Identity Architecture

Okay, let's move on to some of the prerequisites. We'll approach this logically, and by that, I mean that we'll quickly talk about getting your MDI instance created and connected to Active Directory and then on to the prerequisites for domain controllers or AD FS services due to get the sensor. For the full list, refer to these docs: `https://docs.microsoft.com/en-us/defender-for-identity/prerequisites`.

First things first – head over to `https://portal.atp.azure.com/` and get your instance created simply by clicking on **Create**, as shown in *Figure 4.3*. At the time of writing, the MDI portal is in the process of moving to `security.microsoft.com`. From there, go to **Settings > Identities**.

Figure 4.3 – Microsoft Defender for Identity

After the instance gets created, we'll have a few steps to perform. *Figure 4.4* is an example of what you'll see:

1. **Provide a username and password to connect to your Active Directory forest**

2. **Download Sensor Setup and install the first Sensor**

3. **Configure the first Sensor**

Welcome to Microsoft Defender for Identity

Follow these steps to complete the deployment (Note: Integration with Cloud app security has been turned on, click here to Learn more):

● Provide a username and password to connect to your Active Directory forest
◉ Download Sensor Setup and install the first Sensor
○ Configure the first Sensor

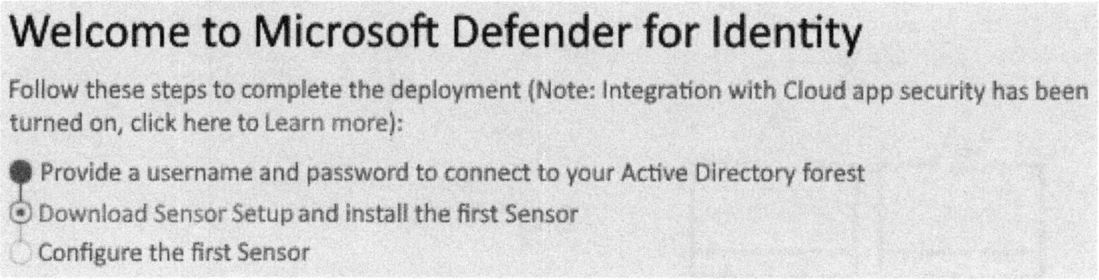

Figure 4.4 – Microsoft Defender for Identity architecture

Now, let's talk about some of the things that your devices and environment will need to have for a successful sensor installation and how to get them. This will be for the sensors installed on domain controllers; we'll cover the standalone sensor following this list:

- **Microsoft .NET Framework 4.7 or later**: If this is not installed on the targeted machines, the sensor setup package will install it for you, as it's included. Keep in mind that installing .NET may require a reboot, so if you're planning a large deployment, I suggest scoping out the `.net` flavors ahead of time.

- As of now, you should know that `Npcap` is the recommendation and can be deployed ahead of time. At the time of writing, when you download the `aatp` sensor package, it includes the `OEM` version that allows you to install silently, which is nice. Maybe, someday, the installation will take care of it – who knows?

- **AD FS servers**: While we won't cover this much at all, there are a few things you'll want to do ahead of time:

  a. **Configure the auditing level to Verbose**: `https://docs.microsoft.com/en-us/defender-for-identity/prerequisites#windows-event-logs`.

  b. If using **Structured Query Language (SQL)** and not **Windows Internal Database (WID)**, the SQL server needs to allow the directory service account to connect, log in, read, and select permissions in the `AdfsConfiguration` database. Go to **Configuration** > **Directory services** > **Username**.

- A **Forest Functional Level (FFL)** of Windows 2003 and above.

The MDI sensor needs a minimum of the following ports, and in case this changes, here's the docs page: `https://docs.microsoft.com/en-us/defender-for-identity/prerequisites#ports`.

The following is the table:

Protocol	Transport	Port	From	To
Internet ports				
Secure Socket Layer (SSL) (`*.atp.azure.com`)	Transmission Control Protocol (TCP)	443	MDI sensor	MDI cloud service
Internal ports				
Domain Name System (DNS)	TCP and User Datagram Protocol (UDP)	53	MDI sensor	DNS servers
Netlogon (Server Message Block (SMB), Common Internet File System (CIFS), and Security Account Manager Remote Protocol (SAM-R))	TCP and UDP	445	MDI sensor	All devices on the network
RADIUS	UDP	1813	RADIUS	MDI sensor
Local host ports*	Required for the sensor update service			
SSL (local host)	TCP	444	Sensor service	Sensor update service
Network Name Resolution (NNR) ports**				
New Technology LAN Manager (NTLM) over Remote Procedure Call (RPC)	TCP	135	MDI	All devices on the network
NetBIOS	UDP	137	MDI	All devices on the network
Remote Desktop Protocol (RDP)	TCP	3389, only the first packet of `Client hello`	MDI	All devices on the network

Table 4.1 – The MDI sensor port requirements

Another consideration is the service account you'll be using. Microsoft recommends that you use a group Managed Service Account (gMSA) for its improved security and automatic password management, not to mention administrative overhead. However, that recommendation comes with some caveats, as follows:

Account type	Windows Server 2008 R2 SP1	Windows Server 2012 or above
Standard AD user account	Yes	Yes
gMSA account	No	Yes

Table 4.2 – Service account considerations

Now, let's talk about the prerequisites for the standalone sensor, which is where you will likely have a scenario where the domain controllers are so locked down that they cannot talk out over the internet. In this case, the sensor is installed on a member server. Before listing what we need to be wary of, let's first list some of the missing features versus the domain controller installation. A full list and additional setup details can be found at the following docs page: `https://docs.microsoft.com/en-us/defender-for-identity/prerequisites#defender-for-identity-standalone-sensor-requirements`:

- It does not support the collection of **Event Tracing for Windows** (**ETW**).

- It requires at least one management adapter and at least one capture adapter.

- The following ports need to be open: `https://docs.microsoft.com/en-us/defender-for-identity/prerequisites#ports-1`.

One last consideration is the operating systems that we can install MDI on, which we can see in *Table 4.3*:

Operating system version	Server with Desktop Experience	Server Core	Nano Server	Supported installations
Windows Server 2008 R2 SP1	✔	✘	Not applicable	Domain controller
Windows Server 2012	✔	✔	Not applicable	Domain controller
Windows Server 2012 R2	✔	✔	Not applicable	Domain controller
Windows Server 2016	✔	✔	✘	Domain controller and AD FS
Windows Server 2019	✔	✔	✘	Domain controller and AD FS

Table 4.3 – The MDI sensor operating system support

Now that we have gone through most of the prerequisites to get our tenant ready, and our devices and environment prepped, we'll want to do one last thing – run the capacity planner. This should only apply to larger environments where you may not know the hardware specs for all of your domain controllers and need to assess whether they're capable or not. Before we start with that, let's look at the minimum hardware requirements:

- A minimum of two cores

- 6 GB of RAM

- Power Option set to High Performance

For a full set of requirements, refer to the following URL: `https://docs.microsoft.com/en-us/defender-for-identity/capacity-planning`.

When you download the capacity tool, which is called `TriSizingTool`, you'll see the following contents:

Name	Date modified	Type	Size
EPPlus.dll	1/21/2018 3:23 PM	Application extens...	1,043 KB
EULA	1/21/2018 7:04 PM	Office Open XML ...	43 KB
Third Party Notices	1/21/2018 7:02 PM	Text Document	35 KB
TriSizingTool	10/16/2018 1:53 PM	Application	188 KB
TriSizingToolResults_20210718_1014.xlsx	7/19/2021 8:12 AM	XLSX File	13 KB

Figure 4.5 – TriSizingTool for capacity planning

Once you initiate `TriSizingTool.exe` from an admin command prompt, you'll see something like the following snippet, where we can see some **Windows Management Instrumentation (WMI)** queries being run on the domain controllers to get some basic information on the machines, and eventually, you'll see it start collecting performance counter samples. Ideally, you'll let this run for 24 hours to ensure you capture the peak hours:

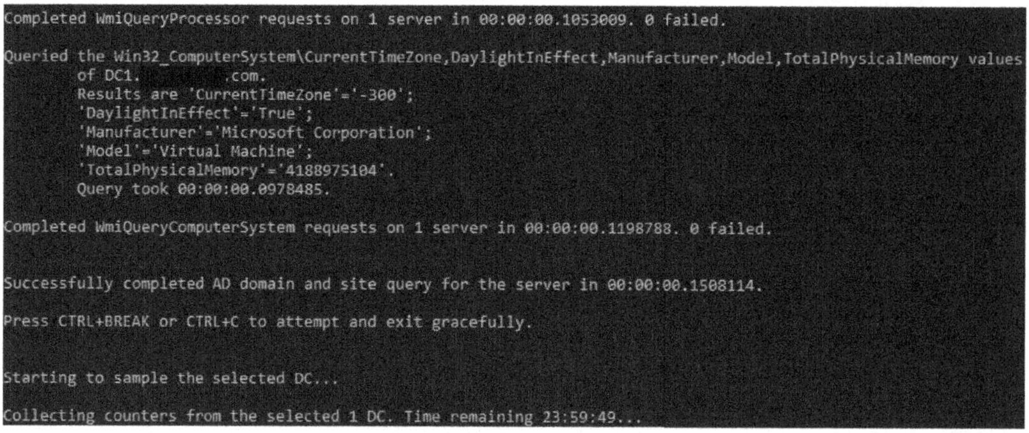

```
Completed WmiQueryProcessor requests on 1 server in 00:00:00.1053009. 0 failed.

Queried the Win32_ComputerSystem\CurrentTimeZone,DaylightInEffect,Manufacturer,Model,TotalPhysicalMemory values
    of DC1.        .com.
    Results are 'CurrentTimeZone'='-300';
    'DaylightInEffect'='True';
    'Manufacturer'='Microsoft Corporation';
    'Model'='Virtual Machine';
    'TotalPhysicalMemory'='4188975104'.
    Query took 00:00:00.0978485.

Completed WmiQueryComputerSystem requests on 1 server in 00:00:00.1198788. 0 failed.

Successfully completed AD domain and site query for the server in 00:00:00.1508114.

Press CTRL+BREAK or CTRL+C to attempt and exit gracefully.

Starting to sample the selected DC...

Collecting counters from the selected 1 DC. Time remaining 23:59:49...
```

Figure 4.6 – A TriSizingTool command prompt example

Once complete or once you exit the command from running, you'll get an Excel file, as shown previously in *Figure 4.5*. Inside the Excel files will be a status on each **Domain Controller (DC)** that was queried, along with some stats on them and any recommendations for hardware changes. Refer to the following as an example:

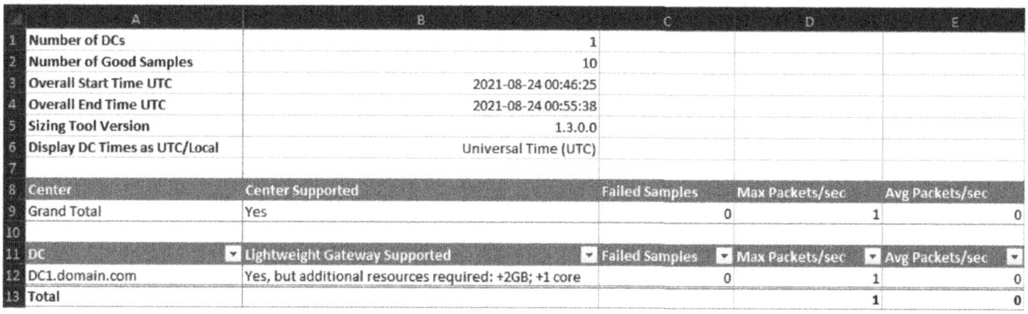

	A	B	C	D	E
1	Number of DCs	1			
2	Number of Good Samples	10			
3	Overall Start Time UTC	2021-08-24 00:46:25			
4	Overall End Time UTC	2021-08-24 00:55:38			
5	Sizing Tool Version	1.3.0.0			
6	Display DC Times as UTC/Local	Universal Time (UTC)			
7					
8	Center	Center Supported	Failed Samples	Max Packets/sec	Avg Packets/sec
9	Grand Total	Yes	0	1	0
10					
11	DC	Lightweight Gateway Supported	Failed Samples	Max Packets/sec	Avg Packets/sec
12	DC1.domain.com	Yes, but additional resources required: +2GB; +1 core	0	1	0
13	Total			1	0

Figure 4.7 – A TriSizingTool output example

That's it as far as considerations for prepping our domain for sensor installations go; now, we can focus on the deployment options. Oddly enough, we'll cover what you can consider as prerequisites when we cover troubleshooting. By that, I mean that you can easily script out some checks for other things you run into when troubleshooting larger deployments so that they can be handled at scale. You'll understand what I mean later on when we get to troubleshooting.

Deployment options

When it comes to deployment options for MDI, it appears limited from a documentation standpoint, as it only talks in the context of manual installations. I don't believe the word *deployment* is even included in the documentation. So, let's list what we're going to cover in terms of *options*:

- A manual installation using the **graphical user interface (GUI)**
- A manual, silent installation
- Microsoft Endpoint Configuration Manager

Most installations will likely be manual, and I say that solely based on experience. I've seen large global companies install it manually on hundreds of domain controllers. Those instances were that way largely because they had the personnel and time and, overall, wanted to be delicate considering the application. It's up to the customer to decide whether they want to deploy it.

With that said, let's cover what manual GUI installation looks like. When you download the sensor package from the portal, you'll see the files shown in *Figure 4.8*:

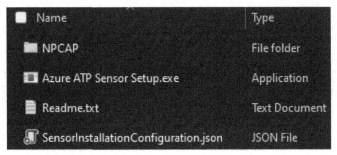

Figure 4.8 – The contents of Azure ATP Sensor Setup.zip

In *Figure 4.9*, you'll see a `json` file example, which contains the information that the executable will use for configuration:

```
SensorInstallationConfiguration.json*  🔒  ⌖  ✕
Schema:  <No Schema Selected>
{
    "$type": "SensorInstallationConfiguration",
    "WorkspaceApplicationSensorApiEndpoint": {
        "$type": "EndpointData",
        "Address": "domainsensorapi.atp.azure.com",
        "Port": 443
    },
    "WorkspaceId": " "
}
```

Figure 4.9 – An example of SensorInstallationConfiguration.json

As we can see in the ZIP file, we get a few things, such as `Npcap`, the sensor executable, a README file, and a JSON file. First up is Npcap, a packet capture library that allows Windows to capture network traffic, which we'll want to install first. Next is `Azure ATP Sensor Setup.exe`, which is the executable for the sensor itself, which uses the `json` file for its configuration details, containing useful things such as the address to the specific `api` URL, the port, and the workspace ID.

Let's go ahead and kick off the executable with admin rights. We'll see the following three screens, shown in *Figure 4.10*, *Figure 4.11*, and *Figure 4.12* in succession:

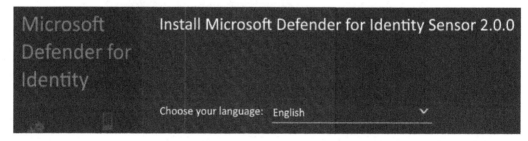

Figure 4.10 – The MDI sensor installation GUI

Here, we can see that it automatically senses what it's being installed on.

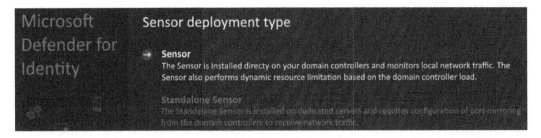

Figure 4.11 – The MDI sensor installation GUI

Lastly, enter the access key that you copied from the portal when you downloaded the sensor package.

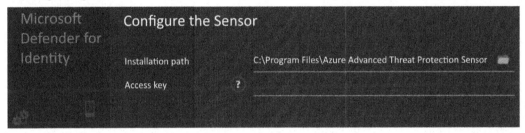

Figure 4.12 – The MDI sensor installation GUI

That's it! The service will go through a few cycles of starting and running now, but that's completely normal. Give a quick check of the services in *Figure 4.13* to see that they're running and you can move on to the next one:

Azure Advanced Threat Protection Sensor	Azure Advanced Threat Protection Sensor	Running	Automatic (Delayed Start)	Local Service
Azure Advanced Threat Protection Sensor Updater	Azure Advanced Threat Protection Sensor Updater	Running	Automatic (Delayed Start)	Local System

Figure 4.13 – MDI sensor services

MDI portal URL: `https://security.microsoft.com/settings/identities?tabid=sensor`.

By this point, you'll see the device in the portal as well, as shown in *Figure 4.14*, where you'll see things such as **Version**, **Service status**, and **Health status**:

Sensor	Version	Delayed update	Service status	Update status	Health status
DC1 ⋮	2.159.14408.6997	Disabled	Running	Up to date	● Healthy

Figure 4.14 – The MDI sensor in the portal

Next, let's talk about the silent installation. The following is an example of the command line that we'd use:

```
"Azure ATP sensor Setup.exe" /quiet
NetFrameworkComma"dLineArguments="/q" AccessKey"Key"
ProxyUrl=http://proxy.domain.com:8080
```

See *Table 4.4* for a breakdown of the different parameters that are being used or that can be used:

Name	Syntax	Mandatory for silent installation?	Description
Quiet	/quiet	Yes	Runs the installer, displaying no UI and no prompts.
Help	/help	No	Provides help and quick reference. Displays the correct use of the setup command, including a list of all options and behaviors.
NetFramework-CommandLineArgu-ments="/q"	NetFrameworkCommandLin-eArguments="/q"	Yes	Specifies the parameters for the .Net Framework installation. Must be set to enforce the silent installation of .Net Framework.
InstallationPath	InstallationPath=""	No	Sets the path for the installation of MDI Sensor binaries. Default path: %programfiles%\ Azure Advanced Threat Protection sensor
AccessKey	AccessKey="**"	Yes	Sets the access key that is used to register the MDI sensor with the MDI instance.

Table 4.4 – MDI sensor silent install parameters

Again, that's it! The service will go through a few cycles of starting and running. Another quick check of the services and we're all set. Like before, this device will show up in the portal as well.

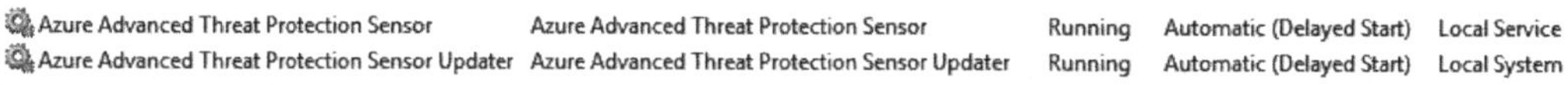

Azure Advanced Threat Protection Sensor	Azure Advanced Threat Protection Sensor	Running	Automatic (Delayed Start)	Local Service
Azure Advanced Threat Protection Sensor Updater	Azure Advanced Threat Protection Sensor Updater	Running	Automatic (Delayed Start)	Local System

Figure 4.15 – The MDI sensor services

MDI portal URL: `https://security.microsoft.com/settings/`
`identities?tabid=sensor`.

You can see the current device status within the security portal link provided below, where we get the full health status of the sensor. Refer to *Figure 4.16* as an example.

Sensor		Version	Delayed update	Service status	Update status	Health status
DC1	:	2.159.14408.6997	Disabled	Running	Up to date	● Healthy

Figure 4.16 – The MDI sensor in the portal

Another installation method that I have been using lately is **Microsoft Endpoint Configuration Manager (MECM)**, provided the customer has it, which most seem to these days. This is a simple standard program, with a command line calling the sensor executable and any switches needed. Let's look at what this looks like as we go through the process.

As I mentioned in the prerequisites, `Npcap` is a recommendation and can be deployed ahead of time, and we'll do exactly that. In *Figure 4.17*, I have started creating a standard program and have set the source folder as the `Npcap` folder that came with the MDI sensor download that we talked about earlier. Of course, I have copied that to a software distribution share that I have in my lab.

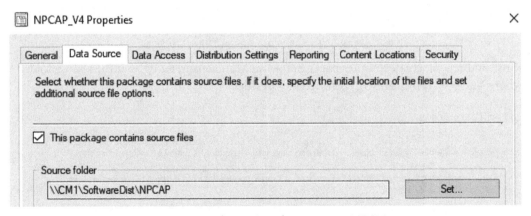

Figure 4.17 – The NPCAP data source in MECM

Next, we set what we want to run as the program, and as you can see in *Figure 4.18*, I have `npcap-1.00-oem.exe` with some parameters. The parameters we use are the following:

- `/S` – silent install and `Npcap` OEM only
- `/loopback_support=no`
- `/winpcap_mode=yes`

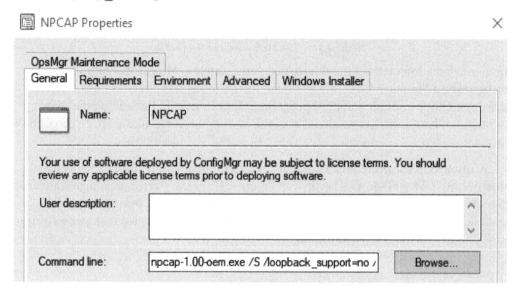

Figure 4.18 – The NPCAP command line in MECM

Rinse and repeat, create another package for the MDI sensor, and give it the source folder where `Azure ATP sensor Setup.exe` resides.

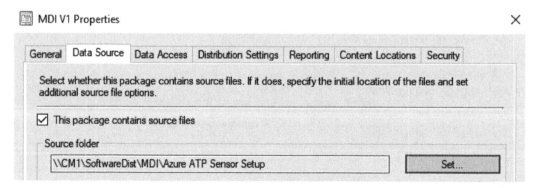

Figure 4.19 – The MDI data source in MECM

Here, we're using the exact same command line that we discussed earlier in the chapter, so revisit that if you need it.

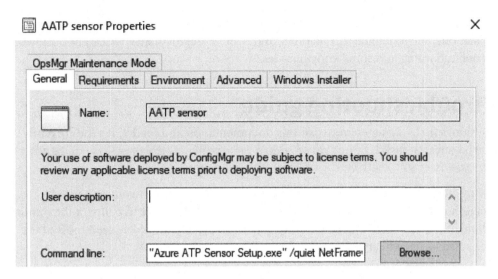

Figure 4.20 – The MDI command line in MECM

Lastly, we'll check the **Run another program first** box so that we can ensure it installs Npcap ahead of installing the MDI sensor. Of course, you don't have to do this and it's completely optional; however, this is a simple way to accomplish your goal. You may have machines in your environment where you need to uninstall WinPcap first as another prerequisite before doing this as well.

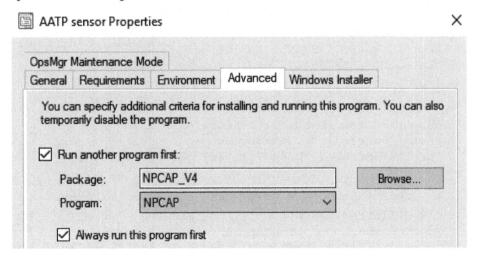

Figure 4.21 – The MDI child program (NPCAP)

We're done! Distribute your content and deploy the package. This is a super-straightforward approach to deploying MDI en masse; just leverage your maintenance windows to handle reboots for domain controllers needing .NET Framework 4.7.

Now that we have wrapped up some basic deployment methods, such as manual installations, silent manual installations, and MECM deployments, we can now move on to troubleshooting and some known issues.

A troubleshooting guide

First things first – I suggest you visit this documentation and read it; it's the currently known issues list for MDI: https://docs.microsoft.com/en-us/defender-for-identity/troubleshooting-known-issues.

Moving along, let's cover some of the known issues that are most common when troubleshooting MDI installations that I've come across. I'd have to ballpark the number of domain controllers I've onboarded to be over 5,000, so I think I've seen most of the wonky issues that will arise.

We'll start with the most common in a bullet-point list, with some information on each:

- **The sensor failed to connect to service**: If you see this when installing, check for the needed root certificates. This can be done by running the following Get-ChildItem cmdlets. It's likely one of them is missing, and if they are, the links to get them are in the URL provided previously for troubleshooting known issues:

```
# Certificate for all customers
Get-ChildItem -Path "Cert:\LocalMachine\
Root" | where { $_.Thumbprint -eq
"D4DE20D05E66FC53FE1A50882C78DB2852CAE474"} | fl


# Certificate for commercial customers
Get-ChildItem -Path "Cert:\LocalMachine\
Root" | where { $_.Thumbprint -eq
"df3c24f9bfd666761b268073fe06d1cc8d4f82a4"} | fl


# Certificate for US Government GCC High customers
Get-ChildItem -Path "Cert:\LocalMachine\
Root" | where { $_.Thumbprint -eq
"a8985d3a65e5e5c4b2d7d66d40c6dd2fb19c5436"} | fl
```

- If you're using Network Interface Card (NIC) teaming on any network adapters, it's necessary to install the Npcap driver before installation. You'll see an error regarding that during installation as well.

- **The GMSA password could not be retrieved**: This will present itself in `Microsoft.Tri.Sensor.Updater.log`, and the entry will look like following the example shown next. With this error, you really need to ensure that you typed in the name of the account correctly and that you set the `PrincipalsAllowedToRetrieveManagedPassword` parameter of `New-ADServiceAccount` to the proper group (the local security group that you can create and to which you can add all built-in domain controller groups, even ones from domains with two-way trust) that contains the domain controllers. Another thing to check is whether you have `Log on as a service` configured in Group Policy, and if you do, you'll need to add this new gMSA account:

```
2020-02-17 14:02:19.6258 Warn
GroupManagedServiceAccountImpersonationHelper
GetGroupManagedServiceAccountAccessTokenAsync failed GMSA
password could not be retrieved [errorCode=AccessDenied
AccountName=account_name DomainDnsName=domain1.test.
local]
```
```
Warn DirectoryServicesClient CreateLdapConnectionAsync
failed to retrieve group managed service account
password. [DomainControllerDnsName=DC1.CONTOSO.LOCAL
Domain=contoso.local UserName=AATP_gMSA]
```

- **Proxy**: If you have a proxy in place, make sure you're running the installer with the proxy parameter. If the sensor can't communicate externally, it's going to fail.

If you put in the work ahead of time, you shouldn't run into a ton of issues while installing, and when you do, it's almost always one of the items shown previously. Get familiar with the logs, which you can find at the following URL. Get used to what entries are in each so that you know where to go if something goes wrong. Feel free to contact me on Twitter (`@trk_rdy`) too with any issues; I'll always try to answer when I'm free: `https://docs.microsoft.com/en-us/defender-for-identity/troubleshooting-using-logs`.

With that said, let's move on to the final part of this chapter – service status and verification!

Service status and verification

Alright, so we've made it to the final part of the chapter. I wish there was a lot more to talk about, but it's quite easy to verify whether the service is running; however, we'll cover them all. First off, we'll check the local services, via `services.msc` or however you like to launch it. Both the sensor and updater should be running. Of course, right after installation, they'll cycle a few times until they are settled on the credentials they can use, as well as some other self-checks. Once that settles, you'll see a steady **Running** state in the following portal:

Azure Advanced Threat Protection Sensor	Azure Advanced Threat Protection Sensor	Running	Automatic (Delayed Start)	Local Service
Azure Advanced Threat Protection Sensor Updater	Azure Advanced Threat Protection Sensor Updater	Running	Automatic (Delayed Start)	Local System

Figure 4.22 – The MDI sensor services

We can check the senor in the portal as well; here, we see it **Healthy** and in a **Running** state. The health status is what you want to look at for any communication issues.

Sensor		Version	Delayed update	Service status	Update status	Health status
DC1	:	2.159.14408.6997	Disabled	Running	Up to date	● Healthy

Figure 4.23 – The MDI sensor in the portal

Summary

Alright, so, **MDI** – what a cool product, and easy to install, right? We'll talk so much more about it in terms of how it works from a threat-hunting standpoint in *Chapter 7, Microsoft Defender for Identity: Alerts and Incidents* where we will discuss alerts, incidents, evidence, and timelines. We just had to get through the setup first to make sure that we set ourselves up for success. So, what did we learn in this chapter? Let's recap together:

- **Understanding prerequisites**: We talked about all the work we need to put in ahead of time to ensure that our deployments are successful and that our environment is in optimal shape.

- **Deployment options**: Here, we talked about the various ways to install, whether that was by manual GUI installation, silent installation, or even an MECM deployment option.

- **Troubleshooting guide**: In this section, we touched on the more common issues you'll run into and what we can do to address them. I also provided the known issues link for you to become familiar with as it updates.

- **Service status and verification**: Lastly, we talked about how we can ensure that our sensors are up and running, reporting in, and keeping us protected.

I look forward to talking more about these subjects in later chapters! Speaking of chapters, next up is *Chapter 5, Understanding and Implementing Microsoft Defender for Cloud (Microsoft Defender for Cloud Standard Tier)* in which you'll be learning about **Defender for Cloud**.

5

Understanding and Implementing Microsoft Defender for Cloud (Microsoft Defender for Cloud Standard Tier)

One of the more cloud-focused tools within the Microsoft 365 Defender suite is **Microsoft Defender for Cloud**. In this chapter, we will be covering numerous topics around Microsoft Defender for Cloud, including ASC, so that you can get a better understanding of how to properly leverage this tool in your role as the Microsoft security operations analyst for your enterprise.

In this chapter, we will cover the following topics:

- Introduction to Microsoft Defender for Cloud and ASC

- Implementing ASC

- Implementing Microsoft Defender for Cloud

- How do ASC and Microsoft Defender for Cloud fit into the security of an enterprise?

By the end of this chapter, you will be able to fully understand all of the steps you need to take to not only be successful in deployment and implementation but also properly plan and utilize Microsoft Defender for Cloud in your role as a Microsoft security operations analyst. Let's go!

Technical requirements

During this chapter, we will be using shortened terms and acronyms we want to ensure you can understand throughout. The following list outlines a few of these terms for your reading and understanding:

- **ASC**: This is an acronym for **Microsoft Defender for Cloud**. Considering Microsoft Defender for Cloud is integrated into ASC, both in this book and within online publishings, you will see ASC used frequently.

- **ATP**: This is an acronym for **advanced threat protection**. Within ASC, many ATP elements will be available for enablement (as you will soon read), so instead of typing it out fully, we will simplify this by presenting it as ATP.

- **KQL**: This is an acronym for **Kusto Query Language**. When we cover monitoring and hunting, KQL will be an acronym you see frequently.

- **LA/LAW**: This will be our acronym for **Log Analytics/Log Analytics workspace**. LA is an *under-the-hood* part of ASC, as you will shortly find out.

- **CSPM**: This is an acronym for **cloud security posture management**. We will dive into what this is specifically later in this chapter.

- **CWP**: This is an acronym for **cloud workload protection**. We will dive into what this is specifically later in this chapter.

Okay! Now that we have covered the shortened terms and acronyms we expect you to encounter within this chapter, let's dive into what Microsoft Defender for Cloud is! Ready? Let's roll!

Introduction to Microsoft Defender for Cloud and ASC

Think about, for a moment, how vast the Microsoft Azure platform can be in your enterprise. Think about all the different resource types, locations, security controls, configurations, baselines, attack vectors, access requirements, authentication methods, and authorization methods. Then, add in the fact that the best practices around securing everything that exists within Azure (and, technically, **Google Cloud Platform** (**GCP**) and **Amazon Web Services** (**AWS**) as well) is ever-changing. How can an organization stay up to date with all of this, on top of what exists on-premises? Microsoft Defender for Cloud and ASC are here to help you with this!

> **Note**
>
> We will no longer be adding in *formerly ASC Standard tier* going forward—we will merely refer to this solution by its current name of Microsoft Defender for Cloud.

So, what is Microsoft Defender for Cloud? We believe, before diving into what Microsoft Defender for Cloud is, you must first know what ASC is. Microsoft Defender for Cloud is integrated into ASC, so let's first dive into ASC a bit so that you have a better understanding of the differences, integration, and enterprise use cases for the solution.

What is ASC?

ASC is Microsoft's CSPM offering. This offering in and of itself is *free* for you to consume in your enterprise. ASC enables you to truly strengthen the security of your Azure environment by identifying where you can potentially perform tasks that will harden your security posture on resources you may or may not even know exist! Each item that has been identified on various resources is a recommendation that is continually evolving as security evolves. This is a living recommendations list that looks at your data, compute, services, and applications in the cloud. Events that are collected from native or installed agents (potentially on-premises or in another cloud) and those that come from assets that live in Azure are correlated on the backend of the tool and are customized and tailored to provide recommendations on how you can improve your security posture on every resource in your environment. These recommendations are designed to secure your workloads and detect threats accordingly. See the following screenshot for an overview of the **Security Center** portal:

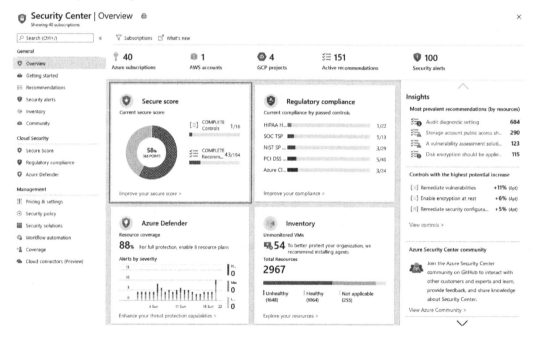

Figure 5.1 – ASC

In summary, ASC provides a solution for the three most prevalent and difficult-to-manage security challenges, which we explore in more detail here:

- **Quickly changing and growing cloud workloads**: Compared to how on-premises resources are created and managed, the cloud brings great simplicity and quickness to resource and workload deployment. While this is great, this wonderful thing is also a challenge for most security teams. How do you, as part of the security operations team, ensure that the team responsible for resource deployment is using the proper and approved (thus secure) templates and patterns? How do you also quickly identify non-compliance or insecure resources in an expeditious manner? This is a challenge.

- **Threat actors are adding increasingly sophisticated attacks to their arsenal**: Whether your workload in the cloud is internal or internet-facing and is basic or complex, there is a foundational and ever-present truth—attacks are getting increasingly sophisticated; attackers are learning the tools and discovery methods that exist in security tools; attackers are using this knowledge to adapt and obfuscate very quickly—many times, quicker than security teams can defend against. This is also a challenge.

- **Staffing properly skilled resources is hard**: Staffing has been a problem for decades in the security space. However, with the introduction of the cloud landscape into your enterprise, you will quickly find out that the number of security alerts and different tools and solutions that are noticing these alerts is far outweighing and outnumbering the number of staffed resources and security administrators. Even worse is the fact that even if you can find the financial means to hire more resources, it becomes even more difficult to find security administrators that possess the proper skillset and experience to defend against attacks properly. Staying up to date with the latest set of attacks being carried out by threat actors is a constant losing battle. This is, once again, a challenge.

With all these challenges present, ASC can help you and your organization prepare against these challenges by providing you with tools to do the following:

- **Improve and harden your security posture**: ASC, by default, will assess and review your resources in your environment and will allow you as a security administrator to fully understand deep insights into your resources and determine whether they are secure, based on best practices per resource type. This is all done automatically, as we will get into in later sections of this chapter when we discuss the deployment of ASC.

- **Protect against threats**: ASC, while assessing your workloads, will also raise awareness through recommendations on additional ways to protect against threats and resolve security alerts that correlate to your workload resources.

- **Expedite your enterprise processes to get secure more quickly**: ASC was born in the cloud, and with that comes simplified processes and expediting implementing recommendations that make your environment more secure! Also, since ASC is natively integrated with Azure cloud resources, deployment of ASC is an absolute breeze (as we will soon cover, later in this chapter). This includes various policy elements (Azure Policy) and auto-provisioning options available for your enterprise right away!

In addition to addressing the most challenging and prevalent issues that are present in your enterprise for you and your team, ASC also provides the following features that can easily be implemented to quickly assist your team:

- **Making managing your enterprise cloud security policies and compliance easy**: ASC works alongside Azure Policy (which is another great security tool that can be described as the Group Policy of the cloud, at a super high level). Each policy that comes with any recommendations of ASC is built on top of Azure Policy controls; these policy controls are key in forming your enterprise security policy posture, along with compliance tracking. As resources in your cloud workloads are spun up and down, these compliance numbers adapt to that and keep you focused on what you need to remediate to maintain compliance and a firm security posture. This is huge for security teams, allowing you to have a tool in place that will constantly be tracking any shadow **information technology (IT)** activities that happen in your cloud workloads without the direct involvement of anyone on the security team. Let the tool work for you!

> **Note**
> We do recommend you begin looking into Azure Policy—there are numerous resources out there for your reading. You will find out that in the cloud, Azure Policy is huge for security administrators and operation teams!

Security policy management in ASC

ASC is continually assessing your workloads and subscriptions for any added resources that have been deployed, reviewing existing resources, and assessing whether they are configured according to various security best practices. See the following screenshot for an example of security policy management:

Policy Management

Choose a subscription or management group from the list below to perform the following tasks:
- View and edit the default ASC policy
- Add a custom policy
- Add regulatory compliance standards to your compliance dashboard

Click here to learn more >

16 MANAGEMENT GROUPS   **40** SUBSCRIPTIONS

🔎 Search by name

Name

∨ [⋏] 72f988bf-86f1-41af-91ab-2d7cd011db47 (12 of 12 subscriptions)

> [⋏] BKG (1 of 1 subscriptions)

∨ [⋏] CnAI Orchestration Service Public Corp prod (4 of 4 subscriptions)

∨ [⋏] Demonstration (2 of 2 subscriptions)

🔑 Contoso Hotels

🔑 Contoso Hotels - Dev

Figure 5.2 – Policy management

What is great is that if any resources are not configured with best practices, they will be flagged and shown as an object that will have recommendations on how to become more aligned with security best practices. Within Azure, there is a specific security benchmark that resources are compared against; this benchmark is called the **Azure Security Benchmark** (**ASB**). This is a benchmark designed and authored by Microsoft and is specifically designed for Azure architecture. This was derived from the **Center for Internet Security** (**CIS**) and the **National Institute of Standards and Technology** (**NIST**) and compiled into a single, easy-to-follow benchmark that resources are assessed against.

Secure Score from assessments in ASC

ASC can monitor the security status of your Azure network. Whether you have an **infrastructure-as-a-service (IaaS)** or a **platform-as-a-service (PaaS)** cloud environment, networking will be a requirement! See the following screenshot for an overview of ASC Secure Score:

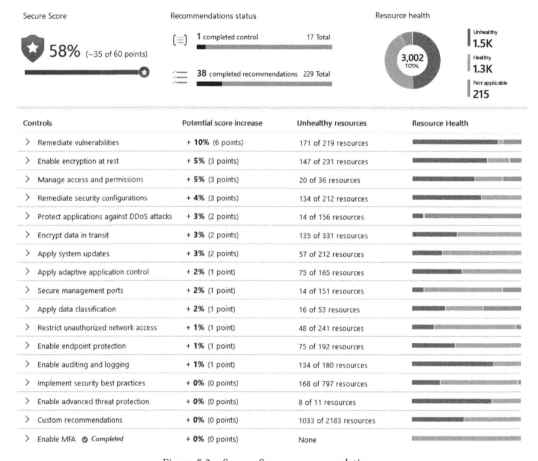

Figure 5.3 – Secure Score recommendations

ASC will analyze any network component in your workload architecture and call out any flaws that lead to security vulnerabilities or implementations that go against best security practices.

Network maps from ASC

One of the core features within ASC is the native ability to provide recommendations that are customized and specific to your workload resources. This is normally a task that is taken up by someone on the security operations team, but the wonderful thing about ASC is that it does this administrative task for you. See the following screenshot for an example of a network map:

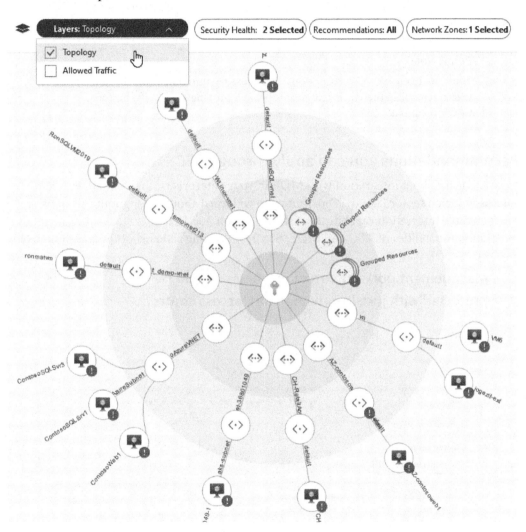

Figure 5.4 – Network map

What is even better is that these recommendations and actions can tie into other parts of the Microsoft 365 Defender stack of tools such as Microsoft Sentinel and **Microsoft Defender for Endpoint** (**MDE**). These recommendations help you reduce improper configurations in your workloads and reduce the attack surface across all your resources. Some examples would be **Azure Virtual Machines** (**Azure VMs**), any PaaS resource, storage accounts, and **Structured Query Language** (**SQL**) resources. Instead of manually doing this review and putting together a list of recommended security tasks for your enterprise, let ASC do this for you!

> **Bonus Note**
>
> There are many *one-click-fix* options with these recommendations that allow you to remediate these configurations through the single click of a button! Check them out!

Recommendations you can apply through ASC

Now let's learn about integration with MDE in your enterprise (when paired with Microsoft Defender for Cloud). One thing you will learn about throughout this book is the incredible integration capabilities of the Microsoft 365 Defender stack—this includes integration capabilities of ASC and MDE. See the following screenshot for an example of an alert:

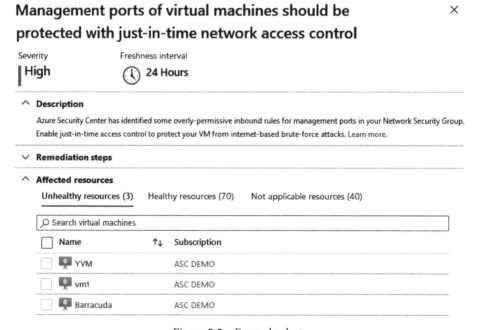

Figure 5.5 – Example alert

You can onboard devices to either service from either portal/tool. You can also view and close out alerts that are generated from either service to the other. This is a great integration capability that proves to be super helpful for security operations teams and analysts alike to ensure you have a single pane of glass to manage and view alerts from both solutions!

Integration settings within ASC

See the following screenshot for an example of integration settings:

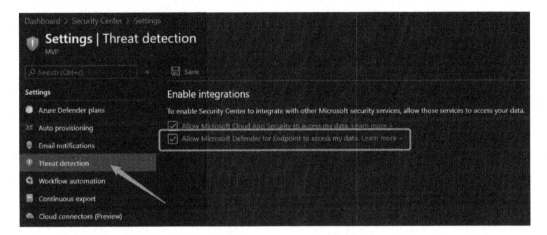

Figure 5.6 – Environment settings

So, back to the original question—what is Microsoft Defender for Cloudr?

What is Microsoft Defender for Cloud?

Remember when we talked about ASC being a CSPM tool? Well, Microsoft Defender for Cloud is integrated into ASC, but it serves a different purpose for your enterprise! Microsoft Defender for Cloud is Microsoft's CWP offering. Microsoft Defender for Cloud integrates into ASC and provides advanced, ever-changing, cloud-driven protection of your Azure and hybrid cloud workloads. In addition to the built-in policies that come with ASC, with Microsoft Defender for Cloud you can enable other custom security policies and compliances (such as NIST, **Payment Card Industry** (**PCI**), **PCI Data Security Standard** (**PCI DSS**), and Azure CIS. In theory, as with ASC, you can enable and extend the capabilities of Microsoft Defender for Cloud into your on-premises environment as well as into multi-cloud environments (AWS and GCP as an example).

> **Note**
>
> Microsoft Defender for Cloud is a *paid* offering that you can enable on resources. There is a different cost of CWP capability coverage (also referred to as ATP) per resource type you want to deploy this on. We will dive into which types of resources support Microsoft Defender for Cloud here in a moment.

Considering Microsoft Defender for Cloud is a part of ASC, to administer it within your enterprise, you will be navigating through ASC, as shown in the following screenshot:

Figure 5.7 – Home dashboard

First, let's start with which types of resources support Microsoft Defender for Cloud, thus allowing you to enable this capability upon such resources within your workloads.

The following resource types support Microsoft Defender for Cloud (as of August 2021 from *Microsoft Docs*):

- Microsoft Defender for Cloud for Servers
- Microsoft Defender for Cloud for App Service
- Microsoft Defender for Cloud for Storage

- Microsoft Defender for Cloud for SQL

- Microsoft Defender for Cloud for Kubernetes

- Microsoft Defender for Cloud for container registries

- Microsoft Defender for Cloud for Key Vault

- Microsoft Defender for Cloudr for Resource Manager

- Microsoft Defender for Cloud for **Domain Name System** (**DNS**)

- Microsoft Defender for Cloud for open-source relational databases

> **Important Note**
> ASC will still provide proactive assessment and recommendations for all of the preceding services for *free*, but if you want protection elements to defend against threat actors, you will need to enable *Microsoft Defender for Cloud, which is paid per resource type* for such protection.

In short: ASC (CSPM) = free; Microsoft Defender for Cloud (CWP) = paid

We want to take some time, as it is something that will come up a lot when applying Microsoft Defender for Cloud in your enterprise, to cover what Microsoft Defender for Cloud brings to the table for each supported resource type. Let's go!

Microsoft Defender for Cloud for Servers

Microsoft Defender for Cloud for Servers is a feature that will add deep threat-detection capabilities and advanced defense mechanisms for your enterprise Windows and Linux workloads. Whenever you onboard servers to Microsoft Defender for Cloud, ASC will present alerts that Microsoft Defender for Cloud finds and give you suggestions on how to rectify known security issues. Remember, Microsoft Defender for Cloud and ASC work together as they are integrated with one another.

Here are some added benefits of Microsoft Defender for Cloud for Servers:

- Whenever you enable Microsoft Defender for Cloud for Servers, **MDE** will also be enabled, which adds excellent value and deep **endpoint detection and response** (**EDR**) capabilities to your servers.

- One of the deep ATP features that comes with Microsoft Defender for Cloud for Servers is **Qualys vulnerability scanning**. Vulnerability assessment scanning on your servers is done through Qualys, and all the outputs of that scanning are shown within the portal! The best part is that you do not even need a Qualys license, as it is included with Microsoft Defender for Cloud for Servers.

- Ever wondered how to secure your access from a Microsoft **Remote Desktop Protocol (RDP)** perspective? Ever been asked to turn off RDP functionality completely because threat actors use it maliciously? Good news! With Microsoft Defender for Cloud for Servers, you will get a feature called **Just-in-Time (JIT)** VM Access, which will allow you to enable RDP through a governed process to certain users, for a set amount of time! This reduces that attack vector in your enterprise right away!

- Typically, whenever a threat actor is making moves within your enterprise, they are changing files and registry settings without your knowledge. With Microsoft Defender for Cloud for Servers, you will have a feature available to you called **File Integrity Monitoring (FIM)**. This feature examines files and registries of the operating system, application software, and other changes that might resemble or be indicative of an attack. This feature is for both Windows and Linux workloads!

- Being able to control which applications run on your servers has historically been a tough task to feat; however, with Microsoft Defender for Cloud for Servers, you will have a feature called **adaptive application controls (AAC)** that will allow you to set a list of known applications that can run on the server. If any application attempts to run, you will get a notification and an alert in ASC accordingly!

- With Microsoft Defender for Cloud for Servers, you will also have a feature available to you that will automatically adapt and manage network complexities based on the behavior of applications and workloads. This feature is called **adaptive network hardening (ANH)**, and Microsoft Defender for Cloud for Servers will automatically modify **network security groups (NSGs)** to only allow traffic that is normal for your application workloads!

- Many times, threat actors inject malicious workloads into memory. With Microsoft Defender for Cloud for Servers, you will have a feature called **fileless attack detection** that will monitor and protect your servers from such adversary activity!

Microsoft Defender for Cloud for App Service

Microsoft Defender for Cloud for App Service is a feature available for enrollment that is designed to deeply protect your App Service deployment in your enterprise. Any application that you have running on Azure App Service will be fully protected by Microsoft Defender for Cloud if you enable it to do so. Learning from already existing processes that Azure possesses around general and deep threat-learning activities, that information is then fed to Microsoft Defender for Cloud for App Service to ensure protection and monitoring are in place to defend against these ever-changing attacks on App Service-based applications.

Here are some added benefits of Microsoft Defender for Cloud for App Service:

- ASC will continually assess your App Service plan and identify security risks, then show these to you as recommendations against your resources within the App Service plan.

- In addition to general assessment, Microsoft Defender for Cloud for App Service will also detect threats to your App Service resources by monitoring numerous fabric-level items, such as the following:

  a. The VM instance that your App Service resource is running on under the hood

  b. Requests to and from your App Service applications

  c. Underlying sandboxes and VMs that your app services might be using

  d. All internal logs of your app service

- Think about the MITRE **Adversarial Tactics, Techniques, and Common Knowledge (ATT&CK)** framework for a moment—think about all the parts of the framework. Microsoft Defender for Cloud for App Service will detect and protect against a good majority of them!

DNS dangling is something that is often overlooked from a process perspective; so, whenever you decommission a site but keep the DNS entry present in your registrar, that can easily be used by a threat actor in a malicious way. Microsoft Defender for Cloud for App Service will alert you whenever you decommission a site and the DNS entry is still present and registered! The following screenshot shows an example of a DNS dangling alert in ASC from Microsoft Defender for Cloud for App Service:

Figure 5.8 – Additional alert details

Microsoft Defender for Cloud for Storage

Microsoft Defender for Cloud for Storage is a feature that will add an extra layer of security to your storage accounts within Azure. We see far too often that an exposed storage account has been compromised or scanned with data being exfiltrated by threat actors. Microsoft Defender for Cloud for Storage is here to solve that for your enterprise.

Here is an overview of Microsoft Defender for Cloud for Storage:

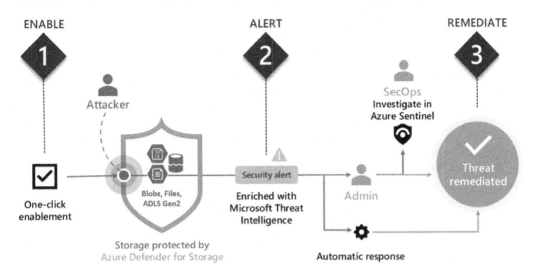

Figure 5.9 – How it all works together

Here are some added benefits of Microsoft Defender for Cloud for Storage:

- If there are any access attempts made to your storage account that match a suspicious access pattern, you will get an alert.

- If Microsoft Defender for Cloud for Storage sees any data exfiltration that appears suspicious, you will get an alert.

- If Microsoft Defender for Cloud for Storage sees any malicious data being uploaded to your storage accounts, you will get an alert.

- Constant guidance on how to better secure your storage accounts will be shown in **ASC's recommendations**.

- All file hashes that are stored, uploaded, or touched within your storage account are analyzed against Microsoft Threat Intelligence Center.

Microsoft Defender for Cloud for SQL

Microsoft Defender for Cloud for SQL is a feature that brings a deep and cloud-backed level of threat protection to your SQL workloads in Azure. This can be either Azure SQL, SQL on an IaaS VM, Azure SQL managed instances, a dedicated SQL pool in Azure Synapse, Azure Arc-enabled SQL servers, and—when configured and supported—even your SQL servers running on Windows on-premises! You might wonder which threat protection features this brings to your enterprise. Let's dive into those a little bit!

Here are some added benefits of Microsoft Defender for Cloud for SQL:

- Whenever you enable Microsoft Defender for Cloud for SQL, you will instantly gain the ability to have vulnerability assessments run on every supported SQL database or instance. This is huge for your enterprise, to assist in detecting and protecting against known vulnerabilities that exist within your SQL enterprise that could lead to data exfiltration or database compromise.

- In addition to the vulnerability assessments being done for best practices from a security standpoint, Microsoft Defender for Cloud for SQL will also bring you ATP elements that will continually monitor your SQL servers for various threats such as brute-force attacks, SQL injection, and privilege abuse. All of these will show in your dashboard as alerts that are then followed up with recommendations for remediation, investigation, and protection!

    Some alert types are listed here:

    - Suspicious database activity

    - Anomalous database access and query patterns

    - Potential SQL injection attacks

Microsoft Defender for Cloud for Kubernetes

Microsoft Defender for Cloud for Kubernetes is a feature that comes with Microsoft Defender for Cloud, should you choose to enable it. Microsoft Defender for Cloud for Kubernetes provides you protection for your Kubernetes clusters, but guess what? It can provide protection wherever they are running, not just within Azure! This includes the following:

- **Azure Kubernetes Service (AKS)**, which—as you know—is Microsoft's managed service within Azure for managing, deploying, and even developing containerized applications.

- **On-premises and multi-cloud environments** that use Kubernetes. This will be achievable by implementing Azure Arc and using the extension for Kubernetes! Super-cool stuff!

Microsoft Defender for Cloud for Kubernetes will assist you in identifying additional ways to harden your Kubernetes environment, as well as providing real-time protection. When this is combined with Microsoft Defender for Cloud for Servers, information on your Linux AKS nodes will also be available! Pretty cool to see these features combine forces to provide you clarity, protection, and best practices to ensure your containerized applications are backed with the ultimate protection and security!

Microsoft Defender for Cloud for container registries

Microsoft Defender for Cloud for container registries is a feature that works alongside **Azure Container Registry (ACR)**, which is a quite common solution used by organizations to manage container images in a centralized manner! If you use ACR in your cloud workloads, you can take advantage of Microsoft Defender for Cloud for container registries. This is a feature that will scan your images whenever they are pushed to your registry, giving you instant visibility into your images and information on any vulnerabilities found. What is great is that this is powered by Qualys, which—as discussed before—is an industry leader in the vulnerability scanning world! Whenever issues are identified by Qualys or ASC, you will get a notification within your ASC dashboard that will provide detailed information about that issue, such as the severity classification, the potential MITRE mapping, and guidance on how to fix the security issue within your images.

When are these images scanned? Great question—the scanning happens here:

- On push

- Recently pulled

- On import

The following screenshot gives you a better visual understanding of how ASC and ACR work together behind the scenes for this protection:

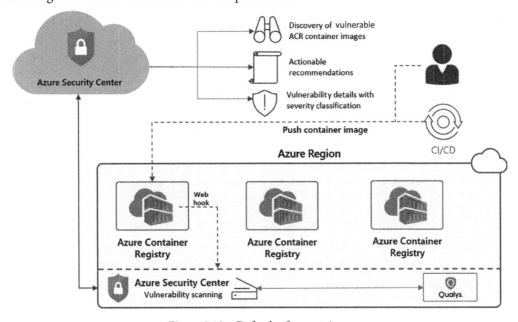

Figure 5.10 – Defender for containers

The preceding screenshot provides an example of Defender for Containers.

Microsoft Defender for Cloud for Key Vault

Microsoft Defender for Cloud for Key Vault is a feature that will provide ATP for any Azure Key Vault instance you have in your environment. When enabled, Microsoft Defender for Cloud for Key Vault will detect any potentially harmful attempts to access or even exploit Key Vault accounts. This is all powered by a vast **machine learning** (**ML**) engine within Microsoft Defender for Cloud. Whenever Microsoft Defender for Cloud suspects any anomalous activities, you will see alerts (such as the one shown in *Figure 5.11*), and if you enable it to do so, Microsoft Defender for Cloud can send emails to whoever needs to be notified about the key vault with this behavior! Considering Azure Key Vault is a critical solution to manage your keys, secrets, and passwords in the cloud, this feature will be well used and appreciated within your security team!

Here is an example of an Azure Key Vault alert in Microsoft Defender for Cloud:

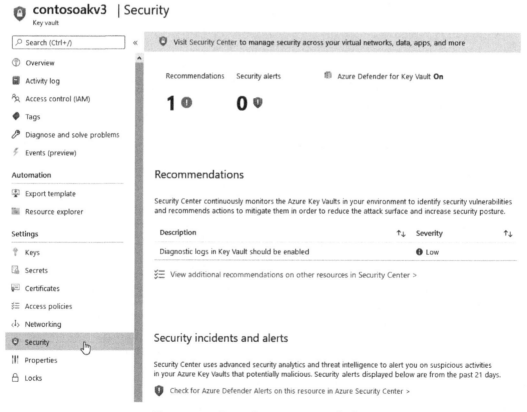

Figure 5.11 – Example Azure Key Vault alert

Microsoft Defender for Cloud for Resource Manager

All your Azure deployments go through an engine called **Azure Resource Manager** (**ARM**), no matter whether you are doing this manually through the Azure portal or programmatically through the **command-line interface** (**CLI**), PowerShell, or even Terraform. ARM is a foundational element within Azure that your deployments rely on. Microsoft Defender for Cloud for Resource Manager is a feature that will automatically monitor all resource management operations that go through ARM. Microsoft Defender for Cloud will run advanced analytics and inspection on this for you, detect any suspicious activity, and follow that up with an alert in ASC.

Here is a screenshot showing how all deployments go through ARM and where Microsoft Defender for Cloud sits within this process:

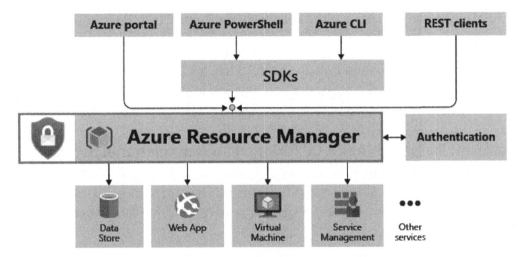

Figure 5.12 – Defender for ARM

What does it detect? Great question! Here are a few of the most important things:

- Suspicious resource management operations
- Lateral movement
- Use of exploitation toolkits

This feature will be beneficial to your organization to automate the security analysis of every deployment and every ARM operation in your Azure environment. Go check it out!

Microsoft Defender for Cloud for DNS

Many organizations take advantage of Azure DNS, which is a hosting service for DNS domains that provide name resolution. Whenever organizations host domains in Azure, you can manage your DNS records and zones, leveraging the same credentials as you would use to manage other Azure resources. If your organization uses Azure DNS, then Microsoft Defender for Cloud for DNS will be a great security feature for you! Microsoft Defender for Cloud for DNS will continually monitor all DNS requests and queries to your Azure resources and provide additional security analytics to allow you to have visibility into any suspicious activity.

Microsoft Defender for Cloud for DNS will protect your resources that are tied to Azure DNS against issues such as the following:

- Malware communicating with a **command-and-control (C&C)** server

- DNS attacks

- Data exfiltration from your Azure resources that use DNS tunneling

- Any known or suspected communication with malicious domains that are associated with phishing and crypto mining

Microsoft Defender for Cloud for open-source relational databases

Microsoft Defender for Cloud for open-source relational databases is much like Microsoft Defender for Cloud for SQL—however, it is intended for open source databases specifically. Microsoft Defender for Cloud for open-source relational databases supports the following database types:

- Azure databases for PostgreSQL

- Azure databases for MySQL

- Azure databases for MariaDB

Here are some added benefits of Microsoft Defender for Cloud for open-source relational databases:

- Whenever you enable Microsoft Defender for Cloud for your open source databases, you will instantly gain the ability to have vulnerability assessments run on every supported open source database or instance. This is huge for your enterprise, to assist in detecting and protecting against known vulnerabilities that exist within your open source database enterprise that could lead to data exfiltration or database compromise.

Some **threat intelligence (TI)** alert types are listed here:

- Suspicious database activity

- Anomalous database access and query patterns

- Brute-force attacks

Now that we have covered each of these rich features within both ASC and Microsoft Defender for Cloud, let's move on to discuss how to implement both solutions in your environment. This information will be crucial for the *SC-200* exam but, more importantly, will enable you to possess the required knowledge to be the best Microsoft security operations analyst in your environment, today!

Implementing ASC

One of the more important parts of your role as a Microsoft security operations analyst, outside of simply knowing what the tools are that make up the overall solution, is to understand the effort and requirements to implement these solutions. We want to take some time and walk through with you how to implement ASC in your enterprise. You will be glad to know that implementing ASC is a simple task—however, we highly recommend that you effectively communicate all the previously shared information to the appropriate parties within your enterprise to ensure you have full alignment on the value this adds to your organization. Often, technology makes implementation so simple that we forget to communicate and follow internal processes. We want you to be successful, so go bridge that communication gap before continuing!

First, to implement ASC, you must have the proper permissions within Azure to do so. This can be applied to your own account, an administrative account, or even a service account you leverage for Azure administration.

Prerequisites

You will need one of the following permissions to implement ASC on a subscription:

- Subscription owner

- Subscription contributor

- Security administrator

All three of these are built-in Azure roles that can be applied to an account. Once you have verified you have these permissions available to you, we can proceed with the remaining steps.

Implementation steps

Now, let's look at the steps to implement ASC. Here they are:

1. Sign in to the Azure portal using the proper account that has the permissions assigned, as discussed in the preceding *Prerequisites* section (`https://portal.azure.com`).

2. Once you are signed in, you will be greeted with the portal menu, as illustrated in the following screenshot. Select **Security Center**, or simply search for it on the top search menu:

Figure 5.13 – General portal navigation to Defender for Cloud

3. Upon clicking **Security Center**, you will be greeted with an ASC overview page that looks like this:

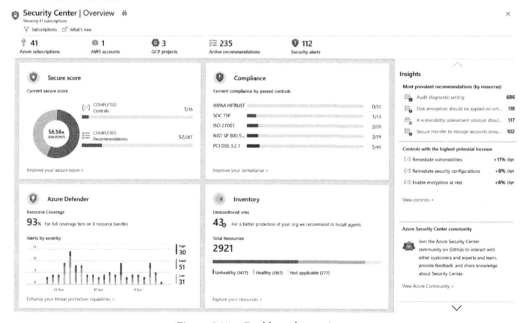

Figure 5.14 – Dashboard overview

Microsoft has made ASC enablement simple by enabling it on all your subscriptions by default. Any subscription that is created by any user in your tenant will automatically be included in all the rich features ASC provides. All you must do is open **Security Center** once, and within minutes, you will begin seeing the following:

- Recommendations for ways to improve the security posture of resources within your subscriptions

- An immediate inventory of all resources within your subscriptions that are now being automatically assessed by **Security Center**, and their security posture

That is it! Simply launch and let the data load!

> **Technical Note**
> One neat technical item to know is that enabling ASC is technically done by Azure Policy.

Here is a screenshot of the Azure Policy initiative that controls ASC enablement:

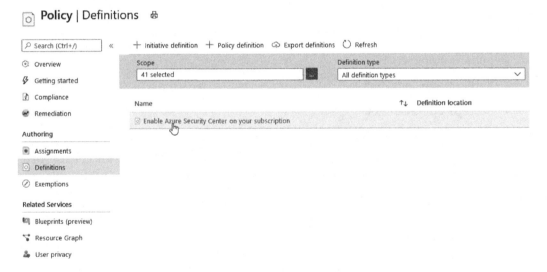

Figure 5.15 – Azure Policy

To take advantage of the additional threat protection features, we will move into showing you how to implement Microsoft Defender for Cloud on supported resource types within your subscriptions, next!

Implementing Microsoft Defender for Cloud

Having ASC enabled in your environment is a great start to strengthen your security posture; however, to protect your environment, you will lean on Microsoft Defender for Cloud. We want to walk through with you how to enable Microsoft Defender for Cloud in your enterprise.

> **Reminder**
>
> Microsoft Defender for Cloud is a solution that comes with various costs, so please review these before enabling.

Enabling Microsoft Defender for Cloud can be either a *carte blanche* task or a very granular task, down to the resource types you want protection on. Just as when you enabled ASC, some prerequisites exist before enablement is an option.

Prerequisites

Permissions are needed within Azure for you to enable Microsoft Defender for Cloud for your enterprise. Here is an outline of the available permission options that must be assigned to your user account, administrative account, or service account:

- Subscription owner
- Subscription contributor
- Security administrator

Outside of the required permissions, we want to state the importance of gaining alignment once again with proper teams. Microsoft Defender for Cloud will come with a charge that varies based on resource types. We do not want you to be shocked by a monthly bill!

So, what's next? Now that you have the proper permissions and alignment internally, we can move on to enabling Microsoft Defender for Cloud for your single subscription and then cover the steps for multiple subscriptions.

Implementation steps (single subscription)

Now, let's take a look at the implementation steps, as follows:

1. Navigate to **Security Center** from the main menu.
2. Select **Pricing and Settings** from the left-hand side of the overview page.
3. Select the subscription you want to enable Microsoft Defender for Cloud on.

4.   Select **Microsoft Defender for Cloud on**.

5.   Select **Save**.

Here is a screenshot of **Pricing and Settings | Microsoft Defender for Cloud on**:

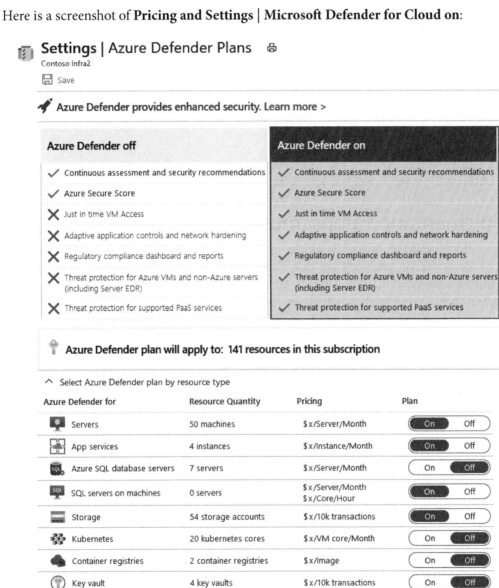

Figure 5.16 – Defender plans

Take note of the slider options you have! You can independently select per preferred resource type which plan each supported resource will have—either the free version of ASC or the paid plan option of Microsoft Defender for Cloud. Discuss these options with your team once again to ensure everyone is aligned on which resource types within your subscription you want to enable Microsoft Defender for Cloud on. You will see the pricing per resource type here as well for your rough cost calculations. Another thing to keep in mind is that what you are seeing from a resource count standpoint is what is currently deployed in your subscription. When you enable Microsoft Defender for Cloud for a specific resource type and you have automatic provisioning turned on (which we will cover a bit later), every new resource that is that same type will also be included in the Microsoft Defender for Cloud plan.

Okay—that was easy enough! But what if you wanted to enable Microsoft Defender for Cloud on multiple subscriptions? Let's cover that quickly.

Implementation steps (multiple subscriptions)

Many enterprises have multiple subscriptions within an Azure tenant—it would become quite a tedious task if you had to go into each subscription simply to enable Microsoft Defender for Cloud plans. Good news—you do not have to! Here, we outline the effortless steps to enable Microsoft Defender for Cloud at a higher level on all subscriptions, as follows:

1. Navigate to **Security Center** from the main menu.
2. Within **Security Center**, find **Getting started** within the **Security Center** sidebar.
3. Once you are in **Getting started**, you will see a list of all your subscriptions and eligible resources for onboarding, as illustrated in the following screenshot:

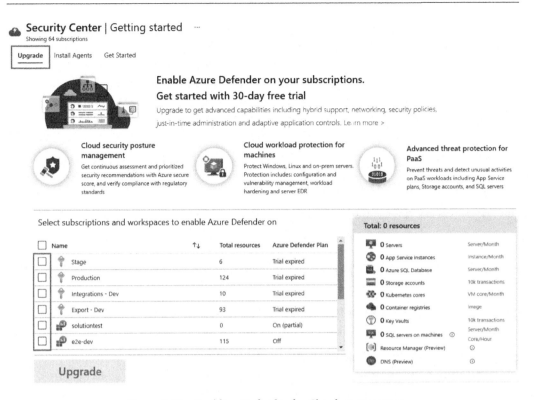

Figure 5.17 – Enabling Defender for Cloud on resources

4.   You can now select multiple subscriptions and workspaces on which to enable your Microsoft Defender for Cloud plan!

5.   Once you select the proper subscriptions and workspaces, all you need to do is select **Upgrade**, as illustrated in the following screenshot:

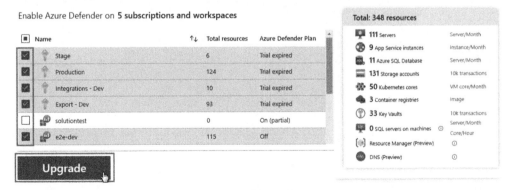

Figure 5.18 – Upgrade process

Once this happens, the necessary changes will happen automatically on your selected resources, and charges will begin.

Pretty easy, right? So, what other considerations should be taken into account when you plan to enable ASC and Microsoft Defender for Cloud in your enterprise? You must consider a plan for provisioning the agents and extensions required on resources to have ASC collect data for analysis. Normally, enterprises prefer to do this in an automatic manner through ASC automatic provisioning. Next, we outline a few key points and steps you should consider before enabling automatic provisioning.

Configuring automatic provisioning for agents and extensions from ASC

Here is a quick set of steps for the prerequisites:

> **Note**
> All the previous prerequisites exist for this step as well.

1. Navigate to **Security Center** and find **Pricing and Settings**.

2. Identify and select the appropriate subscription or subscriptions.

3. Find the **Auto provisioning** page, where you will see assorted options (we recommend turning all of them **on** where applicable). All you need to do—in theory—is turn the **Log Analytics agent for Azure VMs** extension **on**. If you would like other automatic provisioning to be completed for other required extensions based on features, then feel free to turn those settings **on** as well.

Here is a screenshot of the **Auto provisioning** settings:

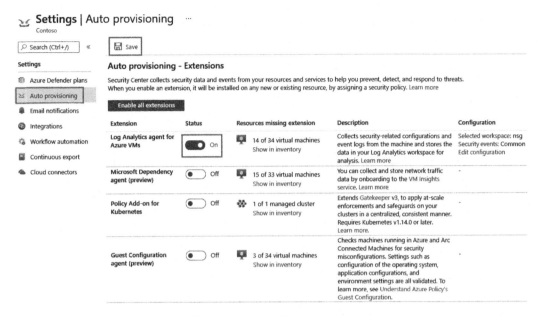

Figure 5.19 – Additional settings

4. Whenever you toggle an extension **on**, you will see a deployment configuration pane slide into view. Use this to choose which workspace you would like the data from the agent to pipe into.

5. Next, from the **Windows security events configuration** page, select the amount of raw data to store from one of the following options:

- **None**: This disables security event storage, and is the default setting.

- **Minimal**: This collects only a small amount of datasets and events for times and configurations where you might want to minimize the event volume.

- **Common**: This is a set of events that from research satisfies most customers when it comes to needing a full audit trail.

- **All Events**: Self-explanatory—this is all events.

6. Once you have decided which level of data you want to store, click **Apply**.

7. Now, you can click **Save**. Please note that this change can take up to 25 minutes to apply as the workspace is provisioned and configured in the backend.

If you previously either intentionally or accidentally configured agents for monitoring on VMs, you will be asked to reconfigure them to be connected to your new workspace. In that case, simply click **Yes**:

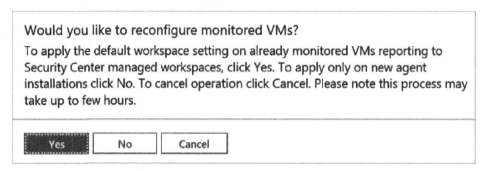

Figure 5.20 – Quick question during onboarding

Okay! You did it! You have successfully learned what ASC brings to the table from a feature standpoint, as well as learning what Microsoft Defender for Cloud brings to the table in terms of protection of your various supported workloads. Not only have you learned this, but you have also learned how to deploy both tools in your enterprise! Now, let's move on to paint a picture of how ASC and Microsoft Defender for Cloud fit into the security mold of your enterprise!

How do ASC and Microsoft Defender for Cloud fit into the security of an enterprise?

As a Microsoft security operations analyst, you will be required to have tools deployed and operational in your enterprise that serve the greater **security operations center** (**SOC**) need. ASC with Microsoft Defender for Cloud enabled provides you the ultimate security posture management and workload protection where supported resource types allow. Think about this for a second—you have this amazing solution that is doing continual assessments and pointing out vulnerabilities as well as sending you alerts on threats present or detected, along with remediation activities. This is invaluable data to have at your fingertips. This data is then able to be simply maintained in ASC, or it can be piped into a **security information and event management** (**SIEM**) tool such as Microsoft Sentinel. You can see where we are going with this—ASC and Microsoft Defender for Cloud will be connected to your Microsoft Sentinel instance for you and your team to have a view into such feeds and alerts. Later, we will get into how to set up Microsoft Sentinel and connect data sources such as Microsoft Defender for Cloud and ASC.

Summary

In summary, Microsoft Defender for Cloud is simply awesome! In this chapter, we were able to cover very important aspects of Microsoft Defender for Cloud to ensure you are not only ready to pass the *SC-200* exam on these topics but can also immediately apply this in your role as the Microsoft security operations analyst in your enterprise, from understanding what Microsoft Defender for Cloud is and how it integrates into ASC to knowing the prerequisites for deployment and implementation, and, finally, fully understanding how this truly fits into the security mold of your enterprise. This chapter is here for you to re-read and review as needed to prepare yourself to implement and utilize this tool in your enterprise today!

Next, we will be diving into chapters that are designed to ensure you can familiarize yourself with dashboards and alerts. Let's go!

Section 3 – Familiarizing Yourself with Alerts, Incidents, Evidence, and Dashboards

The objective of *Section 3* is to ensure you become uniquely familiar with each of the portals, including for alerts, incidents, evidence, and dashboards.

This part of the book comprises the following chapters:

- *Chapter 6, An Overview: Microsoft Defender for Endpoint Alerts, Incidents, Evidence, and Dashboards*
- *Chapter 7, Microsoft Defender for Identity: Alerts and Incidents*
- *Chapter 8, Microsoft Defender for Office: Threats to Productivity*
- *Chapter 9, Microsoft Defender for Cloud Apps and Protecting your Cloud Apps*

6
An Overview: Microsoft Defender for Endpoint Alerts, Incidents, Evidence, and Dashboards

One of the requirements from a skill set standpoint that you will need as the Microsoft security operations analyst for your enterprise will be the skill set in fully understanding the Microsoft Defender for Endpoint portal. You will need to know with quick precision where to go for various alerts, tasks, and reports. This knowledge will prove to be crucial daily, but especially during a time of an active incident or attack. During this chapter, we will go through an in-depth overview of the Microsoft Defender for Endpoint portal so that you are more quickly able to apply this knowledge both in the SC-200 exam and in your role as the Microsoft security operations analyst for your enterprise!

Topics we will cover include the following:

- Creating your lab environment

- General portal navigation

- Alerts and incidents

- How to suppress an alert and create a new suppression rule

We are excited to walk you through this, so now let's get into what incidents and alerts are within the Microsoft Defender for Endpoint portal!

Before we get started – acronyms and creating your lab!

Before we get started, as usual, we would like to give you a starting point for you to follow along with us during this chapter in your own personal portal navigation!

First off, this chapter will be more impactful for you if you were able to have a lab environment handy. Good news! You can get a lab that will suit all the requirements of this chapter and future chapters by signing up for a demo environment.

Creating your lab environment

There are many different routes you can take to create your lab environment that includes all the necessary licensing and configuration for you to begin exploring these solutions. However, the following outlines the steps that are the quickest for you to follow in order to take advantage of this chapter with hands-on learning!

1. Navigate to `Create your Microsoft Defender for Enpoint Trial`.

2. You will be prompted to fill out a form that asks for basic information about you, your organization, and so on. Please go ahead and fill out that information. One of the final steps that you will be asked to complete will be to set up an organization online and go ahead and make it whatever you wish (you will see `packtdemo.onmicrosoft.com` being used in future screenshots within this chapter).

   The following screenshot shows the trial signup:

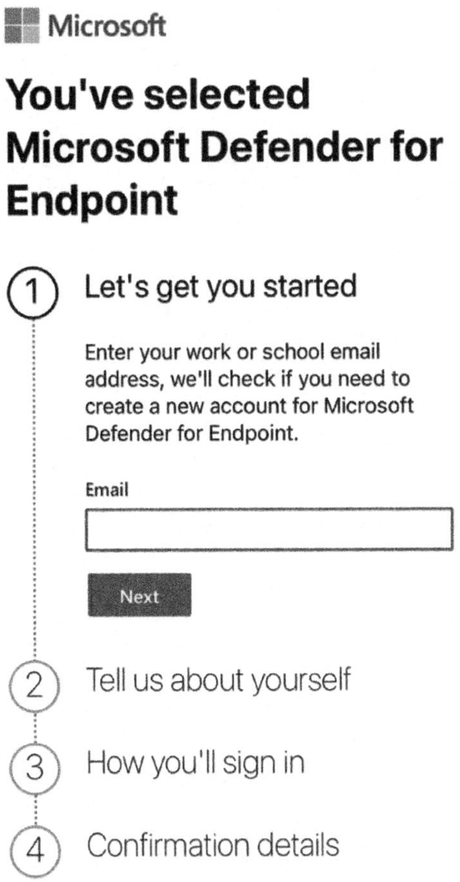

You've selected Microsoft Defender for Endpoint

(1) **Let's get you started**

Enter your work or school email address, we'll check if you need to create a new account for Microsoft Defender for Endpoint.

Email

Next

(2) Tell us about yourself

(3) How you'll sign in

(4) Confirmation details

Figure 6.1 – Trial signup

3. You have now created a lab environment. Give it about an hour for data to be piped into this lab environment before continuing.

4. After some time, you can now log in to your lab environment. To do this, simply go to `https://security.microsoft.com`!

The result

If you are successful in signing up for a Microsoft Defender for Endpoint trial, you will be able to navigate to the portal and log in successfully.

Figure 6.2 – Screenshot of Microsoft 365 Defender's home page

Now that we have covered the steps required for you to create your Microsoft Defender for Endpoint tenant, let's move on to walking through various parts of the portal, to enable you to become familiar with navigation as well as the day-to-day elements that will assist you in not only passing the SC-200 exam but also enable you to use this tool in your role as the Microsoft security operations analyst for your organization today!

General portal navigation

Whenever you head to the portal, you will have a rather long navigation pane on the left-hand side. This pane will be used for quick switching and navigation of the portal on a day-to-day basis. One thing to know about this portal is that it serves as the portal for not only Microsoft Defender for Endpoint, but also Microsoft Defender for Office 365. We want to focus specifically on the navigation elements that relate to Microsoft Defender for Endpoint, as shown in the following screenshot:

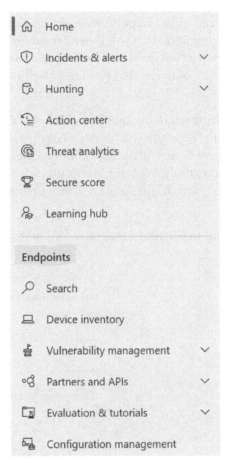

Figure 6.3 – Screenshot of the day-to-day navigation for Microsoft Defender for Endpoint

We will be covering all of the nodes within the top section (**Incidents & alerts**, **Hunting**, **Threat analytics**, **Secure score**), along with the nodes within **Endpoints** (**Device inventory**, **Vulnerability management**, and others). Now that we have your attention focused on the right part of the portal, let's dive into the specifics of each of these nodes!

Alerts and incidents

One of the areas where you will be spending time daily will be the **Incidents & alerts** node within the Microsoft Defender for Endpoint portal. **Incidents & alerts** is an area that will contain detailed information on all the alerts and incidents that are present in your environment. To fully understand the value of this node, we want to break down what each element brings to your security analysis.

First, let's cover alerts.

Alerts within Microsoft Defender for Endpoint are a critical item to bring to your attention. Alerts will be coming into Microsoft Defender for Endpoint for a multitude of reasons, with each alert having a trail for you to investigate and identify the root cause of each. This chapter will dive into both the alert portion as well as the incident investigation and evidence trail.

To begin, alerts will be visible through the **Incidents & alerts** node within Microsoft Defender for Endpoint. From there, you will be able to navigate specifically to the **Alerts** section of the portal. Alerts, by default, are grouped into incidents, and this is something that we will cover more momentarily. We want to cover the alert story; this is exactly what it sounds like – the story and details associated with each alert! Let's dive into this a bit more.

Firstly, selecting any alert within Microsoft Defender for Endpoint will bring up the alert management pane:

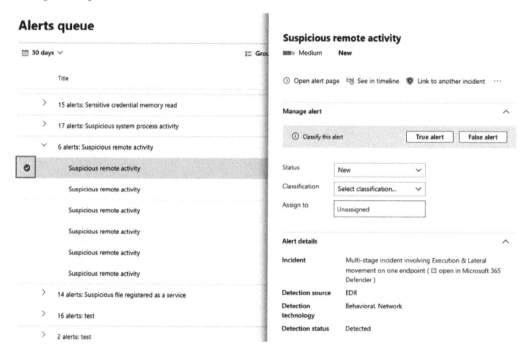

Figure 6.4 – Alert management page

From this pane, you can see quite a bit of useful detail. We will get into incident linking later on in this chapter, but for now, we will cover alert management as a whole.

Alert suppression

So, how would you want to potentially suppress alerts? There might be situations that arise where you have already verified an alert, or know of a business process that proves that the alert present is one that is of standard operations. In these scenarios, having the ability to suppress alerts will be super handy for you and your team. What is really cool is the fact that Microsoft Defender for Endpoint will allow you to create suppression rules for any alerts that are known within your environment to be safe – these can be known tools, processes, or procedures in your environment. Many times, people refer to these as *false positives* – once you onboard devices at large in your enterprise, you will commonly see multiple alerts that are coming into your queue, some valid, but many that are false positives. Do not worry! This is expected. As mentioned before, **Microsoft Defender for Endpoint (MDE)** uses **User Entity Behavioral Analytics (UEBA)** and ML to give you a better understanding of what requires your immediate attention, and with this comes a potential for a learning period for your environment specifically. This is frequently seen in alerts being generated that are not true alerts. Alert suppression will help in this scenario, not only to remove the alert from your queue, but also to train the model in terms of what is normal and what is abnormal in your enterprise.

Suppression rules can be created from any existing alerts, and not only can they be created, but they can also be disabled and re-enabled as you see fit for your environment. One thing to remember is the fact that suppression rules will take effect as soon as you create the rule, but this means only going forward. Any existing alerts that would be grouped into this suppression will not be impacted, so you must go in and clear any existing alerts that correlate to this. Simple enough!

Whenever you create an alert suppression, you will have two different contexts:

- Suppress alert on this device
- Suppress alert in my organization

Context	Definition	Example scenarios
Suppress alert on this device	Only alerts with the same title and description will be suppressed on the device. Any other alerts will continue to light up as designed.	a. A security researcher is investigating a malicious script that has been used to attack other devices in your organization. b. A developer regularly creates PowerShell scripts for their team.
Suppress alert in my organization	Only alerts with the same title on any device in your organization will be suppressed. Other alerts will continue to light up as designed.	A benign administrative tool is used by everyone in your organization.

We want to walk you through how to tactically do this within the Microsoft Defender for Endpoint portal.

How to suppress an alert and create a new suppression rule

Whenever an alert continuously comes into your queue that you have verified is either a false positive or a genuine business process, here are the steps you will take to either suppress the alert or create a suppression rule:

1. Select the alert you would like to suppress; upon doing so, you will be greeted with the alert management pane.

2. Select **Create a suppression rule**:

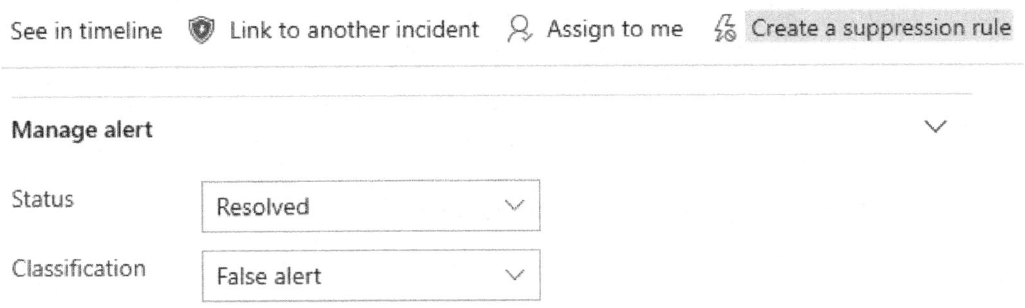

See in timeline   Link to another incident   Assign to me   Create a suppression rule

Manage alert

Status   Resolved

Classification False alert

Figure 6.5 – Creating a suppression rule

You will be able to create a suppression condition that matches the alert fired. An AND operator is applied to each condition, so think of it as this AND this must exist in order for it to match the rule, and therefore be suppressed.

Here is a list of the conditions you can choose from:

- SHA1 file.
- IP address.
- Filename – wildcard supported.
- URL – wildcard supported.
- Folder path – wildcard supported.
- Command line – wildcard supported.
- Select the triggering **Indicator of Compromise (IOC)** from the preceding options.
- Call out what action will be taken on the alert (such as automatically resolving the alert, or hiding it from the portal altogether). Please note that any automatically resolved suppressed alerts will still show in the resolved section of the alerts queue.
- Enter a name for the rule.
- Click **Save**.

You can always view the list of suppression rules by going to **Settings -> Alert suppression** to not only view the list of previously created rules, but you can also add additional comments and modify as needed.

Another important task you will be required to carry out surrounding alerts in your role will be classifying and changing the status of alerts. You can categorize alerts as **New**, **In Progress**, or **Resolved**; these will change during your investigation.

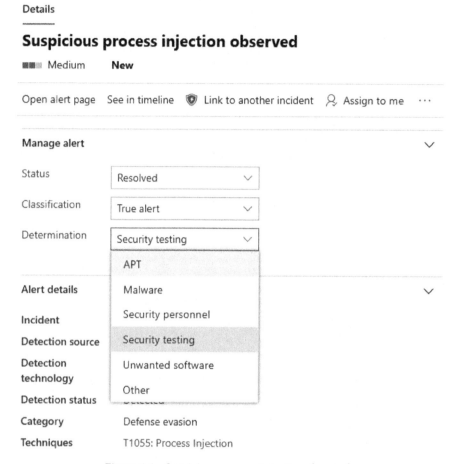

Figure 6.6 – Suspicious process injection observed

This will be helpful from an organizational standpoint! It might depend on your overall team structure, but regardless of who is responsible for changing the status, this will be a critical element to consider implementing as alerts and investigations occur in your environment.

Lastly, in addition to status changes, you will also be responsible for assisting your teams in changing the alert classification. This is immensely helpful in ensuring that only true positives are the alerts that you and your team are spending time investigating. At first, you will be changing this frequently, but as UEBA and ML take over, this will become less and less frequent.

Next, let's cover **incidents**. An incident within Microsoft Defender is a collection of alerts that have been correlated and associated to make up the foundation of an attack.

Here is a good diagram that shows how entities and alerts are analyzed against threat intelligence to become an incident:

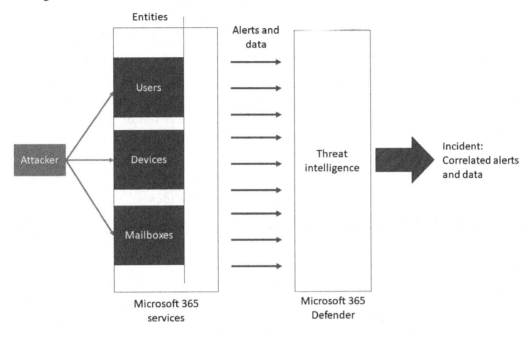

Figure 6.7 – Entities and alerts

Historically as a security analyst, you would be required to do the correlation between alerts manually; however with Microsoft Defender for Endpoint, the product does that for you! Microsoft 365 services and applications create alerts whenever they detect a suspicious or potentially malicious event or activity. You can think of this almost as whenever a door opens that seems suspicious, an alert is triggered. Individual alerts will provide you with informative clues about an ongoing or previous attack. However, typically, an attack will use various techniques against different types of entities or tactics, such as your device, your identity, or even any applications or mailboxes that you use or support. So, what happens when a similar technique is used against multiple objects? The typical result is that you have multiple alerts for multiple entities in your tenant. Think about this for a moment. What if you, along with your team, had to correlate every single alert that came into your SOC? How time-consuming and expensive from a personnel standpoint would that be for your organization? Could you budget this? Because piecing each alert together into a single story that allows you to gain insight into an attack can be challenging, time-consuming, and pricey. Luckily for you, Microsoft 365 Defender automatically aggregates the alerts and their correlated forensics into an incident.

Grouping related alerts into a single incident allows you to have a perspective on the attack. As an example, you can see the following:

- Where within your enterprise did the attack start from?

- What specific tactics and techniques were used by the attacker?

- How far did the attack go within your enterprise (devices, users, mailboxes)?

- All the additional data elements associated with the attack.

While it is great that all of this is considered, Microsoft Defender for Endpoint takes it one step further for you! Where supported, MDE will be able to automatically investigate and resolve alerts through automation and AI. Once the initial investigation is complete, you can perform any additional remediation steps you require to resolve the alert or collect additional information for future analysis.

To manage incidents in your enterprise, you will be doing this from the MDE portal within the **Incidents & alerts** node (**Incidents & alerts -> Incidents**):

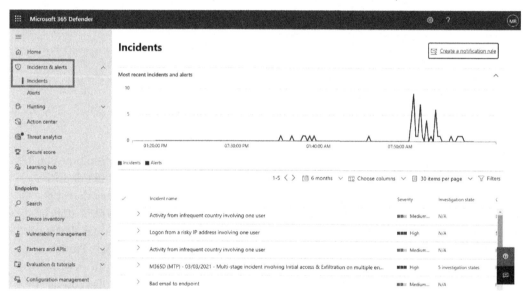

Figure 6.8 – Incidents

Once you select an incident, you will be taken to another screen that has details on that selected incident:

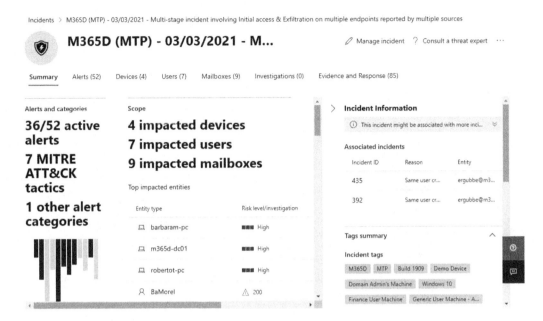

Figure 6.9 – Details on the incident selected

Here you can see that quite a bit of information is presented to you!

There are various tabs available to you, each with its own set of valuable information for your analysis:

- **Alerts**: This tab will show all the alerts related to the incident and the information for your review and analysis.

- **Devices**: This tab will show all the devices that have been identified to be part of, or related to, the incident for your review and analysis.

- **Users**: This tab will show all the users who have been identified to be part of, or related to, the incident.

- **Mailboxes**: This tab will show all the mailboxes that have been identified to be part of, or related to, the incident.

- **Investigations**: This tab will show all the automated investigations triggered by alerts in the incident.

- **Evidence and Response**: This tab will show all the supported events and suspicious entities in the alerts in the incident.

- **Graph (Preview)**: This provides you with a visual representation of the attack. This is a unique feature that can be very helpful in allowing you to map out the breadth of the attack.

While there are so many items that come into play from what alerts are correlated, and against what entities, it might be worth noting the overall relationship of this, from entities to alerts and data, processing through the threat intelligence engine, and ultimately, the result you will see in the MDE portal.

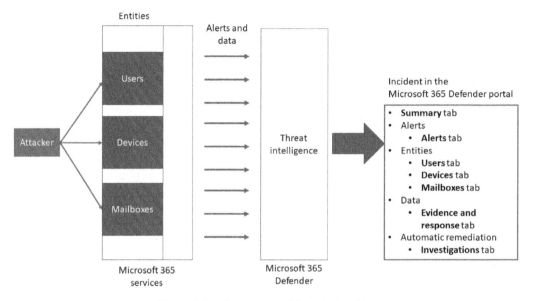

Figure 6.10 – Screenshot of this relationship

So, you might be asking, *What does a normal alert to incident workflow look like for my company?* We would like to spend some time discussing this for your awareness – here is what a typical response workflow would look like:

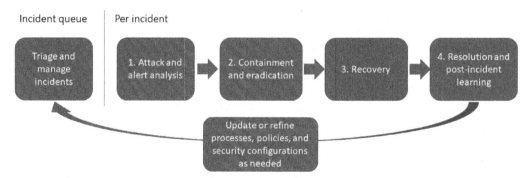

Figure 6.11 – Figure of the process chain

We want to lay this out a bit more for you – one of the largest parts of your role within your organization as the Microsoft security operations analyst is going to be identifying the highest priority incidents not just for mere analysis, but resolution as well. You will be required to put these into a prioritized incident queue and get them ready for response through various techniques (more on this, later, when we talk about Microsoft Sentinel).

This whole process is a combination of many tasks that you and your team will be required to have:

- **Triaging**: There are both manual and automatic ways of beginning the triaging process for your organization. No matter how it is done, triaging is extremely important. This step in the investigation process will allow you to determine the highest priority incident through filtering the incident queue with your team and others.

- **Managing**: Once incidents are created, you will need to manage these by potentially modifying their title and ultimately assigning them to the appropriate analyst on your team, or perhaps even another team altogether.

- There is going to be a common flow for how you manage incidents and, more importantly, work through them. Commonly, you will be required to begin an attack and alert investigation. We want to lay out some high-level tasks you will be required to do whenever an attack happens in your environment, and trust us, it will happen. You must always assume a breach!

For each incident, do the following:

- Start off by taking a look at the summary of the incident to better understand the scope and severity. Ask yourself what entities are being impacted by this attack and then begin to think about what other teams outside of your own security team might need to be involved as you continue the investigation.

- Next, start to determine the origin of this attack. Where did it initiate from? Which user? Which device? Potentially, what inbox? You can do all of this from the **Alerts** tab and within the **Devices**, **Users**, and **Mailboxes** tabs.

- Once you do this, you can then go ahead and check on the status of the overall investigation that has been kicked off by **Automatic Investigation and Response** (where supported). To see this, you will use the **Investigations** tab: if you require additional information on any investigation, you will use the **Evidence and Response** tab. This is a great tab that allows you to dig deeper into what entities were investigated along with evidence for the attack. This helps you better determine what is a true positive compared to a potential false positive. It is basically allowing you to have a single view of all the evidence of the attack, and it even includes a graph! Pretty slick. (Refer to the following *Incident Graph* section for more information.)

Incident Graph

Think about the complexities that exist when mapping out what an attacker hit. Think about being able to see the full story of the attack. Incident Graph is a feature within Microsoft Defender for Endpoint that shows you the entry point, which indicator of compromise or activity was observed (in great granular detail), and where this activity was observed. Microsoft Defender for Endpoint will aggregate threat information into incidents, as we have covered, and then take various data points and create a visual representation of this through Incident Graph:

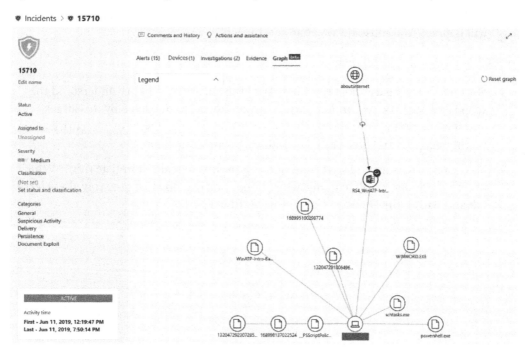

Figure 6.12 – Incident Graph

Once you are in the preceding view, you can click in the circles within Incident Graph to view granular details of the malicious files, associated file detections, how many actual instances there have been worldwide (compared to your environment specifically), and how many instances within your organization:

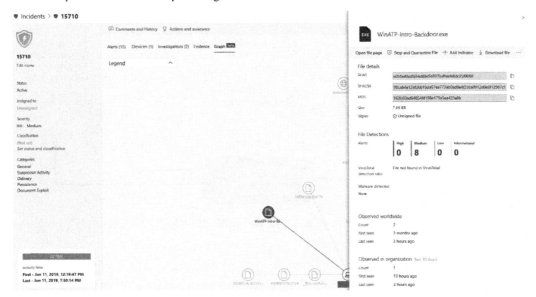

Figure 6.13 – Details within Incident Graph

Once you go through these basic day-to-day steps, you will ultimately be required to recover from this attack. This entails you saving and archiving any forensic data you have obtained by isolating devices and ensuring that you have performed proper containment and cleanup on devices, recreated any users, and quarantined any emails from mailboxes.

Once all of the aforementioned tasks have been completed, you will be able to go into the Microsoft Defender for Endpoint portal and resolve the incident. Do not be hasty here; this is where a lot of post-attack education and lesson learning can take place:

- Think about how security defenses could have been implemented differently in order to prevent this.

- Is any end user education required? For example, was this the result of an end user clicking on a phishing email? If so, how can you better educate your end users?

- Could there have been any areas of investigative improvement? How can you decrease your **Mean Time To Remediation (MTTR)**?

- What can you do daily, monthly, or quarterly to improve your security operations by using these tools?

Microsoft has published a wonderful graphic along with a list of such tasks. Here is an example of security operations for Microsoft Defender for Endpoint:

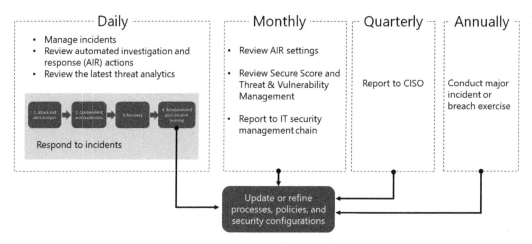

Figure 6.14 – Security operations for Microsoft Defender for Endpoint

Daily tasks

There are so many different daily tasks that you can perform but we want to mention some of the most common that we see in the roles of Microsoft security operations analyst:

- Continually manage your incidents.

- Begin reviewing any automated investigations that have occurred in your environment.

- Stay on top of the latest threat analytics (we will cover this later on in this chapter).

- Most importantly, each day, respond to incidents! Do not let them last longer than they need to. Think of it this way. Every minute during which the incident persists is another minute when the attackers are wreaking havoc in your enterprise, taking data and gaining further control, among other things.

Monthly tasks

Monthly tasks will be a bit different compared to the ones we recommend you do daily. Monthly tasks will predominately entail reviewing settings and reporting back to your management:

- Perform a security review with your IT management and security management teams. This is a great practice for allowing you to highlight current issues and establish where improvements are needed.

- Ensure you are doing a monthly review of your secure score. This score will trend over a month, and you can see what caused it to increase or decrease and modify accordingly.

Quarterly tasks

Quarterly tasks are few and far between. This is normally going to be a time that is set aside to ensure that you are still aligned with your C-levels (CISO). Inform management of the current state of your environment from a security standpoint and point out the next step objectives.

Annual tasks

Annual tasks are normally going to be meant for tests. These tests can be for your end users, or even for your SOC team. These annual tests are meant to gauge the readiness of your SOC team while also testing the educational readiness of your end users to not click the improper links or fall victim to spear-phishing campaigns. Of course, you can do this more often, but at a minimum, we recommend this be an annual task.

Summary

We wanted to ensure that the content is digestible and, quite frankly, there is a lot here to digest. We hope you were able to acquire an in-depth understanding of the importance of alerts and incidents within Microsoft Defender for Endpoint. These will be the first two areas that you will be required to know in your daily life as the Microsoft security operations analyst for your company, and of course, use this knowledge to pass the Microsoft SC-200 exam!

We will cover the following remaining topics in the next chapter:

- MDI concepts
- Understanding and investigating alerts
- Triaging and responding to alerts

We look forward to walking alongside you on the preceding topics. Now, go get yourself a coffee, take a break, and let's get going into the next chapter!

7

Microsoft Defender for Identity, What Happened, Alerts, and Incidents

Alright, folks, it's time. We're going *deep*, deep into **Microsoft Defender for Identity (MDI)**. As I've stated before, MDI is one of or if not my favorite tool in the M365 security stack. It provides so much rich information on your Active Directory environment, including network traffic to and from domain controllers, security logs, sites and subnets, and entity information. All of that is taken in and used to identify indicators of attack. It can also create alerts if an actual attack is detected, as well as providing your **Security Operations Center (SOC)** with threat signals from the network for you to go and investigate. We won't touch on this much, but MDI also supports RADIUS logs for VPN services. Of course, by adding RADIUS logs to your MDI tenant, you get added user information that includes any VPN connection information for that user. Details such as IP address and location with origination – these types of things can help with deeper investigations.

Taking that into consideration, let's look at what we'll cover in this chapter. We're going to cover the following core topics:

- MDI concepts

- Understanding and investigating alerts

- Triaging and responding to alerts

I'm very excited to get into the thick of MDI, covering several key concepts, such as navigating the portal as it relates to MDI, different alert types and activities that are monitored, entity profiles, and **Lateral Movement Paths** (**LMPs**), and understanding fundamentally how MDI uses **Network Name Resolution** (**NNR**). From there on, we'll get into investigating alerts, drilling into the users or devices in question to learn about what might have happened. After that, we'll dive into triaging and responding to alerts, where we'll cover the recommendations **M365 Defender** presents as items to focus on and prioritize, or even what it has automated for you.

Technical requirements

As we move into the later chapters, the technical requirements will start to increase in difficulty for some, but stay with it, we're here to learn together! Let's outline this chapter's requirements with the following:

- Familiarity navigating `Security.Microsoft.com`

- Familiarity with the MITRE ATT&CK framework

- Basic understanding of lateral movement

- Fundamental understanding of Active Directory and authentication methods

MDI concepts

In the next few sections of this chapter, we're going to talk through a handful of core concepts of MDI, from navigating the portal to understanding some of the different monitored activities and how it uses NNR to learn more about entities.

Having these concepts down will give you the information to understand how MDI works and what it's looking for once installed in your environments. Let's keep it moving and start things off by navigating the portal.

Navigating the portal

First things first, let's head over to the `Security.Microsoft.com` portal. From the home page, we're going to scroll down to the bottom and on the lower left-hand side, we'll see **Settings**, as shown in *Figure 7.1*. Go ahead and click that:

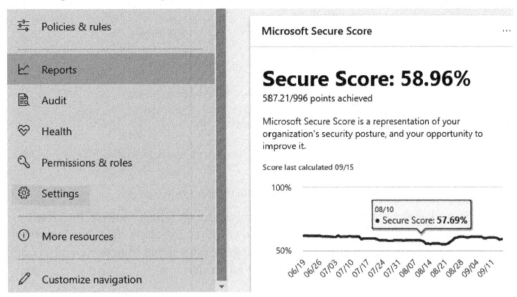

Figure 7.1 – Security portal – Settings location

> **Important Note**
>
> There will be many things in this chapter that you might find confusing to find in your lab. This is because, at the time of writing this book, Microsoft is migrating MDI from the `domain.atp.azure` portal to the `security.microsoft.com` portal. The docs can sometimes refer to something in the older portal, where it's changed or enhanced in the new one.

We should now be at the **Settings** menu, as shown in *Figure 7.2*, for each segment within the M365 security stack, starting with **Security center**. Depending on what licensing you have, you may not see all the options; however, if you're running an E5 demo like me, you'll get the whole kit and caboodle:

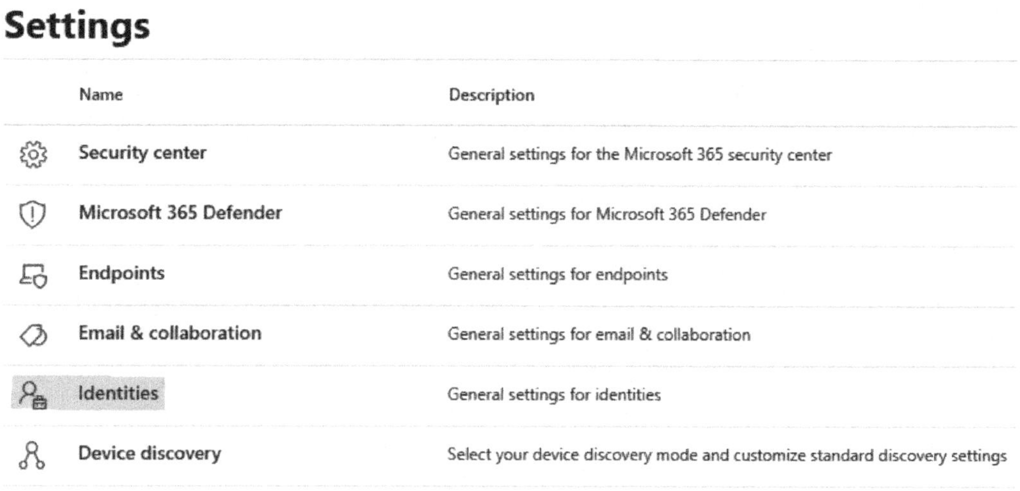

Settings

	Name	Description
⚙️	Security center	General settings for the Microsoft 365 security center
🛡️	Microsoft 365 Defender	General settings for Microsoft 365 Defender
🖥️	Endpoints	General settings for endpoints
🔷	Email & collaboration	General settings for email & collaboration
👤	Identities	General settings for identities
👤	Device discovery	Select your device discovery mode and customize standard discovery settings

Figure 7.2 – Settings menu in the security portal

If we think back to the old portal for a second, `domain.atp.azure.com`, the attack timeline was the landing page (see *Figure 7.3*), so you'd see any alerts right away and from there navigate into your settings. In the new portal, we get a single page to view all of our alerts and the settings are in a dedicated spot for all services:

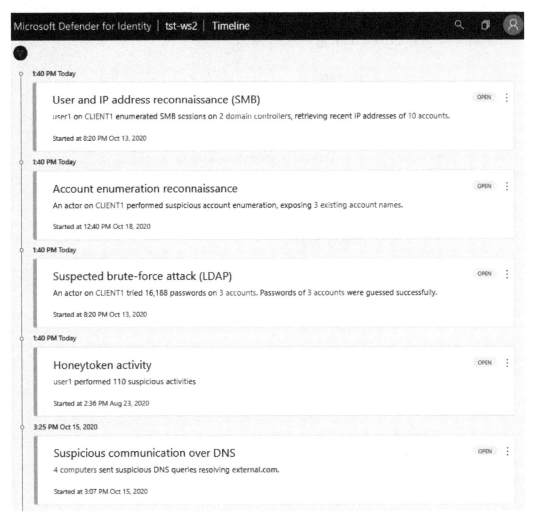

Figure 7.3 – Legacy portal landing page

Getting back to the **Settings** menu, let's cover what we see in *Figure 7.4* from top to bottom so we're comfortable finding what we need:

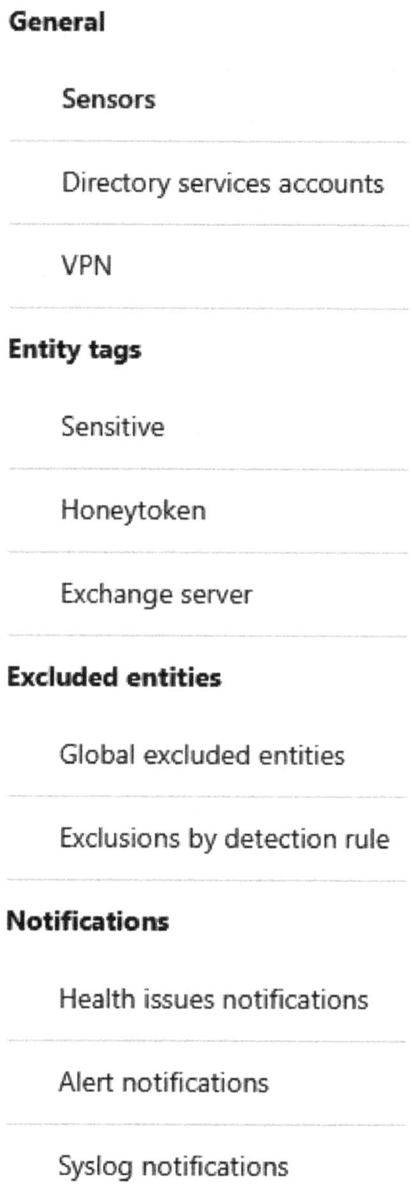

General

Sensors

Directory services accounts

VPN

Entity tags

Sensitive

Honeytoken

Exchange server

Excluded entities

Global excluded entities

Exclusions by detection rule

Notifications

Health issues notifications

Alert notifications

Syslog notifications

Figure 7.4 – MDI settings menu

First up, under **General**, we have **Sensors** (*Figure 7.5*). If we remember from the onboarding part of the book, back in *Chapter 4, Implementing Microsoft Defender for Identity*, we know this is where we'll see all the domain controllers or AD FS servers we onboarded. You'll get all the details of each server, including its name, type, sensor version, update status, service status, and health status. If there are any health issues with a particular server, select it, and the pop-out pane will show, as we see in *Figure 7.6*. We also have **Global health issues** in the upper right-hand corner of *Figure 7.5*, where we can view the alerts on one page for all sensors:

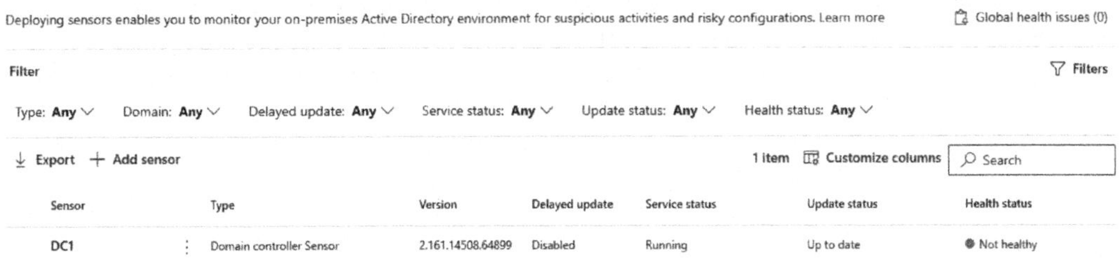

Sensor		Type	Version	Delayed update	Service status	Update status	Health status
DC1	:	Domain controller Sensor	2.161.14508.64899	Disabled	Running	Up to date	● Not healthy

Figure 7.5 – Sensors page

Figure 7.6 shows the popout when you click on **Global health issues**; it shows all sensor issues in the tenant:

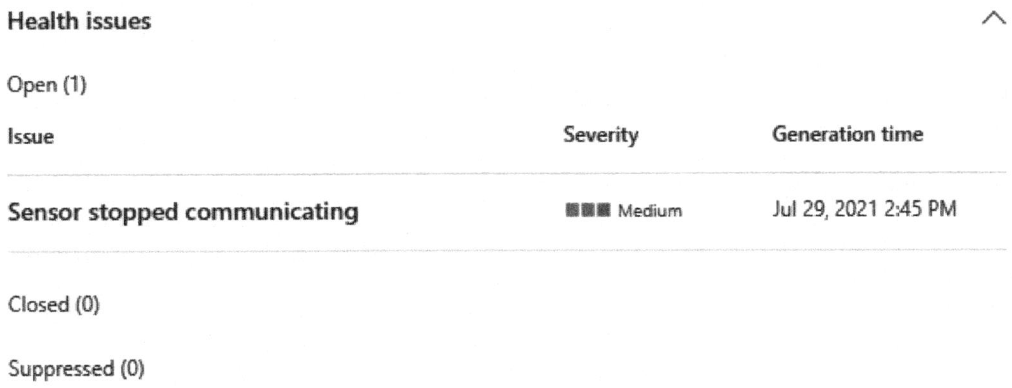

Health issues

Open (1)

Issue	Severity	Generation time
Sensor stopped communicating	▨▨▨ Medium	Jul 29, 2021 2:45 PM

Closed (0)

Suppressed (0)

Figure 7.6 – Domain controller page

Moving on to the next settings page, we have **Directory services accounts** (*Figure 7.7*). This is where we will manage the service accounts used for our sensors to query to Active Directory. These are read-only accounts that you would have created just for this service to use. Depending on how many domains you have, you can add one set of credentials for each. If you have two-way trust between your domains, you can add one account. It's recommended to use a gMSA account for a few reasons: it's more secure and there's no password management – the Windows operating system manages the password for the account instead of the administrator. When adding a gMSA account, remember to check the **Group managed service account** box (see *Figure 7.8*). If you need help creating one, see this doc – `https://docs.microsoft.com/en-us/windows-server/security/group-managed-service-accounts/getting-started-with-group-managed-service-accounts`:

Manage Directory services accounts used to connect sensors with your on-premises Active Directory domains. Learn more

Filter

Domain: **Any** ∨   Group managed service account: **Any** ∨

↓ Export   + Create new account

Account	Domain	Group managed service account ⓘ
IDPMDI	⋮ contoso.com	True

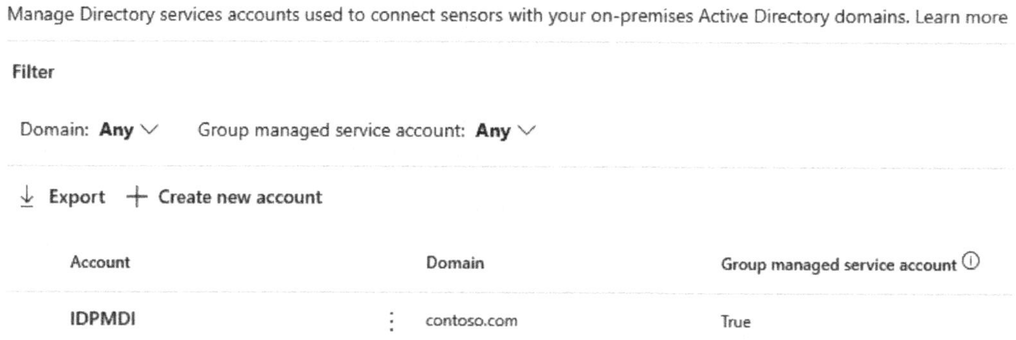

Figure 7.7 – Directory services accounts page

When adding a gMSA account, check the box, as you can see in *Figure 7.7*:

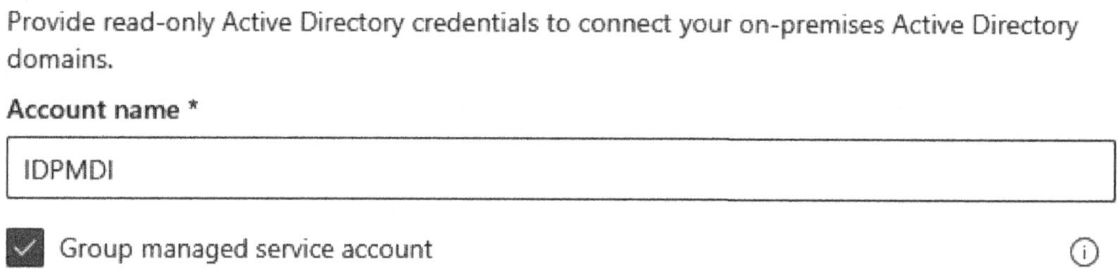

Provide read-only Active Directory credentials to connect your on-premises Active Directory domains.

Account name *

IDPMDI

✔ Group managed service account   ⓘ

Figure 7.8 – Selected service account page

Integrating VPN accounting information from select VPN solutions is another setting that's available to configure. Here, you can pick up additional information from a user's profile page that will include additional information from their VPN connection, such as the originating location and IP address. This can, of course, be useful for investigations as it provides additional information on user activity as well as unusual VPN connections:

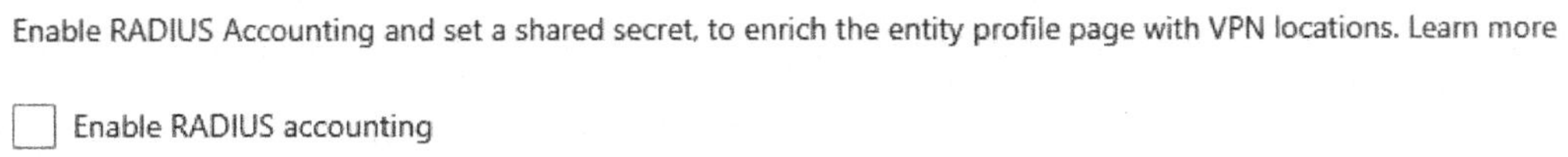

Enable RADIUS Accounting and set a shared secret, to enrich the entity profile page with VPN locations. Learn more

☐ Enable RADIUS accounting

Figure 7.9 – VPN settings page – RADIUS account logs

Moving on, the next section within the MDI settings is **Entity tags**. Under that, the first setting is the sensitive accounts page. This is where you identify and tag high-value accounts in your environment, such as executives or other business decision-makers. Any entity, user, or machine that falls into the following groups will be added for you:

- Administrators

- Power Users

- Account Operators

- Server Operators

- Print Operators

- Backup Operators

- Replicators

- Network Configuration Operators

- Incoming Forest Trust Builders

- Domain Admins

- Domain Controllers

- Group Policy Creator Owners

- Read-only Domain Controllers

- Enterprise Read-only Domain Controllers

- Schema Admins

- Enterprise Admins

- Microsoft Exchange Servers

See *Figure 7.10* for an example of the **Users** page of the sensitive accounts section. As you can see, the two administrator accounts in my lab were automatically added:

Figure 7.10 – Sensitive accounts page

Next, we have honeytoken accounts, which can be used as bait for threat actors. These accounts usually sit inactive but when used will throw specific alerts about honeytoken use. I went ahead and tagged one of the user accounts I don't use often as a honeytoken account as an example. See *Figure 7.11*:

Figure 7.11 – Honeytoken accounts page

Next up after the **Entity tags** section is **Excluded entities**. Here, you can define global excludes, such as users, domains, devices, and IP addresses. This would be used for things such as security scanners that might use DNS for their use. This can help reduce some of the noise and alert fatigue for SOC analysts. *Figure 7.12* shows an example of the exclusion page and the different fields laid out previously:

Figure 7.12 – Globally excluded entities page

Another aspect of exclusions is that you can add exclusions explicitly by detection rule. So, if you wanted to omit alerts for certain entities for something such as suspected NTLM authentication tampering or suspicious VPN connection, you could do so. See *Figure 7.13* for a sample of a few detection rules:

Detection rule		Excluded entities
Suspected overpass-the-hash attack (Kerberos)	⋮	-
Suspected NTLM authentication tampering	⋮	-
Suspicious additions to sensitive groups	⋮	-
Suspected brute-force attack (SMB)	⋮	-
Suspected use of Metasploit hacking framework	⋮	-
Suspected WannaCry ransomware attack	⋮	-
Suspicious VPN Connection	⋮	-
Account enumeration reconnaissance	⋮	-

Figure 7.13 – Excluded entities, exclusions by detection rule

The last section under the settings for MDI is **Notifications**, which should be pretty self-explanatory: you're setting the users or distribution groups for which you want to get alerts for health issues or alerts. There is a section called **Syslog notifications** that would be of use for some teams. Here, you can actually configure one of your sensors to send suspicious activity alerts related to security and health to a Syslog server. *Figure 7.14* shows how easy that setup is:

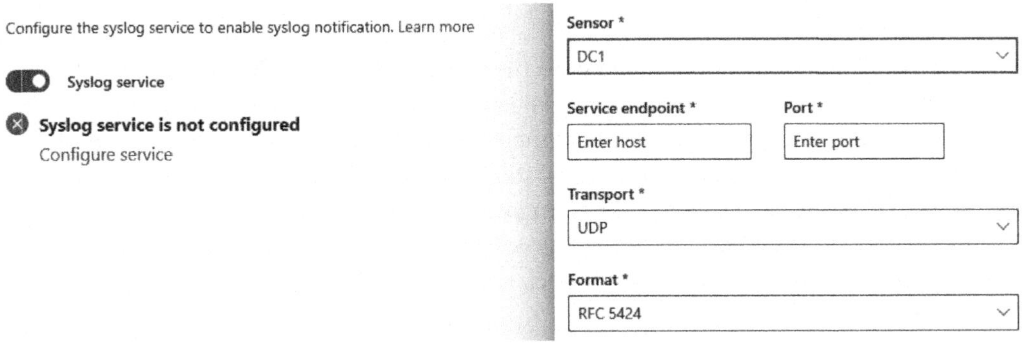

Configure the syslog service to enable syslog notification. Learn more

⬤ Syslog service

⊗ **Syslog service is not configured**
   Configure service

Sensor *
DC1 ⌄

Service endpoint *   Port *
Enter host   Enter port

Transport *
UDP ⌄

Format *
RFC 5424 ⌄

Figure 7.14 – Syslog service configuration page

That's all for the settings aspect of MDI; we've covered all pages at a high level so that you're familiar with where to go as you start building this out. In terms of navigating the portal, beyond configuration settings, it's really just looking at alerts. We won't go deep into that quite yet as we'll cover it in more depth later in the chapter.

At a quick glance, you can either view all the alerts at once or filter specifically on **Microsoft Defender for Identity** for the service source, as shown in *Figure 7.15*:

Alerts

Figure 7.15 – Alerts page, filtered to Microsoft Defender for Identity

Alrighty, that was a pivotal moment here as we started the journey into the goods of MDI. We've covered preparing for and deploying MDI and we've navigated the portal, covering the configuration settings there. Now it's time we talk about what MDI can do!

MDI alert categories and phases

MDI breaks down alerts into different categories, such as reconnaissance, compromised credentials, lateral movement, domain dominance, and exfiltration, that align with the typical phases seen in the Cyber Kill Chain framework. In this next section, we'll go into those phases and explain some of the activities MDI detects for it on the network, which will highlight the actors and machines associated with the alert being raised.

Reconnaissance

So, what is reconnaissance? Plainly put, it's the process of looking for and gathering information that will be useful for a potential attack. Most of the time, this is the longest phase as intelligent threat actors will take their time doing their due diligence finding out everything they can about networks, systems on the network, applications in the environment, as well as the users interacting with everything. The more time they spend, the more success they're likely to have. This phase can go far outside of just the network itself, including things such as social media, websites, blogs, or general search engine results.

Looking at what typically happens on entry for cyber-attacks, it's the low-hanging fruit that gets exploited. Low-privileged accounts are the starting point; from there, they move laterally until they reach something of value. This can be privileged accounts that have access to sensitive data, which could be an assortment of administrator accounts present on machines due to poor Active Directory habits.

One such method for finding low-hanging fruit during reconnaissance would be account enumeration, where they use tools that try to find valid usernames. One such tool is **KrbGuess**, which makes a **Ticket-Granting Ticket** (**TGT**) request to the **Key Distribution Service** (**KDC**) and then looks at the response it gets back. It looks for a response of **Preauthentication required** being returned instead of **Security principal unknown**. The former response means it matched a valid username. *Figure 7.15* shows an example of what that might look like as an alert within MDI:

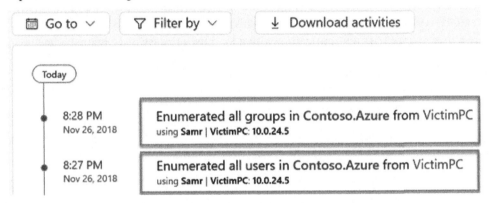

Figure 7.16 – Reconnaissance, account enumeration example

I would recommend you take this a step further and read the following documentation to learn about more attack types for MDI, how to understand them, remediation, and steps to prevent them.

The following link and list will help you learn about reconnaissance phase alerts, Microsoft Docs: `https://docs.microsoft.com/en-us/defender-for-identity/reconnaissance-alerts`.

- Account enumeration reconnaissance (external ID 2003)

- Active Directory attributes reconnaissance (LDAP) (external ID 2210)

- Network mapping reconnaissance (DNS) (external ID 2007)

- Security principal reconnaissance (LDAP) (external ID 2038)

- User and Group membership reconnaissance (SAMR) (external ID 2021)

- User and IP address reconnaissance (SMB) (external ID 2012)

Compromised credentials

When we talk about the compromised credentials phase and alerting, we're looking at things such as activity with honeytoken accounts, brute-force attacks, or detecting tooling known to aid in account compromise. The theme is you're looking for activity in accounts that is out of the ordinary or malicious. Let's cover the previous examples in a little more detail.

Honeytoken accounts, as we mentioned when covering the portal, are decoy accounts used to expose a threat actor. They're accounts created and tagged as honeytoken accounts, not used for anything other than alerting. They're generally given a name of interest to a threat actor to tempt them, which if taken will alert immediately and give them away.

Another alert type you'll see in the compromised credentials phase is an array of brute-force attack types, whether it's with Kerberos, NTLM, LDAP, or SMB. These are attacks where a threat actor tries authenticating with a long list of passwords against a few accounts or a few passwords against a long list of accounts. Eventually, they get a match and can then start logging in with that account and look to move laterally:

Figure 7.17 – Compromised credentials, Mimikatz, credential theft example

As recommended in the *Reconnaissance* section, you should read the documentation on this phase to learn about additional attack types that MDI alerts for in this phase.

The following link and list will help you learn about compromised credentials phase alerts, Microsoft Docs: `https://docs.microsoft.com/en-us/defender-for-identity/compromised-credentials-alerts#suspected-wannacry-ransomware-attack-external-id-2035`

- Honeytoken activity (external ID 2014)

- Suspected brute-force attack (Kerberos, NTLM) (external ID 2023)

- Suspected brute-force attack (LDAP) (external ID 2004)

- Suspected brute-force attack (SMB) (external ID 2033)

- Suspected Kerberos SPN exposure (external ID 2410)

- Suspected Netlogon privilege elevation attempt (CVE-2020-1472 exploitation) (external ID 2411)

- Suspected AS-REP roasting attack (external ID 2412)

- Suspected WannaCry ransomware attack (external ID 2035)

- Suspected use of Metasploit hacking framework (external ID 2034)

- Suspicious VPN connection (external ID 2025)

Lateral movement

Protecting against lateral movement goes beyond having complex passwords or password rotations, hardened machines, or securely stored data. Threat actors can still exploit instances where an account with sensitive privileges logs in to a device where the non-sensitive user that the device belongs to has local rights. They'll start with the low-hanging fruit, then move laterally, gaining credentials for the sensitive account.

There are several methods by which this can be accomplished. Using techniques such as pass the hash, overpass the hash, or pass the ticket, threat actors can use credentials to move around laterally in the environment until they get where they need to perform further initiatives, such as domain dominance, and eventually to exfiltration.

In *Figure 7.18* and *Figure 7.19*, you'll see examples of MDI information when it discovers new activities on an account where an LMP has been discovered:

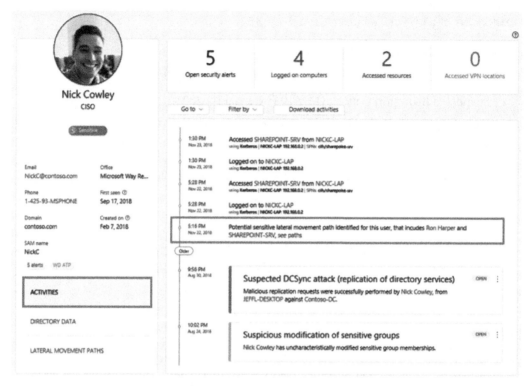

Figure 7.18 – Lateral movement, user profile lateral movement activity

Figure 7.19 shows the path of lateral movement from the user's page:

Figure 7.19 – Lateral movement, user profile LMP

Continuing the recommendations of additional documentation to read for more information on alert types for lateral movement, see the following:

> **Note**
> The following link and list will help you learn about lateral movement phase alerts – https://docs.microsoft.com/en-us/defender-for-identity/lateral-movement-alerts.

- Suspected exploitation attempt on Windows Print Spooler service (external ID 2415)

- Remote code execution over DNS (external ID 2036)

- Suspected identity theft (pass-the-hash) (external ID 2017)

- Suspected identity theft (pass-the-ticket) (external ID 2018)

- Suspected NTLM authentication tampering (external ID 2039)

- Suspected NTLM relay attack (Exchange account) (external ID 2037)

- Suspected overpass-the-hash attack (Kerberos) (external ID 2002)

- Suspected rogue Kerberos certificate usage (external ID 2047)

- Suspected SMB packet manipulation (CVE-2020-0796 exploitation) (external ID 2406)

- Suspicious network connection over Encrypting File System Remote Protocol (external ID 2416)

- Exchange Server Remote Code Execution (CVE-2021-26855) (external ID 2414)

Domain dominance

Domain dominance alerts are ones that generally start to elevate your heart rate if you're unfamiliar with them, especially when you start reading the MITRE ATT&CK technique links provided in the alert. If we're looking at the Cyber Kill Chain framework, this step represents the fact the threat actor has obtained a level of privilege that gives them access to your domain controllers. This level of access means they can do just about anything they want. This is the stage where highly sophisticated attackers will start planting backup persistence so that if their initial entry is found and terminated, they're still in business.

Some examples of these would be the dreaded golden ticket alert, a suspected skeleton key attack where encryption downgrades are offered, DCSync, or DCShadow attacks:

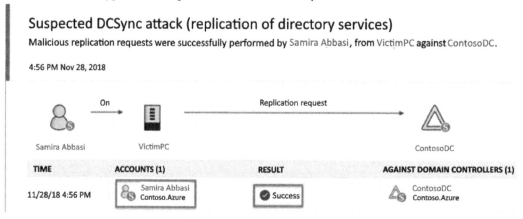

Figure 7.20 – Domain dominance, DCSync attack example

Let's move on to the last phase of alerts for MDI, **exfiltration**. At this stage, the attacker is on their last step: they've come in, snooped around, and gained a foothold. They then found what they were looking for and staged it to be uploaded out of the environment, in what we call exfiltration. This is typically the `NTDS.dit` file that resides on each domain controller, which stores all Active Directory information in it. We're talking all user accounts and their password hashes, the goodies! In this stage, the attacker will often compress and encrypt the files and send it out a **Command and Control (C2)** they have open. Depending on what you know about the timeline at this point, it may be difficult to understand exactly what has been exfiltrated; however, following the alerts should give you some direction for further analysis.

At this point, we've covered a lot: the portal itself and how to get some additional configurations in place. We talked about the different phases and alerts that MDI presents for you and now we'll dive into some of the more granular things, such as entity profiles, followed by the main functional component of MDI, NNR.

Entity profiles

When we talk about entities, or mention entity, we're referring to the array of users, devices, or computers and resources those users and devices can access, as well as the history of them as they move around.

Figure 7.21 provides an example of a user entity page. On this page, the left-hand pane provides some high-level Active Directory information, such as contact information, some information regarding exposure, such as first/last seen, on what devices and what logon types, and any groups they're a part of. What MDI does in the background is bring all this information together to build an activity timeline of up to 6 months of data of interesting events or alerts, which is presented on the right-hand side of the page:

Figure 7.21 – User entity page

To get to a page like you see in *Figure 7.21*, you can search for a particular entity, or you can click any entity hyperlink on the incidents or alert pages, as we see highlighted in red in *Figure 7.22*. See the following URL for updates as the transition to the new portal continues – `https://docs.microsoft.com/en-us/defender-for-identity/entity-profiles`:

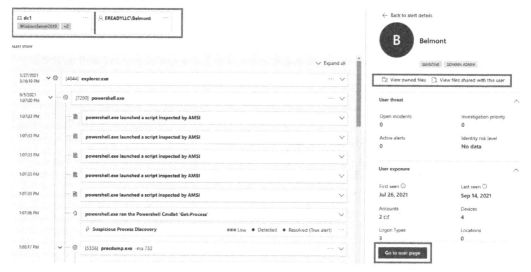

Figure 7.22 – Entities in alerts

Before we get into NNR, let's talk about some of the monitored activities.

Monitored activities

We won't cover all of them as there are a ton, but we'll cover what monitored activities are and some examples. See the following URL to get a complete list: `https://docs.microsoft.com/en-us/defender-for-identity/monitored-activities`.

First, let's break these down into the following categories:

- User account Active Directory attribute changes
- Active Directory security principal operations
- Domain controller-based user operations
- Login operations
- Machine account activities

As you can imagine, with each of these comes very specific changes that are typically, in some way, associated with malicious behavior. Watching for changes in these areas on your domain controllers helps add activities and events to alerts.

Network name resolution

Moving into the last section of core concepts, we are going to cover something called NNR. This component is what aids MDI in capturing activities based on network traffic as well as Windows events and **Event Tracing for Windows (ETW)**. Since these things generally contain IP data, using NNR, Defender for Identity will correlate the activities in the raw data with the computers involved. It's able to get these computer names by using NNR to resolve the IP addresses inside the data captured.

There are three primary methods and one secondary method NNR uses to do this. The primary methods are as follows:

- NTLM over RPC (TCP port 135)
- NetBIOS (UDP port 137)
- RDP (TCP port 3389) – only the first packet of client hello

The secondary method is it queries the DNS server using reverse DNS lookup of the IP address (UDP port 53).

See *Table 7.1* for the prerequisites:

Protocol	Transport	Port	Device	Direction
NTLM over RPC*	TCP	135	All devices on the network	Inbound
NetBIOS*	UDP	137	All devices on the network	Inbound
RDP*	TCP	3389	All devices on the network	Inbound
DNS	UDP	53	Domain controllers	Outbound

Table 7.1 – NNR table – protocols and port information

If you are working in a hardened environment where some, or all, of the primary methods are blocked, reverse DNS lookups of the IP address are performed, but it's recommended that at least one primary is used.

The MDI sensor will throw an alert if it detects that the resolution status has a low success rate due to too many methods and nothing working properly. See *Figure 7.23* for an example:

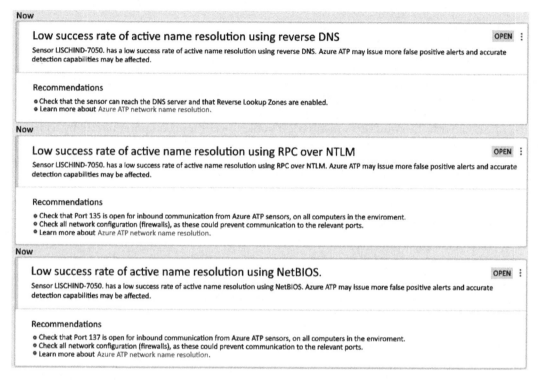

Figure 7.23 – Low success rate MDI sensor error

The process of correlating IP addresses and computer objects goes like this: MDI will analyze the network traffic to determine machine names. From there, the sensor checks Active Directory, comparing what TCP fingerprints it has, to see whether it correlates to an object with the same name. This process helps find machines that are registered to Active Directory as well as ones that are not, providing more accurate information in alerts and investigations. This information is crucial for threats such as the following:

- Suspected identity theft (pass the ticket)
- Suspected DCSync attack (replication of directory services)
- Network mapping reconnaissance (DNS)

Some final configuration recommendations, which can be found at `https://docs.microsoft.com/en-us/defender-for-identity/nnr-policy#configuration-recommendations`, are listed as follows:

- NTLM over RPC:

  - Check that TCP port `135` is open for inbound communication from MDI sensors on all computers in the environment.

  - Check all network configurations (firewalls), as this can prevent communication to the relevant ports.

- NetBIOS:

  - Check that UDP port `137` is open for inbound communication from MDI sensors on all computers in the environment.

  - Check all network configuration (firewalls), as this can prevent communication to the relevant ports.

- RDP:

  - Check that TCP port `3389` is open for inbound communication from MDI sensors on all computers in the environment.

  - Check all network configurations (firewalls), as this can prevent communication to the relevant ports.

- Reverse DNS:

  - Check that the sensor can reach the DNS server and that reverse lookup zones are enabled.

Alright, now that we have covered most of the core concepts, let's switch over to understanding more about alerts so you can make sense of what's in them. Next up is understanding and investigating alerts.

Understanding and investigating alerts

I feel like we're at the cusp of what we've all been waiting for, and that's digging into alerts to see what's going on and what we can do about it. But before we do that, there's one last thing I want to cover and that's ensuring we know all aspects of the alert itself.

When it comes to the structure of the alert, we're presented with *What happened* on the left-hand side of the page, and it reads sort of like a timeline. On the right-hand side of the page, we get more of the details, such as detection source, activity timestamps, description, and entity types involved. You'll often see a link to a docs page that tells you more about that alert type.

Another thing you'll notice is if the alert is a part of an incident, there are mentions of the entities involved. See *Figure 7.24* as an example:

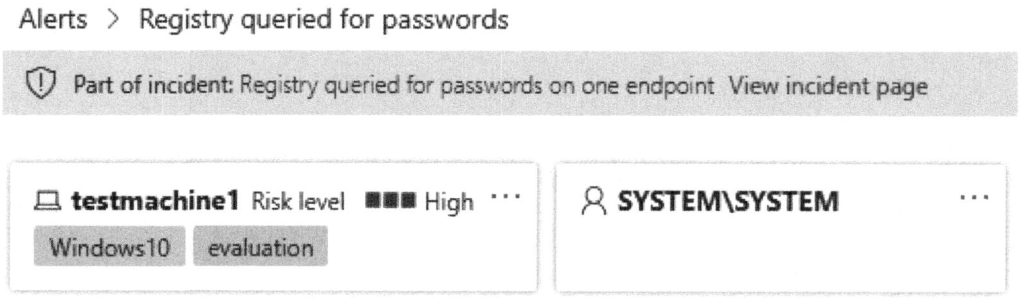

Alerts > Registry queried for passwords

Part of incident: Registry queried for passwords on one endpoint View incident page

🖥 **testmachine1** Risk level ■■■ High ···   A **SYSTEM\SYSTEM**   ···

Windows10   evaluation

Figure 7.24 – Alert structure example

Starting with a breakdown of the right-hand side, you'll see at the top that it's not classified. This is because you'll set that after your initial investigation. *Figure 7.25* shows an example of the alert state and default state of the alert:

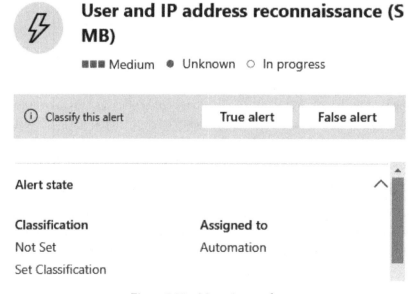

Figure 7.25 – Managing an alert

The following figure is what you're presented with when you set it as a true alert, with a list of options for determination:

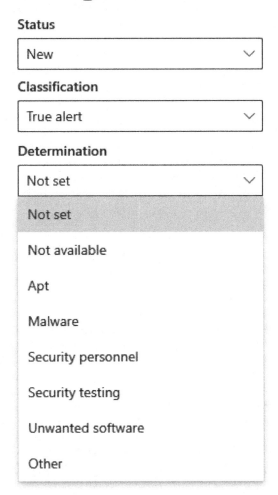

Figure 7.26 – Managing an alert

The next section on the right pane is **Alert details**. This gives us information such as the category of the alert, what MITRE ATT&CK technique it aligns with, along with a link that takes you to the MITRE ATT&CK framework page to learn more. Here is where we'll see what detected the alert: MDI, MDE, Defender Antivirus, and so on. See *Figure 7.27* for an example:

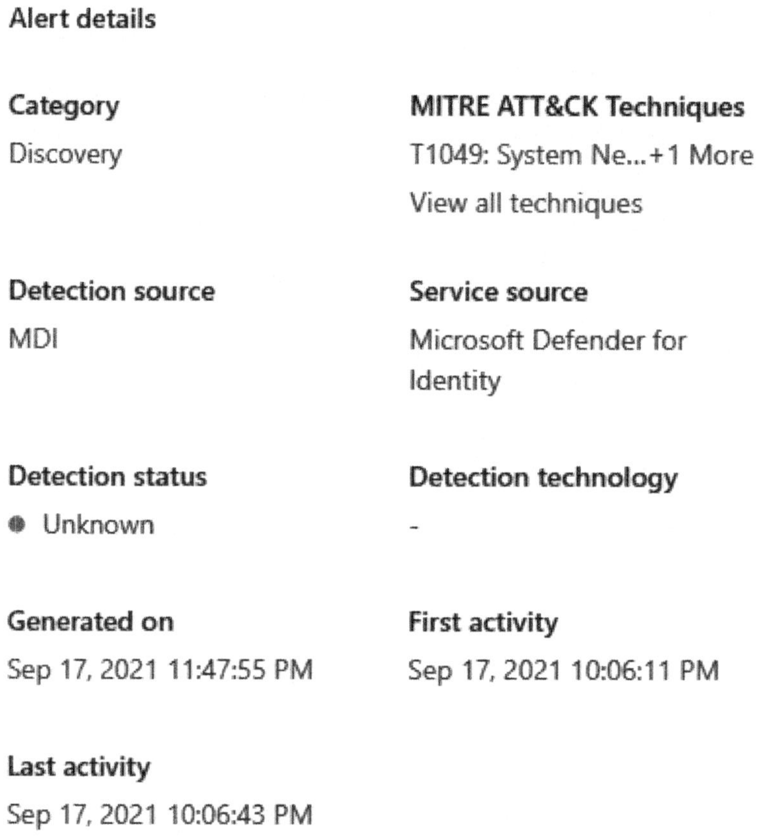

Alert details

Category	**MITRE ATT&CK Techniques**
Discovery	T1049: System Ne...+1 More
	View all techniques
Detection source	**Service source**
MDI	Microsoft Defender for Identity
Detection status	**Detection technology**
● Unknown	-
Generated on	**First activity**
Sep 17, 2021 11:47:55 PM	Sep 17, 2021 10:06:11 PM
Last activity	
Sep 17, 2021 10:06:43 PM	

Figure 7.27 – Alert details

Moving on to the next segment on the right, we have some more alert information, such as a link to the docs page that gives you more information about the alert and some suggestions as well as remediations to help give you direction. See *Figure 7.28* for an example:

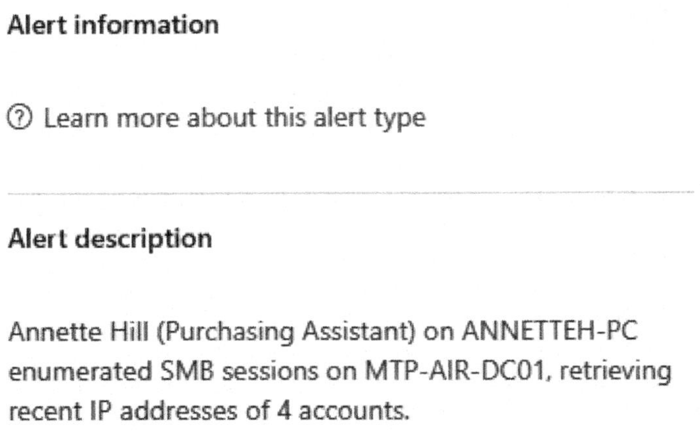

Alert information

⑦ Learn more about this alert type

Alert description

Annette Hill (Purchasing Assistant) on ANNETTEH-PC
enumerated SMB sessions on MTP-AIR-DC01, retrieving
recent IP addresses of 4 accounts.

Figure 7.28 – Alert information

After the alert information, we'll see more information about the incident it's a part of as
well as its severity. You'll also get a link to that incident so you can quickly see the larger
picture. Below that information is a breakdown of the entities included in the incident, as
well as how those items may be linked. See *Figure 7.29* for an example:

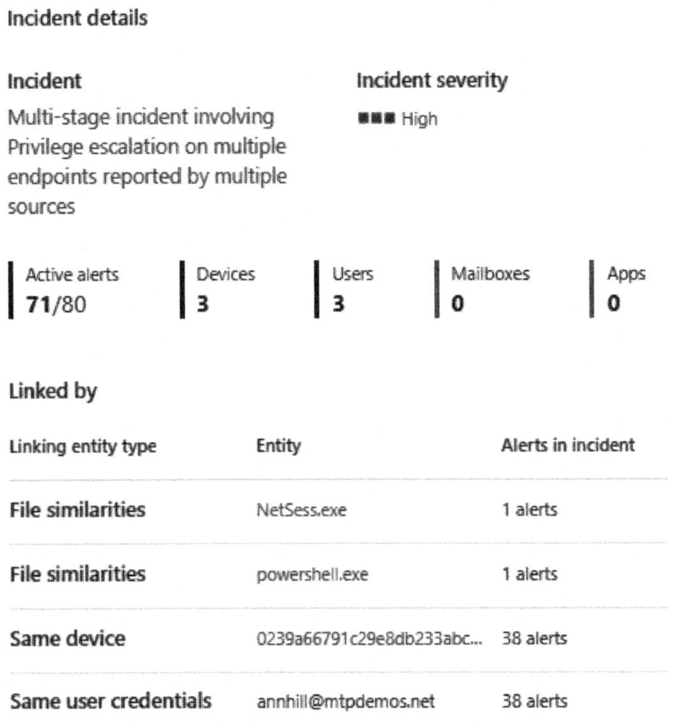

Incident details

Incident

Multi-stage incident involving
Privilege escalation on multiple
endpoints reported by multiple
sources

Incident severity

■■■ High

Active alerts	Devices	Users	Mailboxes	Apps
71/80	**3**	**3**	**0**	**0**

Linked by

Linking entity type	Entity	Alerts in incident
File similarities	NetSess.exe	1 alerts
File similarities	powershell.exe	1 alerts
Same device	0239a66791c29e8db233abc...	38 alerts
Same user credentials	annhill@mtpdemos.net	38 alerts

Figure 7.29 – Incident details

Wrapping up the right-hand alert pane, we have information about the automated investigation, such as status, when it started, and when it ended. Below that, you get another look at the assets impacted in the investigation and its current risk score. Lastly, you get a comment section, where you can add notes from things you've looked at or something you want other analysts to read. Let's also not forget any enrichment data from Defender for Endpoint should you have that integration enabled:

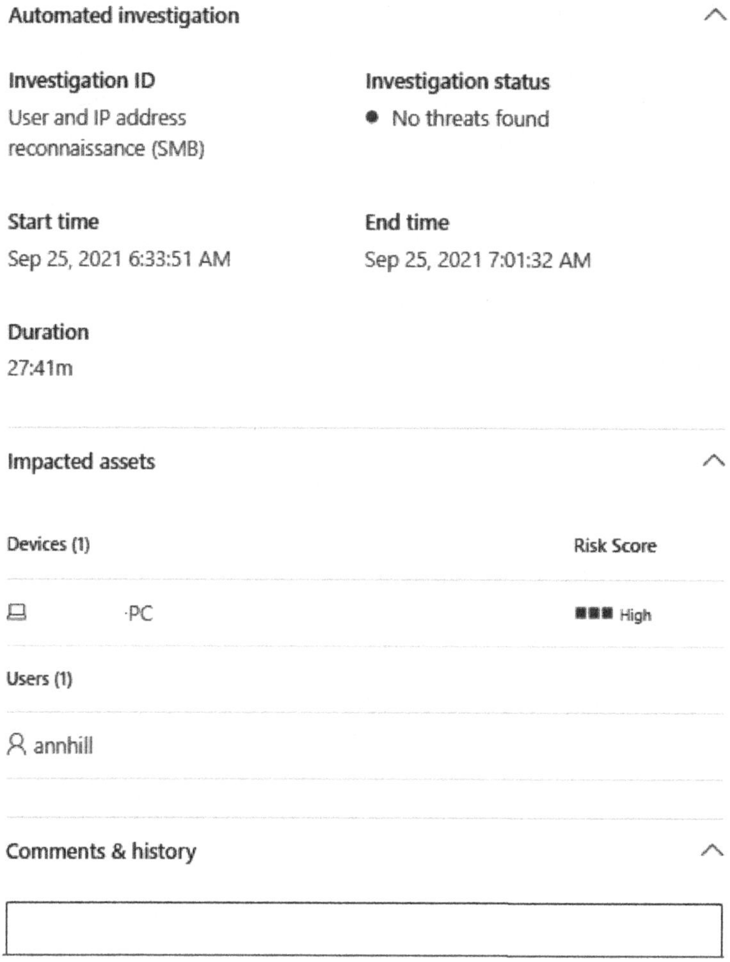

Automated investigation   ︿

Investigation ID   **Investigation status**
User and IP address   ● No threats found
reconnaissance (SMB)

Start time   **End time**
Sep 25, 2021 6:33:51 AM   Sep 25, 2021 7:01:32 AM

Duration
27:41m

Impacted assets   ︿

Devices (1)   Risk Score

🖥   ·PC   ■■■ High

Users (1)

👤 annhill

Comments & history   ︿

Figure 7.30 – Investigation information and assets involved

Moving into the last section of the chapter, let's update and talk about what we just learned. We talked about several of the key concepts of MDI and we covered what an MDI alert looks like, including a breakdown of the alert itself, what information is presented, and how to deal with it. Now we'll take all of that and start looking at sample alerts and how we might respond to them. Let's go!

Triaging and responding to alerts

Triaging and responding to alerts is one of if not the most important part of this whole process. No matter how many security products you have, no matter how well you have them configured, threat actors will always find a way if they have to. This is why responding to and accurately assessing alerts is crucial. Being able to contain a breach quickly and confidently can make or break a company. In this section of the chapter, we'll cover some alerts around the reconnaissance phase. From there, we'll piece together what's happening and how we can respond.

Let's start with some alerts we might see as an attack ensues, and what they might mean. In *Figure 7.30*, we see the beginning of some reconnaissance. Network mapping reconnaissance, for example, is a method to map out the environment and build out a knowledge base for later use. In the following example, we see `srv2012r2` appears to be requesting some suspicious DNS queries from DC1:

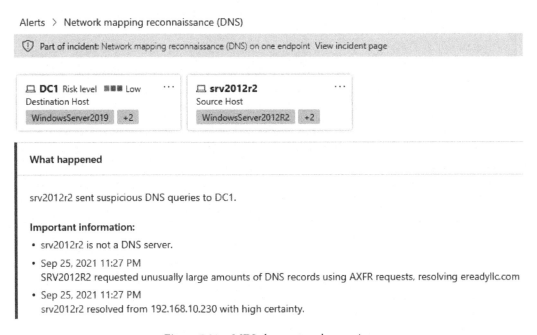

Figure 7.31 – MDI alert, network mapping

Take a look at the evidence at the bottom of the alert in *Figure 7.31* for more details. We get details about the entities involved and what stood out:

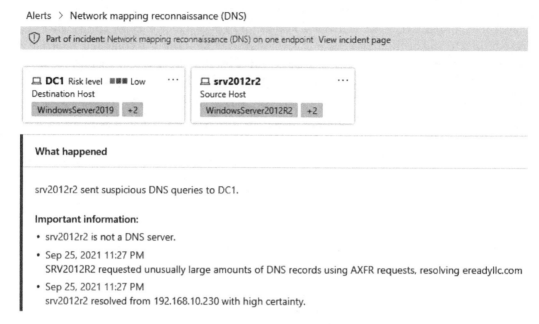

Figure 7.32 – MDI alert, network mapping

Now, if we remember from the previous section, we know that we should see some information in the alert details that tells us more about the detection, such as the service source (MDI). Right below that, we see **Alert information** and a link that says **Learn more about this alert type**. If we click that link, we'll be taken to a docs page that gives us a description and information from the MITRE framework on the tactic and technique it relates to. See *Figure 7.33* for an example:

Important Note

Alert doc – `https://docs.microsoft.com/en-us/defender-for-identity/reconnaissance-alerts#network-mapping-reconnaissance-dns-external-id-2007`:

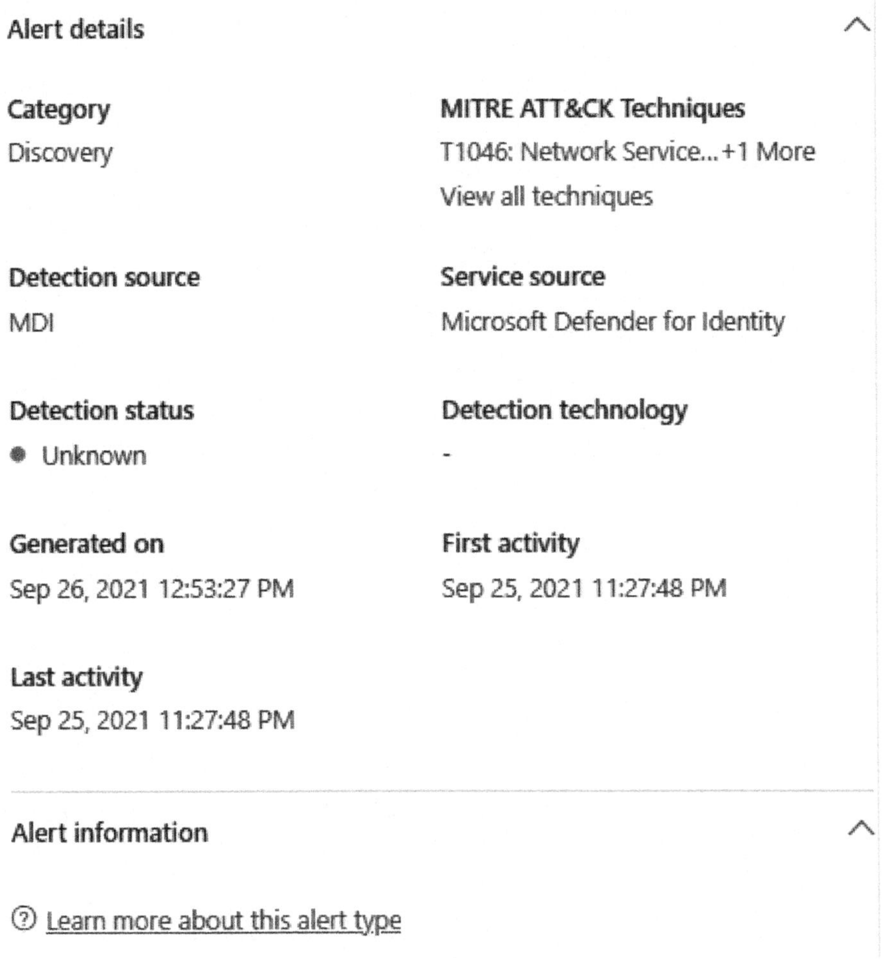

Alert details   ∧

Category

Discovery

MITRE ATT&CK Techniques

T1046: Network Service...+1 More

View all techniques

Detection source

MDI

Service source

Microsoft Defender for Identity

Detection status

● Unknown

Detection technology

-

Generated on

Sep 26, 2021 12:53:27 PM

First activity

Sep 25, 2021 11:27:48 PM

Last activity

Sep 25, 2021 11:27:48 PM

Alert information   ∧

⑦ Learn more about this alert type

Figure 7.33 – Alert details

There are a few things these articles help with, such as helping you decide whether it's a legitimate alert or not. So, in this instance, the first step would be to decide whether the source machine in the alert is a domain controller or not. If it is, we can mark this as a false alert as would be expected. It's worth considering the learning period for this alert, which is provided in the docs, to help you decide as well. Anything within that learning period can lead to false alerts as the sensor is still defining what normal behavior in the environment is.

After deciding that, next we see we should be checking for any security scanners or applications that would be generating DNS queries. If that's the case, you can mark it as a true alert but benign. Beyond that, we get some recommendations for remediation and prevention; see *Figure 7.33* for an example:

Suggested remediation and steps for prevention

Remediation:

- Contain the source computer.
  - Find the tool that performed the attack and remove it.
  - Look for users who were logged on around the same time as the activity occurred, as these users may also be compromised. Reset their passwords and enable MFA or, if you've configured the relevant high-risk user policies in Azure Active Directory Identity Protection, you can use the **Confirm user compromised** action in the Cloud App Security portal.

Prevention:

It's important to preventing future attacks using AXFR queries by securing your internal DNS server.

- Secure your internal DNS server to prevent reconnaissance using DNS by disabling zone transfers or by restricting zone transfers only to specified IP addresses. Modifying zone transfers is one task among a checklist that should be addressed for securing your DNS servers from both internal and external attacks.

Figure 7.34 – Example remediation and prevention

Let's look quickly at how we could help mitigate this reconnaissance attempt with a zone transfer restriction. If you head over to the domain controller in our lab and open DNS manager, you'll be able to see the **Zone Transfer** tab in the properties on either your forward lookup zones or reverse lookup zones. You'll have the following options, as shown in *Figure 7.35*:

- To disable zone transfers, clear the **Allow zone transfers** checkbox and then click **OK.**

- To allow zone transfers, select the **Allow zone transfers** checkbox, and then do one of the following:

  - To allow zone transfers to any server, select **To any server** and then click **OK.**

- To allow zone transfers only to the DNS servers that are listed on the **Name Servers** tab, select **Only to servers listed on the Name Servers** tab and then click **OK**.

- To allow zone transfers only to specific DNS servers, select **Only to the following servers**, add the IP address of one or more DNS servers, and then click **OK**.

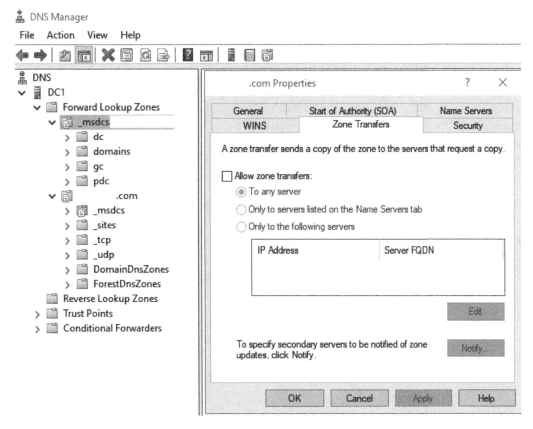

Figure 7.35 – Securing zone transfers

As a test, I tried to transfer the zone to another test box, and I got the following error in *Figure 7.36* showing that's not allowed:

```
> ls -d ████████.com
[dc1.          .com]
*** Can't list domain ███████.com: Query refused
The DNS server refused to transfer the zone ███████.com to your computer. If t
his
is incorrect, check the zone transfer security settings for ████████.com on the
 DNS
server at IP address 192.168.10.101.
```

Figure 7.36 – Securing zone transfers

This is just one example of triaging alerts and evaluating remediations based on the alert type. There are three really good alert labs that you can go through just like this one, as we followed the reconnaissance workflow automation in this example. See the following docs page to get your lab configured with the accounts and tools so that you can follow along and start learning: Alert lab workflow automation – `https://docs.microsoft.com/en-us/defender-for-identity/playbook-lab-overview`.

Summary

Looking back on this chapter, we learned a ton! We covered everything from how to navigate the portal regarding MDI, what all the different settings mean, and why we'd configure them. We talked about a bunch of the core concepts surrounding MDI, the types of activities it tracks, and how the sensor itself looks at that traffic. Then, we dove into what an alert is, the breakdown of it, and everything included in it. After that, we started triaging actual alerts and looking into what they mean and how we can respond to them, from a remediation and prevention standpoint.

Take some time before moving into the next chapter to go through some of the workflow automations that Microsoft provides, so that you can start creating alerts on your own to see how that looks from an offensive and defensive perspective. Learn how those attacks work and what you can do to prevent them or at least make it difficult. You'll learn a ton about your own environment and its posture when you go through these, learning where your gaps in coverage are.

I hope you enjoyed this chapter as much as I did. We could have gone into so much more and deeper into what we did cover, but we must move forward. I'm looking forward to sharing more on **Defender for Office** in *Chapter 8, Microsoft Defender for Office: Threats to Productivity*. See you there!

8
Microsoft Defender for Office – Threats to Productivity

Microsoft Defender for Office (MDO) is the next *Defender* product in our sights, this time for your email and collaboration tools. This seems to be one of the more underutilized sets of tools, and I think that's primarily because a lot of this suite has come into its own recently. Bringing the features of MDO under the `Security.Microsoft.com` portal umbrella has helped shine a light on them for those not familiar with them.

I think there are plenty of exciting things to cover with MDO, such as **Exchange Online Protection (EOP)**, which is included by default as it's really at the core of MDO. Then, there are other features, such as safe links, safe attachments, anti-phishing, and attack simulation training. We'll cover these in detail throughout this chapter. Two licenses can sum up everything we'll discuss, which we'll cover quickly before continuing with this chapter. As I mentioned previously, EOP is included as a core product – it's included in all tenants that have online mailboxes. Once we start looking at the products that provide post-breach, automation, and simulation training, we will move that slider toward the P2 license, as shown in the following diagram. This flow of features is also how you would typically go about configuring them in any environment you work in, starting with EOP and working toward the full MDO suite:

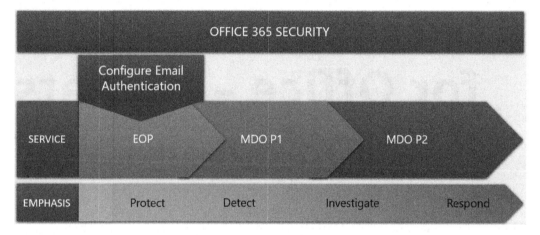

Figure 8.1 – Microsoft Defender for Office license diagram

We'll break these features down into the four categories that Microsoft poses for us. These categories will outline this chapter for us, so let's take a look at the topics we'll be covering:

- Threat protection policies
- Threat investigation and response capabilities
- Automated investigation and response capabilities
- Data loss prevention and insider risk

Technical requirements

The technical requirements for this chapter will be less holistic in terms of environmental variables. What I mean by that is that it's less about operating systems and patch levels and more about the features themselves as they pertain to productivity configurations. Nonetheless, we'll define a few areas you'll want to be familiar with when it comes to this chapter, as follows:

- The `Security.Microsoft.com` portal
- Exchange Online and the **Exchange admin center (AEC)**
- Email authentication
- Safe attachments, phishing, and anti-spam concepts
- Navigating SharePoint OneDrive and Teams documents libraries
- Microsoft information protection and data loss prevention concepts

Threat protection policies

Threat protection policies provide a great way to configure the necessary protection for your organization when it comes to Office 365. They're all conveniently in one spot for you to view. Before we get into the policies themselves, let's highlight what policies there are and the two main ways we can configure them.

First things first, let's head over to `https://security.microsoft.com/threatpolicy`. From here, we'll see two sections for policies: **Templated policies** (*Figure 8.2*) and **Policies** (*Figure 8.3*).

Templated policies, or preset policies, provide a centralized approach to applying a series of policies at once in either a strict or standard fashion. This gives you a bundles approach so that you can apply strict policies leadership and maybe standard policies to everyone else, ensuring the most sensitive communication is protected. Like most things in Windows environments, when you have situations where both are applied, the most restrictive wins that battle. Note that standard policies take precedence over custom ones.

In this section, we'll look at the configuration analyzer, which gives you a breakdown of where all of your current settings fall and whether the recommended protection is being used. This will also show you when new settings arrive, so be sure to check it frequently to get those enabled. A breakdown of the policies it analyzes are as follows:

- EOP policies:
    - Anti-spam policies
    - Anti-malware policies
    - EOP anti-phishing policies
- Microsoft Defender for Office 365 policies:
    - Anti-phishing policies in Microsoft Defender for Office 365, which include the following:
        - The same spoof settings that are available in the EOP anti-phishing policies.
        - Impersonation settings
        - Advanced phishing thresholds:
    - Safe Links policies
    - Safe Attachments policies

The following screenshot shows some templated policies:

Threat policies

Templated policies

🗝	Preset Security Policies	Easily configure protection by applying all policies at once using our recommended protection templates
🗝	Configuration analyzer	Identify issues in your current policy configuration to improve your security

Figure 8.2 – Templated policies for MDO

Moving on from the presets and what those can configure, let's dive into the policies themselves. The next section is where you can configure each policy individually if you wanted more granular control. Looking at the following screenshot, let's start from the top and work our way down:

Policies

↻	Anti-phishing	Protect users from phishing attacks, and configure safety tips on suspicious messages.
✉	Anti-spam	Protect your organization's email from spam, including what actions to take if spam is detected
☠	Anti-malware	Protect your organization's email from malware, including what actions to take and who to notify if malware is detected
📎	Safe Attachments	Protect your organization from malicious contect in email attachments and files in SharePoint, OneDrive, and Teams
🔗	Safe Links	Protect your users from opening and sharing malicious links in email messages and Office apps

Figure 8.3 – Policies for MDO

Let's delve deeper into these policies, starting with anti-phishing policies.

Anti-phishing

Anti-phishing policies help protect against phishing attempts, which are attacks where the main objective is to bait you into giving up sensitive information. This is generally accomplished by sending messages that look legitimate and from trusted senders. Phishing is often broken into a few different categories, such as the following:

- Spear phishing, which is usually specifically tailored to the recipient.

- Whaling, which is meant for executives and other high-value targets.

- Business email compromise, where trusted senders are forged and trick people into giving up information or even approving payments or fund transfers.

- Ransomware, which is one of the worst kinds. Detecting these kinds of phishing emails can stop large-scale campaigns from hitting companies.

The following screenshot shows an example of what the policy pane looks like when it's selected for edits:

Figure 8.4 – The Anti-phishing policy window

Looking at the protection that's provided in this policy, we have things such as spoof intelligence, which allows you to review detected senders in messages that come in from external or even internal domains and manually mark them as **Allow** or **Block**. Other protection includes implicit email authentication, which enhances standard email authentication by checking for things such as SPF, DKIM, and DMARC. These can help you decipher sender reputation, sender history, and receipt history:

- **Sender Policy Framework (SPF)**: This is the process of updating DNS so that you can use the SPF's email authentication with your domain. It's a way to help validate outbound emails so that it's easier to prove that they came from your domain.

- **DomainKeys Identified Mail (DKIM)**: This is the second form of authentication that helps prevent threat actors from sending messages that look like they're from your environment. DKIM adds a signature to your outbound mail inside the header as extra validation.

- **Domain-based Message Authentication Reporting and Conformance (DMARC)**: This works as the third authentication protection. It works alongside SPF and DKIM to authenticate senders to make sure the destination email systems trust messages from your domain.

To learn more about email authentication and what it can do, go to `https://docs.microsoft.com/en-us/microsoft-365/security/office-365-security/email-validation-and-authentication?view=o365-worldwide`.

Anti-spam

Anti-spam policies are designed to help reduce the amount of junk email a domain receives. It's comprised of a proprietary filtering technology to identify and separate mail to do just that. Let's look at some of the things that make up the anti-spam policy:

- **Connection Filtering**: This is a feature that determines good email sources from bad ones based on what's defined in the IP Allow or Block list, as well as the safe list.

- **Spam Filtering**: Using the spam filtering verdicts from EOP, it classifies messages as spam, bulk email, or phishing.

- **Outbound Spam Filtering**: This works on the outbound side of things to ensure people aren't sending spam out.

Spam filtering is configured by default to send messages marked as spam to your junk folder. However, if the environment you're working in has a hybrid configuration, you'll need to configure mail flow rules to get this same behavior.

The following screenshot shows what the policy pane looks like when it's been selected for edits:

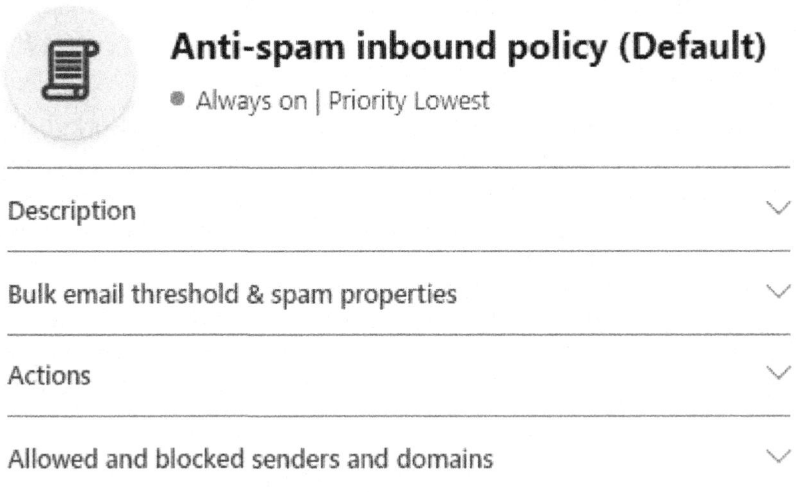

Anti-spam inbound policy (Default)

● Always on | Priority Lowest

Description	∨
Bulk email threshold & spam properties	∨
Actions	∨
Allowed and blocked senders and domains	∨

Figure 8.5 – The Anti-spam inbound policy (Default) window

Now that we have covered anti-spam policies, let's delve into anti-malware policies.

Anti-malware

Anti-malware policies help you defend against messages that may contain malware; any such message that's found is immediately quarantined. These types of messages can be broken into three different categories:

- **Viruses**: These traditionally infect other programs and data, speeding through the network looking to do the same thing where it can.

- **Spyware**: This is something that can gather information, such as sign-in details or personal information, to then send it back to its author.

- **Ransomware**: This, as we've mentioned many times so far in this book, aims to encrypt your data and demand payment for decryption.

Three main forms of protection are working behind the scenes with this policy when it's enabled, in a layered approach for optimal protection. These features are as follows:

- **Layered Defenses Against Malware**: This consists of several anti-malware scanning engines that provide self-learning detection in an attempt to give early detection during an outbreak.

- **Real-Time Threat Response**: This is an incredible service that works behind the scenes. The anti-malware team can use it to provide policy rules that detect threats before any definitions are written and deployed for use in the anti-malware engine. Rules of this kind are published to a global network every 2 hours for organizations to leverage.

- **Fast Anti-Malware Definition Deployment**: This is similar in concept to real-time protection on the AV side of things. This service leverages relationships with several close partners of Microsoft who also develop anti-malware engines to provide updated definitions by the hour.

The following screenshot shows what the policy pane looks like when it's been selected for edits:

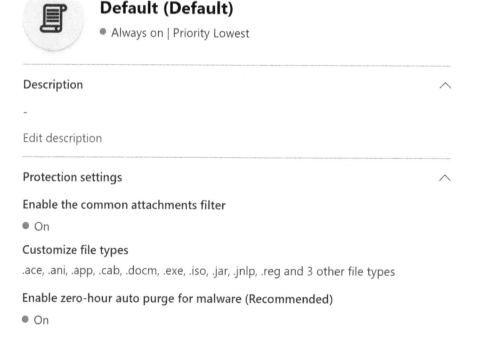

Figure 8.6 – Anti-malware policy window

Before we get into **Safe-Attachment** and **Safe-Links**, I wanted to talk about **zero-hour purge** (**ZAP**), which is something that's used in anti-phishing, anti-malware, and anti-spam. ZAP is a feature that can retroactively detect and remove malicious messages that were already delivered to a mailbox. It does this by leveraging the spam and malware signatures that are updated in real time daily, to continuously monitor messages even when they've already been delivered. Owners of the mailbox are not even aware of this service; it's seamless and will remove messages without the user knowing.

One caveat of this is that the safe sender lists override this protection, which is why it's very important to be careful when you're configuring what messages can bypass filtering. Overdoing it with additions can remove some of your protection, such as ZAP. To learn more about ZAP and where and how it's used, go to `https://docs.microsoft.com/en-us/microsoft-365/security/office-365-security/zero-hour-auto-purge?view=o365-worldwide#zero-hour-auto-purge-zap-for-phishing`.

Safe attachments

Moving onto the last two topics now, let's talk about **safe attachments**. Safe attachments is yet another layer of protection that's provided by MDO. This is an additional scan beyond what the anti-malware service may have already done. It does this by something called detonation, where it opens the attachment in a virtual environment before it's delivered to see if it's malicious. It does this in a data center in the same region where your tenant resides for the best performance.

An important note about safe attachments is that, unlike the other policies, there is no default policy – you need to create one to get this protection. Visit the following URL for additional information on it and its policies: `https://docs.microsoft.com/en-us/microsoft-365/security/office-365-security/safe-attachments?view=o365-worldwide`.

Safe links

Finally, there's **safe links**. This is a URL scanning form of protection that provides protection when emails contain URLs that could be obscured to encourage users to click on and give up sensitive information. This is done in addition to the anti-spam and anti-malware protection that's performed on incoming messages. This protection is available for Office 365 apps, as well as Microsoft Teams. To learn more about safe links, visit the following URL: `https://docs.microsoft.com/en-us/microsoft-365/security/office-365-security/safe-links?view=o365-worldwide`.

Now that we've covered the threat policies and what protection they can provide, let's discuss investigating threats and what response capabilities we have to combat them!

Threat investigation and response capabilities

When it comes to threat investigation and threat response in MDO, Microsoft provides a suite of best-in-class tools, with things such as threat trackers, Threat Explorer, real-time detection, and attack simulation training, which helps train users to learn the dos and don'ts of mail security. With that said, we'll break this section down into the following categories:

- Threat trackers
- Threat Explorer (real-time detection)
- Attack simulation training

You'll find these sections under **Email & collaboration** in the `security.microsoft.com` portal, as shown in the following screenshot:

Figure 8.7 – Email & collaboration

Let's dive into the first category: threat trackers.

Threat trackers

Threat trackers are specific views about trending malware campaigns, broken into trending campaigns and noteworthy campaigns, as well as **Saved** or **Tracked** queries, which allow you to get back to saved view filters, as shown in the following screenshot:

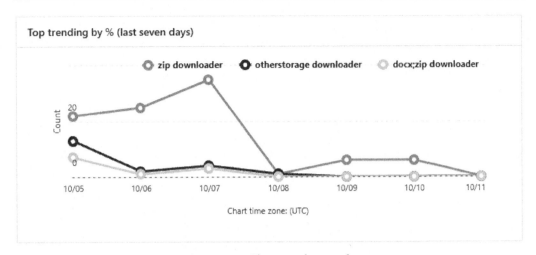

Figure 8.8 – Threat tracker trends

These are updated periodically to help you understand what trends are affecting your environment over time, which may help you implement stricter policies or other changes to cut down on those attack types. The following screenshot shows the chronological trend view:

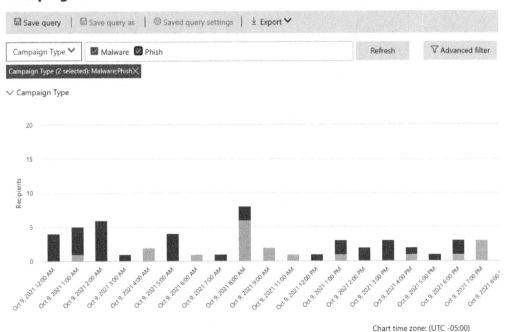

Figure 8.9 – Threat tracker trends

Below the graph, you get to see the breakdown of these campaigns and look at the messages that fall into the different categories. In the following screenshot, you can see an example of this, where there are categories regarding what percentage of the environment was targeted, the type, the recipients that got it, how many clicked it, and the click rate:

Name	Sample subject	Targeted	Type ↑	SubType	Recipients
Malware.D852CA15	[EXTERNAL] Re: PO000037189.xls	0.2%	Malware	Malicious Payload	6

Figure 8.10 – Threat tracker – campaign breakdown

You can choose one of the examples and you'll see a pane slide out, as shown in the following screenshot. Here, you can see some more granular information, as well as a link that takes you right to the Explorer:

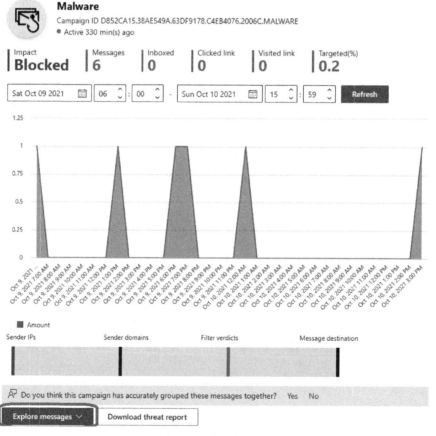

Figure 8.11 – Threat tracker – campaign example

Circling back to some terms we mentioned earlier, let's cover the **Noteworthy** and **Trending** trackers in more detail. Noteworthy trackers are going to be the more prominent threats that Microsoft feels you should have awareness of. These are going to be related to things that are potentially happening in your environment, as well as how they may impact you. Some of the topics here are around bigger campaigns that you should be reviewing continually with your security team.

When it comes to trending trackers, that's more related to new things that are coming into your environment. These will be things you need to understand and ensure you have the proper protection in place to protect against.

No matter what you're reviewing within Office 365 from a threat perspective, whether that's email or content and, soon to come, Office activities, threat trackers can help with your investigation as you track certain risks and threats within an organization. Next, we'll talk about Threat Explorer, which also compliments the threat trackers.

Threat Explorer (real-time detection)

Threat Explorer is another security tool your SOC can use when they're investigating and responding to threats. It gives you a view of what features you have enabled are blocking, as well as phishing URL verdict data on clicks. It also lets you start an automated investigation on a threat you see, as shown in the following screenshot:

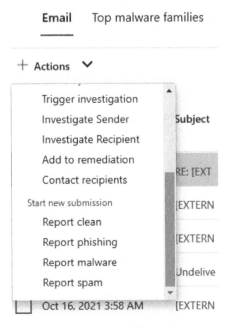

Figure 8.12 – Actions in Threat Explorer

One thing I like to use is the **Detection technology** filter because it shows you which protection you have configured and the work it's doing. The following screenshot shows an example of this:

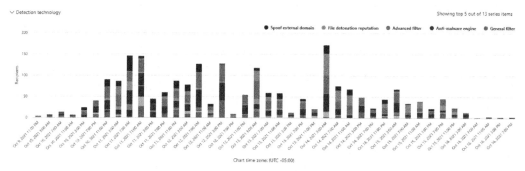

Figure 8.13 – Detection technology – Threat Explorer

To wrap up this section, we'll talk about some of the information on emails that's provided, such as pre-delivery and post-delivery information. This includes the actions that are taken by the ZAP process, which we covered earlier, as well as spam verdict, threat level, and the delivery locations of said message. All of this gets put into a single view for you to review as needed.

Attack simulation training

Something that is talked about a lot when it comes to Office 365 is its attack simulation feature. There's a handful of third-party tools out there that we could all name, but today, we'll be focusing on the Microsoft version of it. This allows you to run realistic scenarios in your environment that help you identify areas where you need to increase training for your end users.

The following screenshot shows the dashboard section. Here, you can see what simulations are in progress or have been completed, along with their behavior impact, if they were successful:

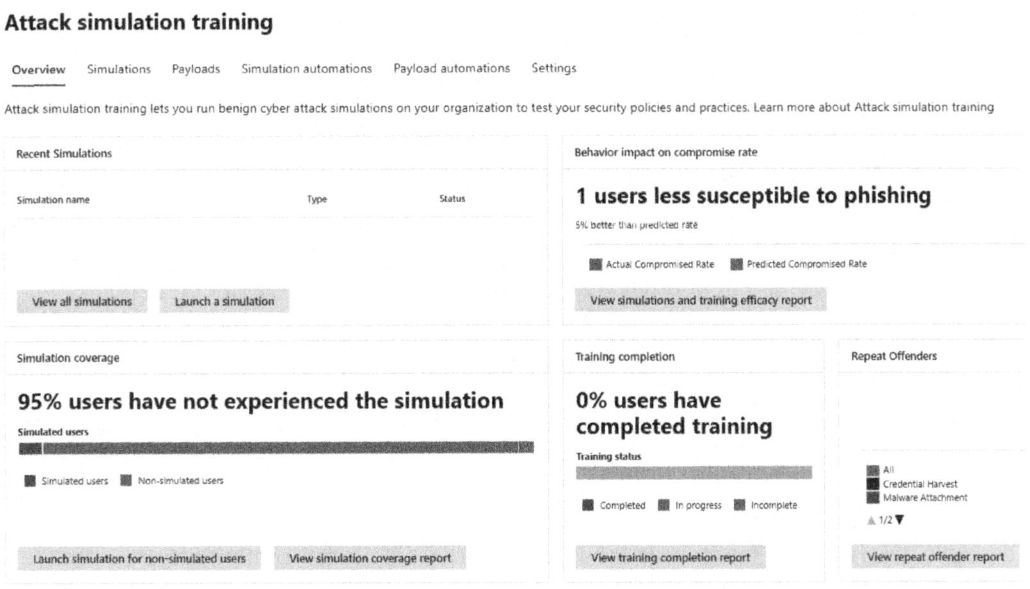

Attack simulation training

Overview   Simulations   Payloads   Simulation automations   Payload automations   Settings

Attack simulation training lets you run benign cyber attack simulations on your organization to test your security policies and practices. Learn more about Attack simulation training

Recent Simulations			Behavior impact on compromise rate
Simulation name	Type	Status	**1 users less susceptible to phishing**

5% better than predicted rate

■ Actual Compromised Rate   ■ Predicted Compromised Rate

View all simulations   Launch a simulation

View simulations and training efficacy report

Simulation coverage	Training completion	Repeat Offenders
95% users have not experienced the simulation	**0% users have completed training**	

Simulated users

Training status

■ Simulated users   ■ Non-simulated users

■ Completed   ■ In progress   ■ Incomplete

■ All
■ Credential Harvest
■ Malware Attachment
⚠ 1/2 ▼

Launch simulation for non-simulated users   View simulation coverage report

View training completion report

View repeat offender report

Figure 8.14 – Attack simulation training

The bottom part of the dashboard, as shown in the following screenshot, shows the percentage of your users that have not experienced any simulations, as well as the percentage of users that have completed training:

Attack simulation training

Overview   Simulations   Payloads   Simulation automations   Payload automations   Settings

Attack simulation training lets you run benign cyber attack simulations on your organization to test your security policies and practices. Learn more about Attack simulation training

Recent Simulations			Behavior impact on compromise rate
Simulation name	Type	Status	**1 users less susceptible to phishing**

5% better than predicted rate

■ Actual Compromised Rate   ■ Predicted Compromised Rate

View all simulations   Launch a simulation

View simulations and training efficacy report

Simulation coverage	Training completion	Repeat Offenders
95% users have not experienced the simulation	**0% users have completed training**	

Simulated users

Training status

■ Simulated users   ■ Non-simulated users

■ Completed   ■ In progress   ■ Incomplete

■ All
■ Credential Harvest
■ Malware Attachment
⚠ 1/2 ▼

Launch simulation for non-simulated users   View simulation coverage report

View training completion report

View repeat offender report

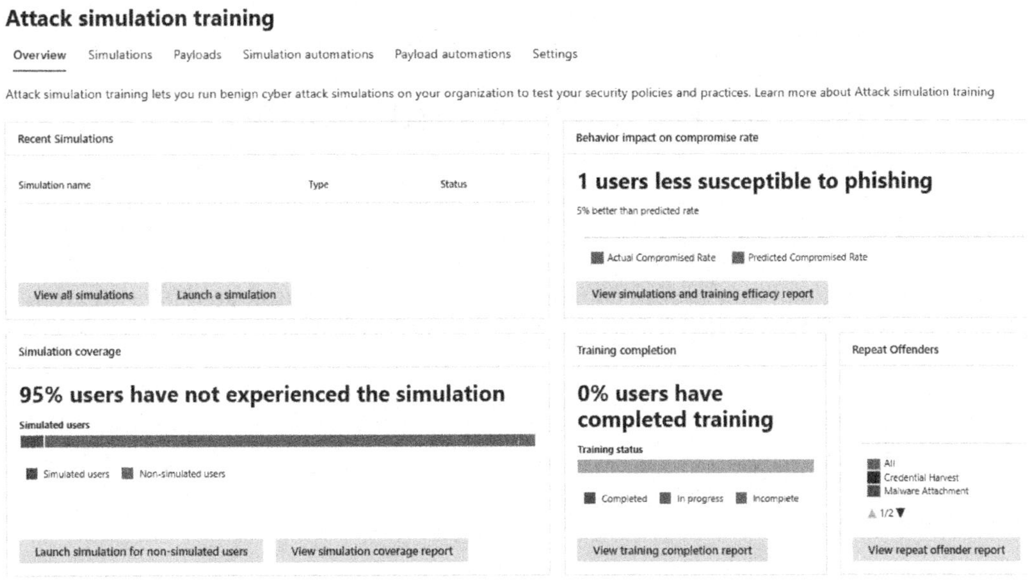

Figure 8.15 – Attack simulation dashboard, coverage, and training

There are five different types of campaigns you can run, as follows:

- **Credential harvest**: This typically contains a URL that tries to encourage you to enter credentials by mimicking a site you may or may not use.

- **Malware attachment**: This is an email that contains an attachment that, when run, can launch malicious code and compromise a machine.

- **Link in attachment**: This is similar to credential harvest but is contained within a document that acts as another method to try to entice you to enter credentials.

- **Link to malware**: Generally, this is a URL that directly takes you to a malicious file that can be downloaded and run malicious code as well.

- **Drive-by-URL**: Also referred to as a watering hole attack, this email contains a URL that takes a user to a site, where the site tries to run code to gather information or even run code on the device itself.

Once you get through a few simulations, you'll start seeing improvement actions – the same actions that can be found in Microsoft Secure Score. These are based on the payloads that you use in your simulations and are geared toward helping protect your users against those types of attacks.

To learn more about attack simulation, check out the following URL to get started: `https://docs.microsoft.com/en-us/microsoft-365/security/office-365-security/attack-simulation-training-faq?view=o365-worldwide`.

Automated investigation and response capabilities

When it comes to investigating and responding to alerts, it can be exhausting. Having some level of automated investigation and response capabilities can save your SOC from burnout and give them time to focus on deeper investigations. **Automated investigation and response**, or **AIR**, can help your team operate more effectively. Let's cover an example of this feature.

In this example, the alert is from a user submitting a suspicious email as a phishing attack, as shown in the following screenshot. On top of the message being sent to Microsoft for further analysis, it also gets sent to your administrators and is visible in Threat Explorer, under **Submissions**:

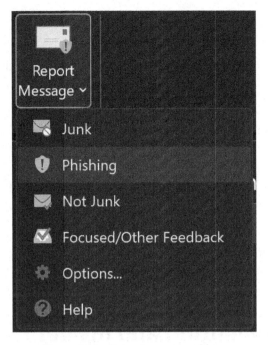

Figure 8.16 – Report message add-on

Once this submission comes in, it kicks off an investigation workflow automation, which includes the following phases:

- Determining what type of threat it might be and who sent it
- Where the email was sent from
- Whether other instances of the email were delivered or blocked
- An assessment from our analysts
- Whether the email is associated with any known campaigns

Once this has been done, recommendations are provided as actions to take on the email, as well as any entities involved. Once those investigations are done, there are a series of threat hunting steps that take place:

- Similar email messages are identified via email cluster searches.
- The signal is shared with other platforms, such as Microsoft Defender for Endpoint.
- A check is done to see if any users have clicked any malicious links in suspicious email messages.

- A check is done across EOP and Microsoft Defender for Office 365 to see if other, similar messages have been reported by users.

- A check is done to see if a user has been compromised. This check leverages signals across Office 365, Microsoft Defender for Cloud Apps, and Azure Active Directory, correlating any related user activity anomalies.

You can find other examples at `https://docs.microsoft.com/en-us/microsoft-365/security/office-365-security/automated-investigation-response-office?view=o365-worldwide#example-a-user-reported-phish-message-launches-an-investigation-playbook`.

The final step in this process is approving pending actions such as soft deleting email messages or clusters, as well as turning off external mail forwarding.

To learn more about remediation actions, go to `https://docs.microsoft.com/en-us/microsoft-365/security/office-365-security/air-review-approve-pending-completed-actions?view=o365-worldwide`.

Data loss prevention and insider risk

Finishing on protection within Microsoft 365 as it pertains to the productivity suite, let's talk a little about **data loss prevention (DLP)** and insider risk, as these are two more topics that are covered in the exam. We'll cover each topic at a high level as they are much smaller parts of the exam topics, but they're still important.

DLP

DLP policies are there to help you monitor activities that users perform on sensitive items, both at rest and in transit. Once you've done this, you can perform actions on them. A simple example of this is when a user tries to copy something marked as sensitive to an unapproved location or application. When DLP policies have been applied, actions can be taken automatically. This includes things such as the following:

- Showing a pop-up policy tip to the user that warns them that they may be trying to share a sensitive item inappropriately.

- Blocking sharing capabilities and, via a policy tip, allowing the user to override the block and capture the users' justification.

- Blocking sharing capabilities without the override option.

- For data at rest, sensitive items can be locked and moved to a secure quarantine location.

- For Teams chat, sensitive information will not be displayed.

DLP policies can be applied across the Microsoft 365 productivity stack, which includes locations such as the following:

- Exchange Online email

- SharePoint Online sites

- OneDrive accounts

- Teams chat and channel messages

- Microsoft Defender for Cloud Apps

- Windows 10 devices

- On-premises repositories

To learn more about preparing for and deploying DLP policies, go to `https://docs.microsoft.com/en-us/microsoft-365/compliance/dlp-learn-about-dlp?view=o365-worldwide#prepare-for-dlp`.

To take DLP a little further, you can read about endpoint DLP, where you can learn how actions on Windows devices can be reported to the security portal, as well as how to leverage MDE: `https://docs.microsoft.com/en-us/microsoft-365/compliance/endpoint-dlp-learn-about?view=o365-worldwide#whats-different-in-endpoint-dlp`.

Insider risk

Insider risk is the last topic we're going to cover before we wrap up this chapter. It's not a part of the MDO suite of tools per se, but it's still very relevant when it comes to protecting your productivity suite. It's a compliance suite that helps protect against insider risk by defining a policy that looks for malicious activities inside the organization when it comes to data. The following screenshot shows the head of the **Insider risk management** dashboard in the compliance.microsoft.com portal, which shows all the immediate options, as well as alerts below that:

Figure 8.17 – Insider risk management

There are a few behaviors that come to mind when it comes to insider risk, such as confidential data being leaked, confidentiality violations, IP theft, and insider trading. The amount of data that's being moved around in different areas across many applications can be challenging to govern. Here, you can identify potential risks with analytics, a feature that's in preview at the time of writing. Scans run daily and are a great way to keep on top of potential risks as new things are added to the Office 365 suite.

It can scan from sources such as the following:

- Microsoft 365 audit logs
- Exchange Online
- Azure Active Directory

The following screenshot shows the dialog to get those scans going. You'll see this in your recommendations when you get started, as shown here:

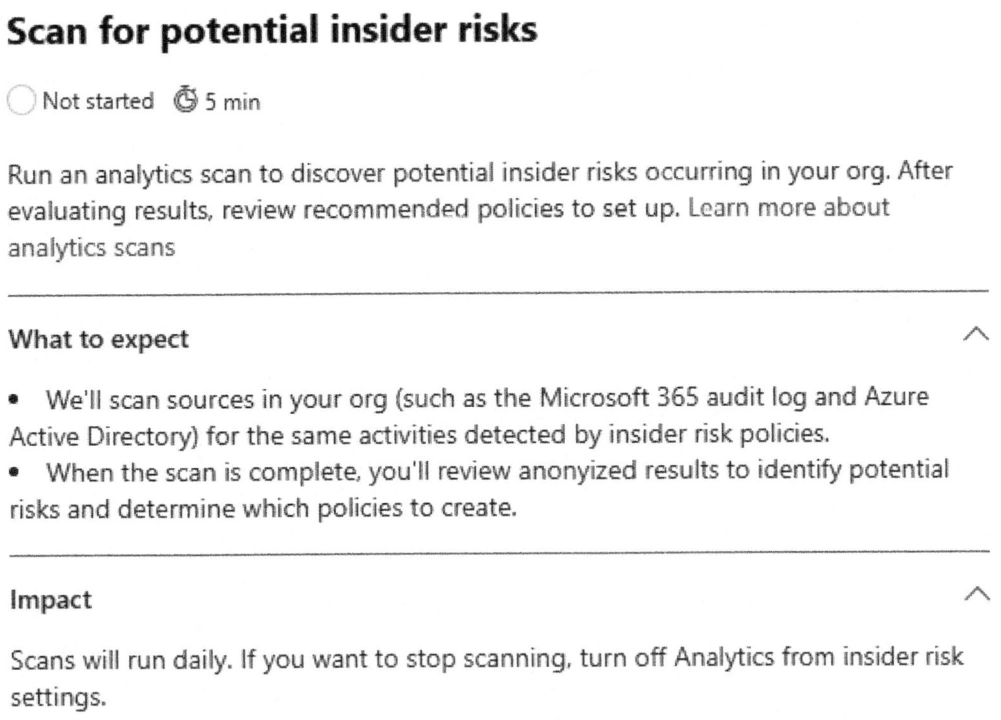

Scan for potential insider risks

◯ Not started ⏱ 5 min

Run an analytics scan to discover potential insider risks occurring in your org. After evaluating results, review recommended policies to set up. Learn more about analytics scans

---

What to expect   ∧

- We'll scan sources in your org (such as the Microsoft 365 audit log and Azure Active Directory) for the same activities detected by insider risk policies.
- When the scan is complete, you'll review anonyized results to identify potential risks and determine which policies to create.

Impact   ∧

Scans will run daily. If you want to stop scanning, turn off Analytics from insider risk settings.

Figure 8.18 – Insider risk analytics scan

To learn more about the analytics piece, go to `https://docs.microsoft.com/ en-us/microsoft-365/compliance/insider-risk-management- settings?view=o365-worldwide#analytics-preview`.

Let's cover the templates that are provided out of the box before we finish up; see the following screenshot for an example of what you get to start with. These categories can be broken into the following templates:

- Data theft by departing users

- General data leaks

- Data leaks by priority users (preview)

- Data leaks by disgruntled users (preview)

- General security policy violations (preview)

- Security policy violations by departing users (preview)

- Security policy violations by priority users (preview)

- Security policy violations by disgruntled users (preview):

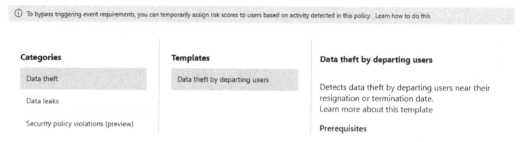

Figure 8.19 – Insider risk policy wizard

There is a lot more to insider risk, but as I stated earlier, it's not a huge part of the exam, so we don't need to spend a ton of time here. I would still recommend that you go and read the documentation if you end up working in that area more: `https://docs.microsoft.com/en-us/microsoft-365/compliance/insider-risk-management?view=o365-worldwide`.

Summary

In this chapter, we looked at Defender for Office and made sure our productivity suite is ready for the world. We covered a lot. You could read into all the topics we covered in much more detail, and I encourage you to. These products change monthly, with new features already in preview. We covered various topics, from the various threat policies MDO offers, how you can perform investigations and respond to threats, the automated investigation and response capabilities of MDO, and DLP and insider risk. This chapter has hopefully helped you understand what needs to be protected outside of endpoints and servers. If this is an area you specialize in or want to specialize in, spend some time going through the documentation – it's great and it's endless. Get in the lab, play with it, break it, fix it, and so on, but more importantly, have fun with it.

Moving into *Chapter 9, Microsoft Defender for Cloud Apps and Protecting your Cloud Apps*, we'll cover what MDCA can do for your cloud apps with its rich visibility and control over data.

9

Microsoft Defender for Cloud Apps and Protecting Your Cloud Apps

One of the biggest headaches companies have when migrating to the cloud is dealing with all of the new avenues that open up in terms of data travel and access. This can cause complications, but it's the way of the world and we need to adjust as security professionals. This new way of working has to be dealt with, with a mix of supporting access that isn't traditional for most IT teams and yet protects critical data. **Microsoft Defender for Cloud Apps (MDCA)** helps navigate these challenges by providing great visibility and control over your data as it's accessed and moved around, as well as analytics to help you identify security threats or attack vectors that need to be closed.

The great thing about using a **Cloud App Security Broker (CASB)** is that it provides safeguards for your employees to do their job wherever they are, all while being protected from accidental and unwanted data exposure. If we think about the name for a second, *broker*, we can understand its fundamental purpose, which is to manage access between your users and the cloud resources they're accessing.

CASBs are always discovering and providing insights into what we call **shadow IT**, which is apps that are being used that were not deployed or provided by the organization. By doing this, CASBs can monitor access to those sites and apps, as well as prevent potential data exfiltration by classifying sensitive data. They can even block access to it altogether.

In this chapter, we're going to cover a broad array of topics concerning MDCA. Although it's an extremely robust product, it accounts for a smaller portion of the exam so, at the same time, we won't go super deep into all of them. We're going to cover the following topics:

- The MDCA framework
- Cloud Discovery
- Conditional Access App Control
- Classifying and protecting sensitive information
- Detecting, investigating, and responding to application threats

Technical requirements

By now, you should be familiar with Conditional Access to some extent. For the proxy-related topics, it helps to know how they work conceptually when we get to some of the MDCA features such as Conditional Access App Control. The following are the technical requirements for this chapter:

- Conditional Access
- Proxies and reverse proxies
- M365 data connectors

The MDCA framework

Before we get into the MDCA framework, let's talk about the architecture behind this fantastic tool and then tie that into the framework. If we break down the core components, we get the following topics:

- **Cloud Discovery**: Discovering the cloud apps that are accessed in the organization
- **App Connectors**: APIs from cloud providers to integrate with other cloud apps
- **Conditional Access App Control**: Controlling data access outside of corporate networks
- **Granular control by policy**: Defining user behavior with cloud apps

Taking into consideration what the industry considers a CASB, we can enforce security policies between cloud services and providers to inject enterprise policies while accessing cloud-based resources. Think of them as an intermediate step between your users and their cloud resources, helping you monitor and implement security controls such as firewalls in a network.

The following diagram is a great representation of the data flow within the context of MDCA, as well as the paths it can take through different scenarios:

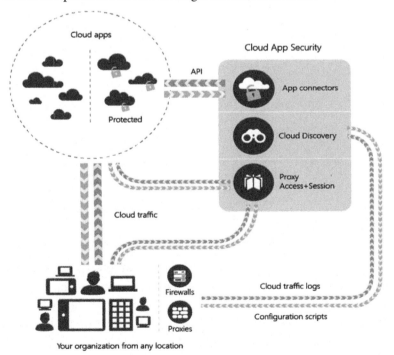

Figure 9.1 – The MDCA architecture

Let's break down the four elements of the MDCA framework, as follows:

- Shadow IT
- Protecting sensitive data
- Detecting anomalies
- Cloud app compliance

Discovering and controlling shadow IT is best done sooner rather than later since a lot of these apps are not controlled and regulated. MDCA provides a detailed set of information on apps that users are using, as shown in the following screenshot, where we can see two of the four categories for an app. From these two alone, we can see some untrustworthy fields, such as no MFA requirements.

At this point, you must take into consideration what the app is and what it does. Apps can get low ratings and we don't need to have some of these security controls. This is where admins need to do some homework to understand the app's intent and how it can be used before deciding if you'll sanction it or not:

SECURITY

Latest breach: —	Data-at-rest encryption method: N...	☒ Multi-factor authentication	☒ IP address restriction
✔ User audit trail	☒ Admin audit trail	✔ Data audit trail	✔ User can upload data
☒ Data classification	✔ Remember password	☒ User-roles support	✔ File sharing
✔ Valid certificate name	✔ Trusted certificate	Encryption protocol: TLS 1.3	✔ Heartbleed patched
HTTP security headers: **Partial**	☒ Supports SAML	✔ Protected against DROWN	☒ Penetration Testing
✔ Requires user authentication	⊖ Password policy		

COMPLIANCE

☒ ISO 27001	☒ ISO 27018	☒ ISO 27017	☒ ISO 27002
⊖ FINRA	⊖ FISMA	⊖ GAAP	⊖ HIPAA
☒ ISAE 3402	⊖ ITAR	☒ SOC 1	☒ SOC 2
☒ SOC 3	⊖ SOX	☒ SP 800-53	☒ SSAE 16
⊖ Safe Harbor	⊖ PCI DSS version	⊖ GLBA	FedRAMP level: Not supported
CSA STAR level: Not support...	☒ Privacy Shield	⊖ FFIEC	⊖ GAPP
☒ COBIT	☒ COPPA	☒ FERPA	☒ HITRUST CSF
☒ Jericho Forum Commandm...			

Figure 9.2 – MDCA app discovery information

Protecting sensitive data anywhere cloud apps are accessed is a huge benefit, given how mobile everyone and everything is getting. One great example of this protection is the ability to provision policies to block uploading or downloading if your users are not on corporate devices. The following screenshot shows the policy template for blocking downloads based on real-time inspection. Let's look at this template in more detail:

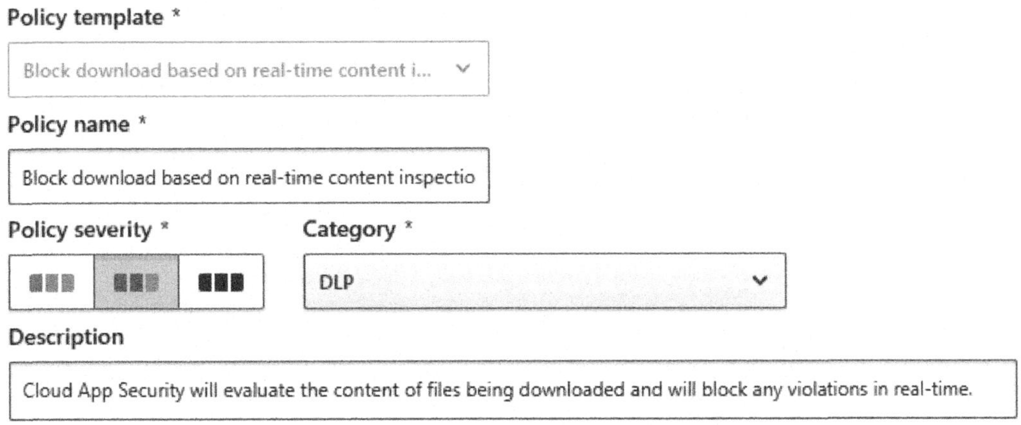

Policy template *

Block download based on real-time content i...   ⌄

Policy name *

Block download based on real-time content inspectio

Policy severity *   **Category** *

▪▪▪   ▪▪▪   ▪▪▪   DLP   ⌄

Description

Cloud App Security will evaluate the content of files being downloaded and will block any violations in real-time.

Figure 9.3 – MDCA policy for file blocking

The following screenshot shows the session control type for the policy, where we can choose to monitor activities to see what's happening in the organization. So, think of that as an audit mode that's comparable to Conditional Access or attack surface reduction rules. We can also block activities outright, which means we can't upload or download them, no questions asked. Then, we can see that we can control how files are uploaded and downloaded via inspection, which means it inspects the content for any internal DLP policies that have been applied. This ensures you're not uploading or downloading sensitive information to untrusted locations:

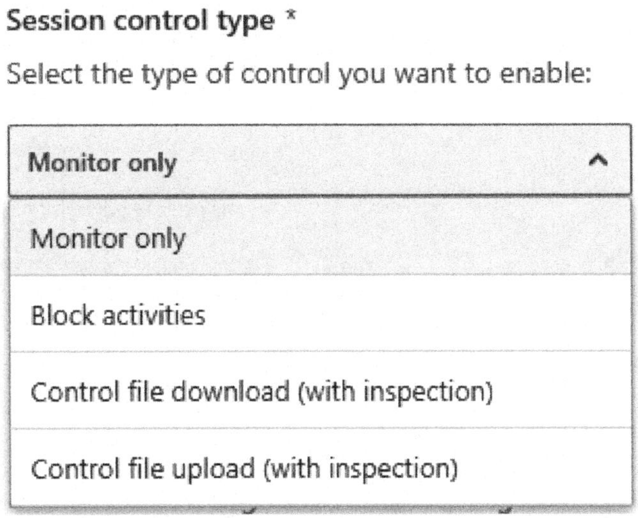

Session control type *

Select the type of control you want to enable:

Monitor only   ⌃

Monitor only

Block activities

Control file download (with inspection)

Control file upload (with inspection)

Figure 9.4 – MDCA policy – Session control type

Next, we get the option to set our filters, as shown in the following screenshot. Here is where we would say that if the activity source doesn't match this criterion, fire the policy off. By setting any of these options, you're saying that if the device isn't managed and compliant per the company policy, session control should be applied:

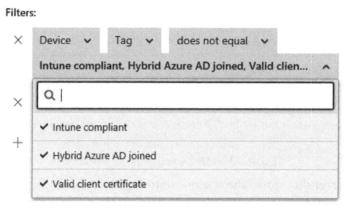

Figure 9.5 – MDCA policy – Filters

Lastly, if you were to select either of the last two options – that is, to inspect on upload or download – you would get the file filters section shown in the following screenshot. Here, you select what sensitivity labels you want to search for. If they are found, it will block the download:

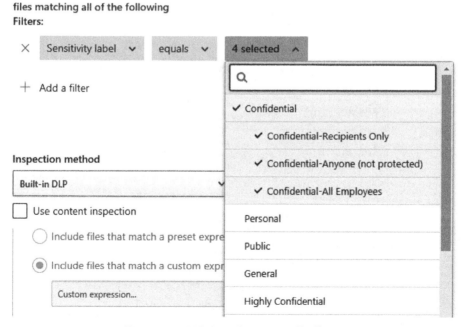

Figure 9.6 – MDCA policy – DLP file filers

If you're curious to learn more about this, there is a cool tutorial you can follow about blocking sensitive information at `https://docs.microsoft.com/en-us/cloud-app-security/use-case-proxy-block-session-aad`.

We'll come back to this example later in this chapter when we talk about Conditional Access App Control since it's part of what we'll configure.

Detecting anomalies in app behavior is another feature of MDCA, where activities are detected outside what has been normal in the past. One of the main components behind that is **user entity behavioral analytics** (**UEBA**). The policies that are a part of this are enabled by default and start detecting results on behaviors right away, except for the 7-day learning period, where not all the alert types are available.

Once that time has passed, data from the API connectors that you have configured starts getting collected and analyzed. This includes the time a user is active, from what IP address and on what device, and a risk score for each. All of these types of things start to build a baseline for your organization. From there, machine learning algorithms profile user patterns to reduce false alerts. There are many risk indicator categories that get evaluated in this process and they are grouped into the following risks factors:

- Risky IP address
- Login failures
- Admin activity
- Inactive accounts
- Location
- Impossible travel
- Device and user agent
- Activity rate

Based on the results of the evaluations, alerts will be generated. There are many anomaly detection policies that you can go read about here: `https://docs.microsoft.com/en-us/cloud-app-security/anomaly-detection-policy#impossible-travel`.

The last element of the MDCA framework is **cloud app compliance**. Simply put, MDCA does the work for you to understand the compliance of apps that are being used. The following screenshot shows what it can report on, which is helpful for decision making when an app needs to meet a certain industry standard:

Figure 9.7 – MDCA app compliance reporting

Now that we've covered the MDCA framework at a high level, let's look at Cloud Discovery and what that process entails!

Cloud Discovery

Cloud Discovery is made up of four different discovery methods, in which traffic logs are digested and analyzed so that the apps that are being accessed can be scored. Let's cover these four methods and dive into each one.

Microsoft Defender for Endpoint (MDE) integration

If your devices are enrolled into **Microsoft Defender for Endpoint** (**MDE**), MDCA will use the traffic information about the apps and services that are being accessed. This is an integration that is native to the MDCA platform and requires toggling it on from the security portal, as shown in the following screenshot:

Figure 9.8 – MDCA integration within Security.Microsoft.com

Then, to enforce app access, which allows access to sanctioned apps or blocks access to unsanctioned apps, there is another checkbox in the settings within MDCA, as shown in the following screenshot:

Figure 9.9 – MDCA integration for MDE app enforcement

Again, this is the most native way to get traffic logs into MDCA without having to upload logs or set up automatic log uploads, about which you can read more in the next section (`https://docs.microsoft.com/en-us/cloud-app-security/discovery-docker`).

Log Collector

Log Collector, the second method you can leverage for log collection if MDE is not an option currently, is where you set up a dedicated device to collect and upload network logs. To learn more about setting one up, check out the following article, which walks you through the process of using a Windows box as the collector. You can use Windows, Ubuntu on-premises or in Azure, Red Hat on-premises, or CentOS: `https://docs.microsoft.com/en-us/cloud-app-security/discovery-docker-windows#set-up-and-configuration`.

Secure Web Gateway

Secure Web Gateway (SWG) is another option for uploading network traffic logs, which also lets you discover cloud apps, block access to unsanctioned apps, and assess risk within the SWG's portal. The four supported SWGs are as follows:

- **Zscaler integration**: `https://docs.microsoft.com/en-us/cloud-app-security/zscaler-integration`
- **iboss integration**: `https://docs.microsoft.com/en-us/cloud-app-security/iboss-integration`
- **Corrata integration**: `https://docs.microsoft.com/en-us/cloud-app-security/corrata-integration`
- **Menlo Security integration**: `https://docs.microsoft.com/en-us/cloud-app-security/menlo-integration`

Now let's have a look at what the Cloud Discovery API is about.

Cloud Discovery API

The Cloud Discovery API is the last method you can use to enable Cloud Discovery and block access to unsanctioned applications. Here, you generate a script block and import it into your security appliance to call. To read more about this method, check out the following article: `https://docs.microsoft.com/en-us/cloud-app-security/api-discovery`.

Once you have your Cloud Discovery set up, it's time to start going through everything at a high level, including reviewing the apps that are being used and their profiles. You can see cloud app usage stats such as the top users, devices, and basic traffic stats. Between understanding your industry, the compliance guidelines you need to stay within, and conversations with your end users, you can start to filter down the apps that should and shouldn't be allowed.

Next, let's dive into Conditional Access App Control, where we'll talk about protecting data in apps on the fly!

Conditional Access App Control

Conditional Access App Control is an incredibly powerful tool when it comes to protecting data for your organization. It lets you monitor access and retrieve information in real time to help protect against data leaks and potential breaches. Let's take, for example, the policy we created earlier in this chapter when we talked about protecting sensitive data.

We started creating a policy that could be used to block sensitive data from being downloaded and inspected that it matched DLP-protected data, such as documents that have been classified as confidential because they contain personal customer data.

The following screenshot shows our starting point; that is, **Azure Active Directory** > **Security** > **Conditional Access**. In this example, we're creating a policy that's targeting a test user, which is targeting Office 365, and then specifying **Use Conditional Access App Control** to leverage the MDCA reverse proxy backend:

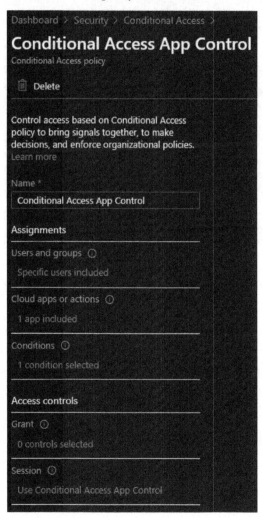

Figure 9.10 – AAS CA policy

In the following screenshot, we're setting it to **custom policy**, where it's going to leverage the custom policy we created earlier in this book.

If we were to set it to **Monitor only (Preview)** or **Block downloads (Preview)**, it would use a built-in template that's not been defined in the UI anywhere, all while still leveraging the MDCA backend:

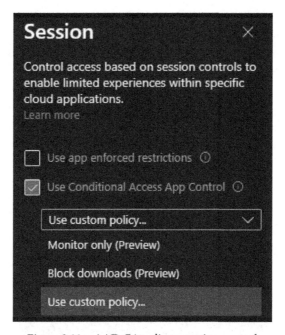

Figure 9.11 – AAD CA policy – session control

To learn more about this, I suggest watching the video provided here, as well as reading the article on how session control works:

- Session control walkthrough video: `https://docs.microsoft.com/en-us/learn/modules/microsoft-cloud-app-security/walkthrough`

- How session control works: `https://docs.microsoft.com/en-gb/cloud-app-security/proxy-intro-aad#how-session-control-works`

Next, we will look at Microsoft Information Protection, where we'll discuss labeling data so that it behaves as expected when on the move.

Classifying and protecting sensitive information

Simply put, MDCA can leverage **Microsoft Information Protection (MIP)** to automatically scan new files for sensitivity label applicability, as well as apply labels for you. This can be enabled in the MDCA settings portal, under **Information Protection**. Check the two boxes shown in the following screenshot. If you want it to inspect an already protected file, you can grant MDCA that access in this same setting pane.

Some of the benefits of this integration are as follows:

- You can apply classification labels as a governance action to files that match specific policies.

- You can view all the classified files in a central location.

- You can investigate according to your classification level, as well as view sensitive data within your cloud applications.

- You can create policies to make sure that the classified files are being handled properly:

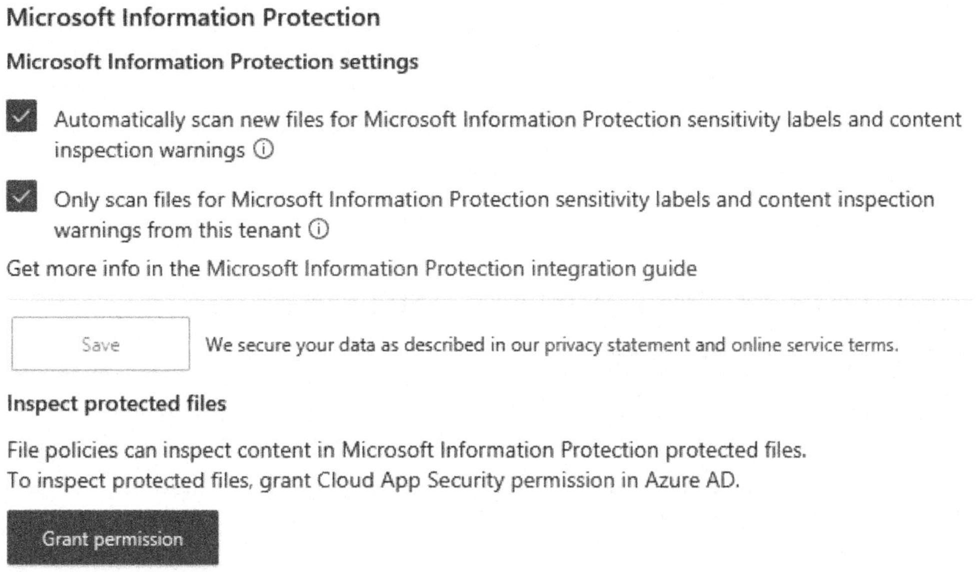

Microsoft Information Protection

Microsoft Information Protection settings

☑ Automatically scan new files for Microsoft Information Protection sensitivity labels and content inspection warnings ⓘ

☑ Only scan files for Microsoft Information Protection sensitivity labels and content inspection warnings from this tenant ⓘ

Get more info in the Microsoft Information Protection integration guide

| Save | We secure your data as described in our privacy statement and online service terms. |

Inspect protected files

File policies can inspect content in Microsoft Information Protection protected files.
To inspect protected files, grant Cloud App Security permission in Azure AD.

Grant permission

Figure 9.12 – MDCA settings – MIP settings

To learn more about this integration, go to https://docs.microsoft.com/en-us/cloud-app-security/azip-integration.

One other feature to mention here is the ability to create file policies, which create and detect sensitive information and trigger defined alerts with governance actions. Some of these actions are as follows:

- Triggering alerts and email notifications
- Changing sharing access for files
- Quarantining files
- Removing file or folder permissions
- Moving files to a trash folder

Lastly, you could simply filter your alerts on DLP, as shown in the following screenshot, and see what's coming in from the newly configured policies:

Figure 9.13 – MDCA – The Alerts dashboard

Now, it's time for one of my favorite topics – detecting and responding to threats! Let's dive in!

Detecting, investigating, and responding to application threats

At the core of detecting threats with MDCA, we have anomaly detection policies. Anomaly detection policies evaluate and detect threats by evaluating over 30 different indicators of risk. We listed these earlier when we talked about UEBA. It looks at all users' sessions to evaluate whether the behavior deviates from normal behavior. These policies include the following:

- Impossible travel
- Activity from unusual countries
- Malware detection

- Ransomware activity

- Activity from suspicious IP addresses

- Suspicious inbox forwarding

The following screenshot shows the portal where you can filter on different statuses and severity levels for these alert types, as well as the alert counts for each:

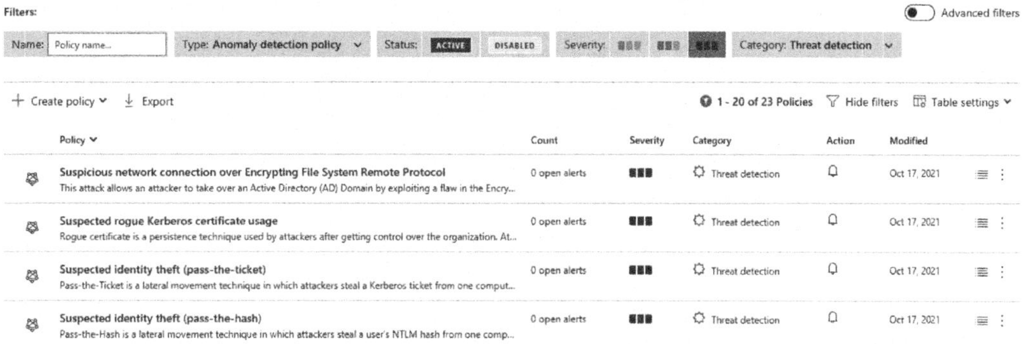

Figure 9.14 – MDCA settings and MIP integration

When it comes to investigating applications, MDCA provides many different dashboards for you to use while digging into alerts. Check out the following URL for the full list: `https://docs.microsoft.com/en-us/cloud-app-security/investigate#dashboards`.

The following screenshot shows the options under **Investigate** within MDCA, which is where we'll head next. The activity log is a great place to start when you're looking for oddities and you can check who is accessing your cloud environment and from where, as well as on what devices. From there, you can go to **Files** and check who is sharing files with a link, essentially leaving them open for potential leaks, or even who is sharing information with personal accounts.

Users and accounts are a good place to check account roles, revoke permissions, or even require MFA for a user if you notice something out of the ordinary. It's also a place to view associated accounts and connected applications.

Connected apps identifies which apps have been connected to MDCA so that accounts, activity logs, and files can be ingested. **Activity log** shows you things such as the activities that have been performed on files, logons, group changes, and a host of Azure operations:

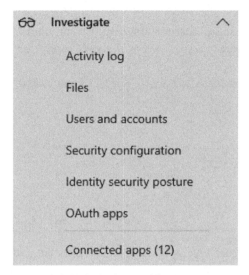

Figure 9.15 – MDCA settings – The Investigate menu

By looking through these dashboards, you should start recognizing areas where you can create policies to monitor for anomalies. As you start creating policies, you'll also want to start looking at the workflow automations you can create with Power Automate. For example, if you have a particular alert, you can create an automated response to kick off, such as an antivirus scan, or even isolate machines until you can investigate. This can be seen in the following screenshot:

Figure 9.16 – Power Automate workflow automation examples

Summary

That wraps up this chapter! MDCA could truly be a book all on its own, as with many topics in this book, but we covered a good amount at a high level to arm you with both a good starting point to jump in and learn more, as well as enough to take on any MDCA exam questions.

We learned about the MDCA framework, what Cloud Discovery is and how it works, and Conditional Access App Control and where we can apply it. We also talked about how MDCA integrates with Microsoft Information Protection to help protect sensitive data by classifying it on the fly. Finally, we looked at some of the policies you have at your disposal to help detect and investigate threats in your cloud environment. In the next chapter, we'll look at Microsoft Defender for Cloud in more detail.

Section 4 – Setting Up and Connecting Data Sources to Microsoft Sentinel

The objective of *Section 4* is to guide you through the initial configurations required to set up Microsoft Sentinel, and then begin connecting data sources from a data ingestion perspective.

This part of the book comprises the following chapter:

- *Chapter 10, Setting Up and Configuring Microsoft Sentinel*

10
Setting Up and Configuring Microsoft Sentinel

Welcome to *Chapter 10*! This chapter is all about Microsoft Sentinel. We want to make sure you have a great starting point in your Microsoft Sentinel journey, and that all begins with understanding what it takes to successfully set up and configure Microsoft Sentinel for your organization! The good news is that this is a relatively straightforward process and that it can be configured quickly. Are you ready? We are looking forward to covering this topic, so let's get into what you can expect to learn.

In this chapter, we will cover the following topics:

- Pre-deployment activities
- Azure tenant-level prerequisites
- Enablement/onboarding
- Connecting data sources

First, let's look at the pre-deployment activities within Microsoft Sentinel!

Pre-deployment activities

As with almost any technical implementation, there will be a few pre-deployment activities you will like to consider and plan for. This section is meant to get these ironed out and assist you in acquiring any internal assistance you might need. Generally speaking, the pre-deployment activities for Microsoft Sentinel are straightforward. Let's take a look:

1. One of the first items you will need to tackle before deploying Microsoft Sentinel will be to determine which data sources you need to monitor from a security standpoint. This will help you get a rough understanding of the overall data size requirements. If you happen to work for an organization that has an existing SIEM, ask the team for the daily average ingestion that they see and divide that out by topic type or source! This will be a great conversational starting point.

    As you may have assumed, this conversation is truly budget-driven. You will be able to review Microsoft's public documentation on data source ingestion costs. One thing to remember is that with Microsoft Sentinel, there are various free data sources you can begin your journey with!

    > **Note**
    >
    > The following table has been taken directly from `https://docs.microsoft.com`. While the tool names have changed, the documentation still refers to known older naming conventions (Advanced Threat Protection).

The following are the free data sources you can use:

Microsoft Sentinel Data Connector	Data Type	Free or Paid
Azure Activity Logs	AzureActivity	Free
Azure AD Identity Protection	SecurityAlert (IPC)	Free
Office 365	OfficeActivity (SharePoint)	Free
	OfficeActivity (Exchange)	Free
	OfficeActivity (Teams)	Free
Microsoft Defender for Cloud	SecurityAlert (Defender for Cloud)	Free
Microsoft Defender for IoT (Internet of Things)	SecurityAlert (Defender for IoT)	Free
Microsoft 365 Defender	SecurityIncident	Free
	SecurityAlert	Free
	DeviceEvents	Paid
	DeviceFileEvents	Paid
	DeviceImageLoadEvents	Paid
	DeviceInfo	Paid
	DeviceLogonEvents	Paid
	DeviceNetworkEvents	Paid
	DeviceNetworkInfo	Paid
	DeviceProcessEvents	Paid
	DeviceRegistryEvents	Paid
	DeviceFileCertificateInfo	Paid
Microsoft Defender for Endpoint	SecurityAlert (**Microsoft Defender Advanced Threat Protection**) (**MDATP**)	Free
Microsoft Defender for Identity	SecurityAlert (**Azure Advanced Threat Protection**) (**AATP**)	Free
Microsoft Defender for Cloud Apps	SecurityAlert (Defender for Cloud Apps)	Free
	MCASShadowITReporting	Paid

2. One of the underlying technologies that runs in Sentinel is Log Analytics. One of your pre-deployment activities will be to design your Log Analytics workspace. So, what does this mean? You will need to decide if you are going to use a single workspace or multiple. Also, from a tenant standpoint, you must consider whether you are going to use a single tenant or multiple tenants. The following are some additional considerations:

a. Think about your internal compliance requirements. Where can you collect and store data? Items such as **General Data Protection Regulation** (**GDPR**) will come into discussion when you're deciding on your pre-deployment activities.

b. Then, there's **role-based access control** (**RBAC**). How will you control access to Microsoft Sentinel data? As we mentioned earlier in this book, RBAC can be very granular. Will you use built-in or custom RBAC objects?

3. Now that you have a few basic items accounted for, one of the final pieces to the pre-deployment preparation puzzle will be to ensure you have discussed and educated yourself on the various aspects of pricing associated with Microsoft Sentinel. This will be key from a budgetary perspective to get approval and align the project with your implementation. Budget is king, is it not? The following are some final items you must review:

    a. Microsoft Sentinel costs and billing (to get an understanding of what is free versus what is not)

    b. Log Analytics pricing

    c. Logic Apps (these are used for workflow automations/any automation) pricing

    d. Understanding if you will need Azure Data Explorer for long-term log retention, and calculating the costs if this applies to your enterprise

4. Lastly, as you would suspect, you will need to identify someone to lead the deployment; this could be you or another colleague. We also highly recommend that you have a decision-level sponsor to keep everyone on track!

That will do it from a pre-deployment planning prerequisite perspective. Now, let's look at the Azure tenant-level requirements! Are you ready? Let's go!

Azure tenant-level prerequisites

Now that we have covered the pre-technical planning items for your deployment, we want to quickly cover the Azure-related prerequisites you should have so that you can successfully deploy and configure Microsoft Sentinel:

> **Note**
> In most enterprises, some of these will already be taken care of. Nonetheless, we want to look at all the prerequisites accordingly.

1. First off, you will need to have a valid Azure Active Directory Tenant with the appropriate licensing and billing. This will be a requirement for any resources to be deployed. You have probably already done this in your enterprise, but if this is your lab, certainly consider this.

2. Once you have a tenant configured and accessible, you will need to create an Azure subscription. Again, this should already be configured in most enterprises unless your company is brand new to Azure – nonetheless, we wanted to remind you of this fact.

3. Next, it's permission time! There are various permissions you will need to review and obtain. First, we start with the subscription. If you are using a new subscription, you will need an administrator or someone with higher permission to grant you the minimum role of Contributor. Often, we see Owner being given; however, as security experts, we want to ensure you are following the least privileged approach as follows:

a. To maintain the least access possible, only assign yourself permissions at the resource group level.

b. Keep in mind that you can also create very granular custom roles from an RBAC standpoint in Azure – leverage that to your benefit!

4. From a resource standpoint, you will need to create a Log Analytics workspace. This is a requirement for all of the data that Microsoft Sentinel will be analyzing, ingesting, and leveraging for general detections and analysis, plus so much more!

> **Note**
>
> We recommend that you create a dedicated resource group for Microsoft Sentinel and any other resources that Microsoft Sentinel may use (such as Logic Apps for automation, workflow automations, workbooks, and so on). This will also come in handy from a permissions standpoint because you will be able to set permissions at the resource group level, which will aid in ensuring you are using Microsoft Sentinel securely from an access standpoint. This will be much more efficient compared to having to manage multiple resource groups and associated permissions. Think of a resource group as a tier – you can have multiple resource groups/tiers for more granular RBAC needs.

Once you have both the pre-deployment activities and the Azure tenant-level prerequisites completed, you can start enabling configuration and other settings to deploy Microsoft Sentinel! Are you ready?

Enabling and onboarding Microsoft Sentinel

At this point, all of the heavy prerequisite lifting is complete! You will be thrilled to know that enabling and onboarding Microsoft Sentinel is rather easy! It normally comes down to the planning and costing discussions you have already had, which makes this a bit more time-consuming.

To begin, we recommend leveraging the wide variety of connectors that Microsoft provides from its solutions, as well as gallery-based connectors (for example, Palo Alto Network Firewalls). This will be the quickest way to onboard your data source into Microsoft Sentinel.

Some recommended starting points are as follows:

- Microsoft 365 Defender (formerly Microsoft Threat Protection)
- Microsoft 365 data sources
- Office 365 data sources
- Microsoft Defender for Cloud Apps
- Microsoft Defender for Cloud
- Azure Active Directory Identity Protection
- Azure Activity
- Syslog
- **Common Event Format (CEF)** connectors
- REST APIs

Of course, there are many more, but generally speaking, this list is a great place to start for your lab or enterprise!

Global requirements and prerequisites for Microsoft Sentinel

Let's look at some Sentinel-specific requirements so that you can continue onboarding and deploying Microsoft Sentinel:

- As we mentioned previously, you will need an active Azure subscription.
- You will also need a Log Analytics workspace.
- You will need Contributor permissions to the subscription or resource group where Log Analytics exists and where you plan to enable Microsoft Sentinel (remember the recommendation and guidance previous).
- Ensure you have any required permissions at the individual data source level as well. This becomes very granular but is necessary in some large enterprises.

Often, you will need to know the general information on availability and data residency for your compliance and regulatory purposes. Let's get into that!

Data residency

Generally speaking, Microsoft Sentinel can run on Log Analytics workspaces in most of the **General Availability (GA)** regions. There are a few exceptions in the China and Germany regions, but other than that, you will be good to go!

The data that is generated by Microsoft Sentinel will contain items about any incidents, bookmarks, analytics rules, and potentially your tenant-related data that's within your Log Analytics workspace. You may be asked where this data is being stored for various audit-related/regulatory compliance needs. We want to provide you with that answer, straight from Microsoft's documentation:

> **Note**
> This table has been taken from Microsoft's documentation.

Workspace Geography	Microsoft Sentinel-Generated Data Geography
United States India	United States
Europe France	Europe
Australia	Australia
United Kingdom	United Kingdom
Canada	Canada
Japan	Japan
Asia Pacific	Asia Pacific
Brazil	Brazil
Norway	Norway
Africa	Africa
Korea	Korea
Germany	Germany
United Arab Emirates	United Arab Emirates
Switzerland	Switzerland

Now that we have covered this from a documentation standpoint, just in case you are asked, let's learn how to enable Microsoft Sentinel. Let's go!

Enabling Microsoft Sentinel for your organization

This process is pretty cut and dry! You will need to follow these steps for either your enterprise or lab:

1. Sign into the Azure portal (`portal.azure.com`) and ensure that you select the proper **Subscription** if you are greeted with that message.

2. Search for `Microsoft Sentinel` (this may appear as `Azure Sentinel`, depending on your tenant):

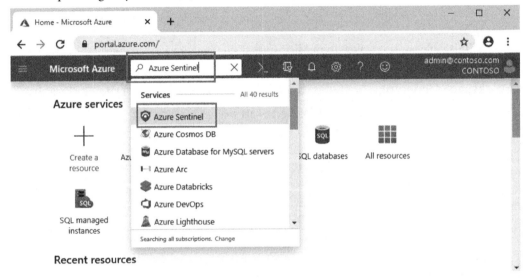

Figure 10.1 – Microsoft Sentinel (formerly known as Azure Sentinel)

3. Click the **Add** button.

4. You will be asked to select a workspace to add Microsoft Sentinel to. Go ahead and select the option that allows you to create a new one (this aligns with the best practices):

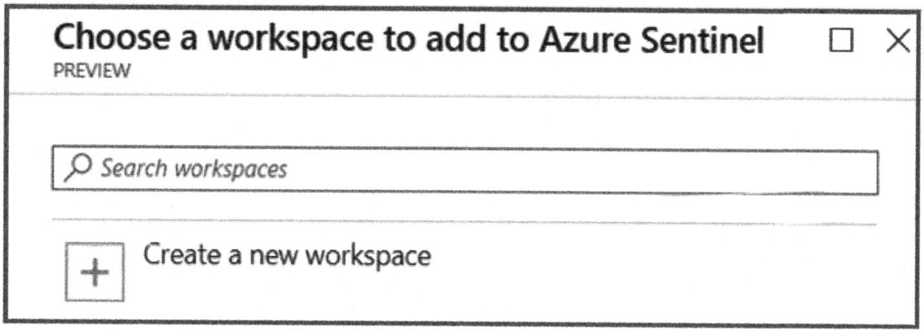

Choose a workspace to add to Azure Sentinel   □ ✕

PREVIEW

🔍 *Search workspaces*

⊞ Create a new workspace

Figure 10.2 – Choose a workspace to add to Microsoft Sentinel (formerly known as Azure Sentinel)

> **Note**
>
> If you have Microsoft Defender for Cloud, the workspace that's attributed to that will not appear, so you will not be able to install and integrate Microsoft Sentinel with that workspace.

5. Choose the **Add Microsoft Sentinel** option.

That's it! Pretty simple, right? Give this some time on the backend and you will soon have Microsoft Sentinel ready to go! Remember that items will go into your Log Analytics workspace and that Microsoft Sentinel will then take that data and ingest it accordingly to detect and analyze your feeds appropriately!

Now that you have Microsoft Sentinel technically up and running, we want to walk you through connecting data sources to Microsoft Sentinel for ingestion.

Connecting data sources to Microsoft Sentinel

Microsoft Sentinel will ingest data from sources and apps whenever you connect the service and decide to forward any events to Microsoft Sentinel. If you happen to have any servers that are either physical or virtual, you will be able to achieve very similar results if you install the Log Analytics agent. This will collect the required logs and send it to Microsoft Sentinel. Additionally, if you have any firewall and proxies, you will be able to use Syslog servers and have those servers forward the logs to Microsoft Sentinel.

Let's learn how to connect these data sources accordingly:

1. From the main menu, find the **Data Connectors** option. Go ahead and click it to be taken to the data connectors gallery.

2. This gallery contains a list of all the built-in data sources you can connect to! Choose the data source you would like to connect to and, in the bottom right-hand corner, select **Open connector page**:

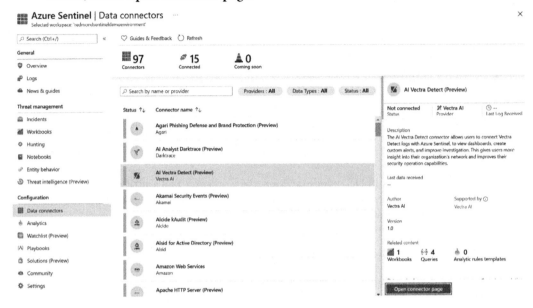

Figure 10.3 – Data connectors

3. The connector page will then provide you with the required information to successfully connect the data to Microsoft Sentinel:

Figure 10.4 – Connecting data to Microsoft Sentinel

4. You will notice a **Next Steps** tab on the **Data connectors** page. This is a great place for you to see any relevant built-in workbooks, queries, and analytics rule templates that will be useful in conjunction with the data coming from this data connector. You can choose to use these as-is or modify them as your organization needs!

Once connected, you will see a count of the data sources that are connected, as shown in the following screenshot:

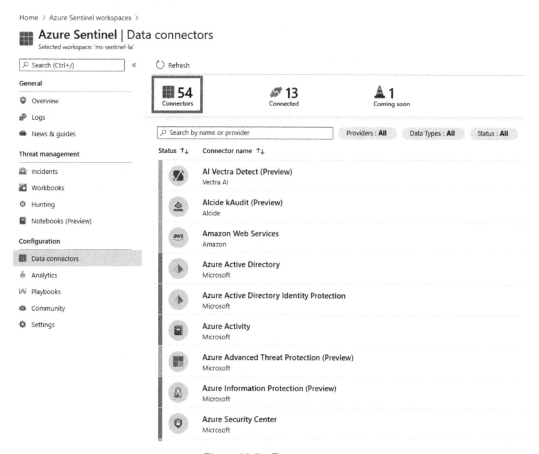

Figure 10.5 – Data sources

After you verify them, they appear in the **Connectors** section with a green indicator next to them. The data will begin to stream into Microsoft Sentinel and will be available for you to work with and query.

Summary

Congratulations! All you have to do is repeat this process for every data source you have. By doing this, you will be on your way to building out your SIEM on Microsoft Sentinel! Next, we will take you on a journey into that data and show you the ways of the hunter! Stay tuned!

Section 5 – Hunting Threats within Microsoft 365 Defender and Microsoft Sentinel

The objective of *Section 5* is to guide you through using Microsoft Sentinel to hunt threats in the enterprise. There are numerous ways to threat hunt, and in this section, those options will be covered.

This part of the book comprises the following chapters:

- *Chapter 11, Advanced Threat Hunting, Microsoft 365 Defender Portal, and Sentinel*
- *Chapter 12, Knowledge Check*

11

Advanced Threat Hunting, Microsoft 365 Defender Portal, and Sentinel

To me, **advanced threat hunting** is one of the most exciting parts of the **Microsoft 365 (M365)** Defender portal as it involves diving into data with **Kusto** – I mean, that's what we all came for, right? I'm kidding, but seriously, I could spend all day learning queries to pull what I want, learning what data is there as a whole, and figuring out what's normal and what's not.

We have lots planned for this chapter, including covering higher-level areas such as the basics of Kusto queries, advanced hunting in the M365 Defender portal and Microsoft Sentinel, and leveraging some of its additional hunting features, such as Livestream, notebooks, and bookmarks. The focus is to make sure you have what you need for the exam, but at the same time, we've been trying to provide more than that so that you can be as successful as possible in the real world as you get started in the M365 stack.

In this chapter, we will be covering the following topics:

- Kusto query overview

- Advanced threat hunting and M365 Defender portal

- Hunt for threats in Microsoft Sentinel

Technical requirements

As I mentioned previously, we're going to get into the query language that's used across the M365 stack, which is the **Kusto query language** (**KQL**). We're going to break down a few things to help get you up to speed on it, then dive into leveraging it for advanced hunting in the M365 Defender portal, as well as inMicrosoft Sentinel. With that said, let's look at the list of technical requirements for this chapter:

- A basic understanding of KQL

- The ability to work with custom queries

- The ability to work with custom detections

- Microsoft Livestream, notebooks, and bookmarks

Kusto query overview

Let's talk about **Kusto queries**. These are read-only requests for data that you define in the query itself, so think of it as a PowerShell `get` cmdlet. You're simply asking to retrieve information, as defined in the query. If you're familiar with SQL, then Kusto should be easy for you to pick up as it's similar to the database, table, and column hierarchy.

First, we need to figure out a place to start. Looking at the schema, we have a handful of table descriptions that show the available tables. We have **Alerts**, **Apps and Identities**, **Email**, **Devices**, and **Threat and Vulnerability Management**. Let's start with **DeviceEvents**, which can be found under **Devices**, as shown in the following screenshot:

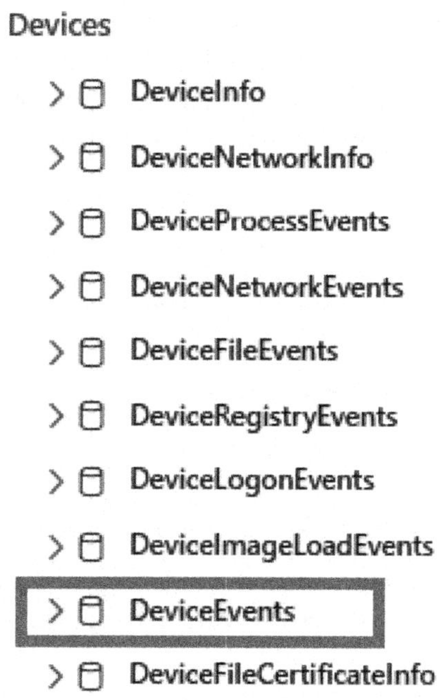

Devices

> 🗂 DeviceInfo

> 🗂 DeviceNetworkInfo

> 🗂 DeviceProcessEvents

> 🗂 DeviceNetworkEvents

> 🗂 DeviceFileEvents

> 🗂 DeviceRegistryEvents

> 🗂 DeviceLogonEvents

> 🗂 DeviceImageLoadEvents

> 🗂 DeviceEvents

> 🗂 DeviceFileCertificateInfo

Figure 11.1 – Advanced hunting column categories

The following is a sample query that we'll break down quickly. We'll start with a table called `DeviceEvents` that contains all sorts of events that take place on devices that are onboarded to MDE, including anything that's triggered by security measures. Some examples include **Windows Defender AV** and, as shown in the following code, **Attack Surface Reduction** rules. Now that we have the table, let's figure out what columns we want:

```
DeviceEvents
| where Timestamp > ago(30d)
| where ActionType  startswith "ASR"
```

As shown in the following screenshot, if we don't get more specific in our query, we get a ton of columns – just look at the scroll bar at the bottom. What I like to do when I'm unfamiliar or simply poking around is enter the table `and then do | Take 10 under that,` and then look through everything I want and pick the columns I'm interested in. The `take` operator is just saying, "give me x number of rows" – there is no order to the records that are returned unless the source is sorted already. It's an easy way to quickly return some examples so that you can start narrowing down what you're looking for.

So, continuing with the previous example, let's say we want to set the timeframe for results – in this case, we'll use the last 30 days. I'm also only interested in any attack surface reduction rules that may have been triggered, so I'll use a `Where` operator to filter the `DeviceEvents` table on the `ActionType` column, and then set the `startswith` operator to **ASR**:

ccountObjectId	InitiatingProcessVersionInfoCompanyName	InitiatingProcessVersionInfoProductName	InitiatingProcessVersionInfoProductVersion	InitiatingProcessVersionInfoInternalFileName	InitiatingProcessVersio
	Microsoft Corporation	Microsoft ® Windows ® Operating System	10.0.14393.2155	Wmiprvse.exe	Wmiprvse.exe
	Microsoft Corporation	Microsoft ® Windows ® Operating System	10.0.14393.206	POWERSHELL	PowerShell.EXE
	Microsoft Corporation	Microsoft ® Windows ® Operating System	10.0.14393.206	POWERSHELL	PowerShell.EXE
	Microsoft Corporation	Microsoft ® Windows ® Operating System	10.0.14393.206	POWERSHELL	PowerShell.EXE
	Microsoft Corporation	Microsoft ® Windows ® Operating System	10.0.14393.206	POWERSHELL	PowerShell.EXE

Figure 11.2 – Advanced hunting query results pane

Let's look at our example in the editor and what kind of results we get back. The following screenshot shows that we had some devices with ASR rules enabled, which are triggered with block actions:

```
1    DeviceEvents
2    | where Timestamp > ago(30d)
3    | where ActionType  startswith "ASR"
4
```

↓ Export

ctionType	FileName	FolderPath
srUntrustedExecutableBlocked	outlook.exe	C:\Program Files (x86)\Microsoft Office\Office16
srUntrustedExecutableBlocked	outlook.exe	C:\Program Files (x86)\Microsoft Office\Office16
srUntrustedExecutableBlocked	outlook.exe	C:\Program Files (x86)\Microsoft Office\Office16
srUntrustedExecutableBlocked	outlook.exe	C:\Program Files (x86)\Microsoft Office\Office16
srUntrustedExecutableBlocked	outlook.exe	C:\Program Files (x86)\Microsoft Office\Office16
srUntrustedExecutableBlocked	outlook.exe	C:\program files (x86)\microsoft office\office16
srUntrustedExecutableBlocked	outlook.exe	C:\program files (x86)\microsoft office\office16

Figure 11.3 – Advanced hunting query results pane

At this point, we're interested in looking deeper, so let's look at the columns list. Either scroll through the screen in the results pane or use the filters popup, as shown in the following screenshot:

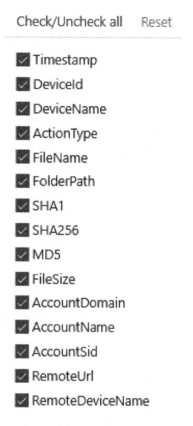

Figure 11.4 – Advanced hunting results – available columns

Let's clean this up using the project operator. You can use this operator for a few things, but for now, we'll use it to select the columns to include in the results. Let's say we want to grab the ActionType, FileName, FolderPath, InitiatingProcessFolderPath, and InitiatingProcessCommandline columns. Here is what we end up with:

```
DeviceEvents
| where Timestamp > ago(30d)
| where ActionType  startswith "ASR"
| project ActionType, FileName, FolderPath,
InitiatingProcessFolderPath, InitiatingProcessCommandLine
```

Kicking that off, we get the results shown in the following screenshot. It's much easier to deal with this without scrolling to see what we're interested in:

ActionType	FileName	FolderPath	InitiatingProcessFolderPath	InitiatingProcessCommandLine
AsrOfficeProcessInjectionBlocked	notepad.exe	C:\Windows\System32	C:\Program Files\Microsoft Office\root\Office14	"excel.exe" 4abc7b5e-4a18-4ac4-8ccd-e69634fc452f True
AsrPsexecWmiChildProcessBlocked	powercfg.exe	C:\Windows\System32	C:\Windows\System32\wbem	wmiprvse.exe -Embedding
AsrPsexecWmiChildProcessBlocked	powercfg.exe	C:\Windows\System32	C:\Windows\System32\wbem	wmiprvse.exe -Embedding
AsrUntrustedExecutableBlocked	outlook.exe	C:\Program Files (x86)\Microsoft Office\Office16	C:\Users\JoeAnich\Downloads	"ASRtool.exe"
AsrUntrustedExecutableBlocked	outlook.exe	C:\Program Files (x86)\Microsoft Office\Office16	C:\Windows\System32	svchost.exe -k NetworkService -p -s CryptSvc
AsrUntrustedExecutableBlocked	outlook.exe	C:\Program Files (x86)\Microsoft Office\Office16	C:\Windows	Sysmon64.exe
AsrUntrustedExecutableBlocked	outlook.exe	C:\Program Files (x86)\Microsoft Office\Office16	C:\Program Files (x86)\Microsoft Office\Office16	"outlook.exe" ff16072c-fc4f-4f70-9887-8a1ce21c63be True

Figure 11.5 – Advanced hunting results

This was a pretty straightforward example of a query and how to quickly build one out to get started; you saw how it would be easy to start building upon that to add more or start filtering it better. As we mentioned at the beginning of this chapter, in the Technical requirements section, we're hoping you have the basics down. To learn more about working with queries, check out the following document: Kusto query overview – https://docs.microsoft.com/en-us/azure/data-explorer/kusto/query/.

Applying query best practices

Once you start becoming proficient at writing queries, you'll see that some take longer than others. The goal of this brief section will be to cover some pointers to ensure your queries are running efficiently and without errors. When you run a query, you'll get a timer, as shown in the following screenshot, that shows the time it took to run, as well as the resource usage rating of **Low**, **Medium**, or **High**:

Figure 11.6 – Advanced hunting query execution time example

When it comes to optimizing your queries, Microsoft outlines a lot of them to get you started. Let's take a look at a few of them:

- **Size new queries**: If you know what you're querying will yield a lot of results, add the count operator to see how many rows it would return, or limit, to cap the number of rows that are returned.

- **Apply filters early**: Apply time filters and other filters to reduce the dataset before using transformation and parsing functions.

- **Has operator over contains**: To avoid searching substrings within words unnecessarily, use the `has_cs` operator instead of `contains_cs`.

- **Case-sensitive for speed**: Case-sensitive searches are more specific and run quicker. Names of case-sensitive string operators, such as `has_cs` and `contains_cs`, generally end with `_cs`.

- **Project selectively**: Try projecting only the columns you need, as we discussed earlier. Projecting specific columns before running `join` or similar operations also helps improve performance.

Here is the link to the full list: `https://docs.microsoft.com/en-us/microsoft-365/security/defender/advanced-hunting-best-practices?view=o365-worldwide#general-optimization-tips`.

Another area for optimization is when you're using the `join` operator. This operator merges the rows from two tables when you have a matching value in the column. The main thing to look for here is making sure you put the smaller table on the left of the `join` operator. That way, there is less to match in the right-hand table.

The following is an example from the Microsoft documentation that sums up exactly what we're talking about here. `DeviceLogonEvents` is the smaller table because it's been limited to three devices. This has been done so that when the right table is queried, it only has to return for those matches:

```
DeviceLogonEvents
| where DeviceName in ("device-1.domain.com", "device-2.domain.com", "device-3.domain.com")
| where ActionType == "LogonFailed"
| join
    (IdentityLogonEvents
    | where ActionType == "LogonFailed"
    | where Protocol == "Kerberos")
on AccountSid
```

For the full list of join operator optimizations, refer to the following documentation: `https://docs.microsoft.com/en-us/microsoft-365/security/defender/advanced-hunting-best-practices?view=o365-worldwide#optimize-the-join-operator`.

There are numerous other ways to optimize your queries and better ways to use the `summarize` operator, including using query command lines, ingesting data from external resources, or even using parsing strings. I highly recommend that you read about them here: `https://docs.microsoft.com/en-us/microsoft-365/security/defender/advanced-hunting-best-practices?view=o365-worldwide`.

Now that we've learned about queries and the best practices to follow with them, let's look at advanced threat hunting.

Advanced threat hunting and the M365 Defender portal

Now that we have a set of results to play with, let's start looking at what we can do with that data to gain further insight into the activity or possible indicator.

We can do things such as the following:

- View results in the form of a table or chart

- Export the table and chart

- Drill into the entities that are returned in the results

Let's add `DeviceName` to the project line so that we can see what I mean when I say "drill into the entities that are returned." Can you see the icon next to the device name in the following screenshot? The square with an arrow? That and the name is a clickable URL that takes us to the device page of that entity:

Figure 11.7 – Advanced hunting results

If you project the specified `DeviceId`, that will also become a link in the results, which takes you to the exact event in the timeline, within the device's page:

Figure 11.8 – Device page timeline

Getting back to what you can do with results, let's look at some of the ways you can view the data. Here are a few of the available view types:

- Table (default)
- Column chart
- Pie chart
- Donut chart
- Line chart
- Scatter chart

One thing to keep in mind when you want to use charts is that you need to filter your results down to numerical values. Looking back at our example where we were tracking ASR rule hits, let's add two new lines to change it up to look more like this:

```
DeviceEvents
| where Timestamp > ago(30d)
| where ActionType  startswith "ASR"
| summarize EventCount=count() by ActionType
| render piechart
```

As you can see, we had to take what would have been returned and use the `summarize` operator to give us the counts for each `ActionType`. If we ran this without the last line, it would give us a row for each `ASR` rule type and the number of times it was triggered. This gives us the numerical result we need to be able to use a chart. Now, we can take that and put it into a pie chart, as shown in the following screenshot:

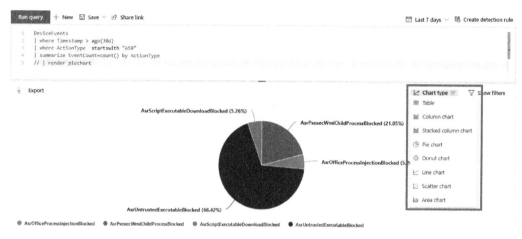

Figure 11.9 – KQL pie chart

One last note about rendering is that if you see the chart type outlined in red, as shown in the preceding screenshot, you'll see you can hit the dropdown and change the charts on the fly.

One other cool thing you can do with the results is **Inspect record**. So, when you select a row, as shown in the following screenshot, you get a pane that slides out where you get all the columns in a nice window, as well as has the option to kick off device actions:

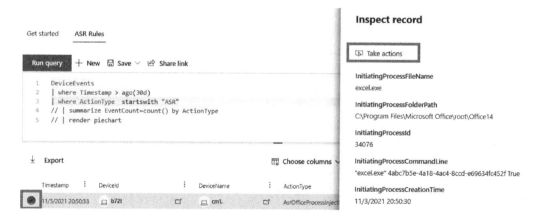

Figure 11.10 – Inspect record example

That's all that we'll cover regarding this topic. If you'd like to learn more, check out the following document as a starting point: Working with advanced hunting query results – `https://docs.microsoft.com/en-us/microsoft-365/security/defender/advanced-hunting-query-results?view=o365-worldwide`.

Now, let's look at the community and shared queries within advanced hunting.

Community and shared queries

In this section, we're going to talk about community and shared queries within **Advanced Hunting**, as shown in the following screenshot:

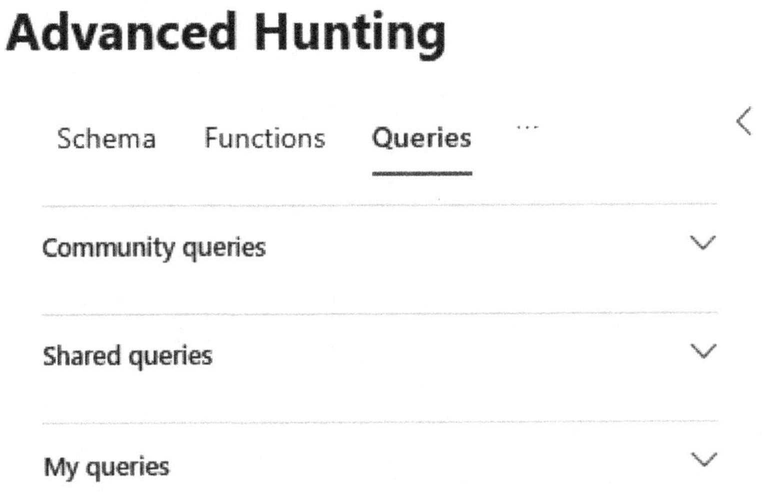

Advanced Hunting

| Schema | Functions | **Queries** | ··· | ‹ |

Community queries ⌄

Shared queries ⌄

My queries ⌄

Figure 11.11 – Advanced Hunting

Microsoft security researchers share advanced hunting queries from time to time and publish them in a GitHub directory where the community can contribute to them. These are also available in the community queries within advanced hunting. The following screenshot shows some of the categories that these queries fall into. Keep in mind that these are sample queries and they are designed to be a starting point for you to become experienced in advanced hunting. It's an incredible asset to have these at your disposable as someone who may be starting as a SOC analyst and new to KQL and the M365 security stack:

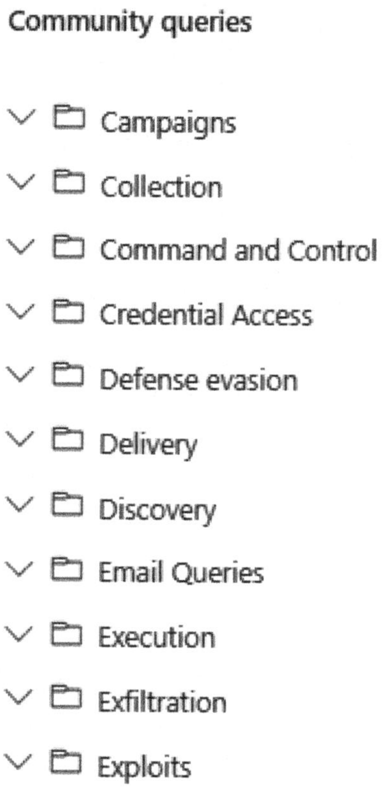

Community queries

∨ ⊟ Campaigns

∨ ⊟ Collection

∨ ⊟ Command and Control

∨ ⊟ Credential Access

∨ ⊟ Defense evasion

∨ ⊟ Delivery

∨ ⊟ Discovery

∨ ⊟ Email Queries

∨ ⊟ Execution

∨ ⊟ Exfiltration

∨ ⊟ Exploits

Figure 11.12 – Sample community queries

The Advanced Hunting GitHub repository can be found at https://github.com/microsoft/Microsoft-365-Defender-Hunting-Queries.

> **Important Note**
>
> Most of these queries can also be used in Microsoft Defender ATP. However, queries that search tables containing consolidated alert data, as well as data about emails, apps, and identities, can only be used in M365 Defender.
>
> Microsoft Defender ATP schema: `https://docs.microsoft.com/windows/security/threat-protection/microsoft-defender-atp/advanced-hunting-schema-reference`.
>
> M365 Defender schema: `https://docs.microsoft.com/microsoft-365/security/mtp/advanced-hunting-schema-tables`.

To get started with one, just click the ellipses next to the query you want to test out and choose **Open in query editor**. This will launch a new tab in the editor, populated with the query you selected:

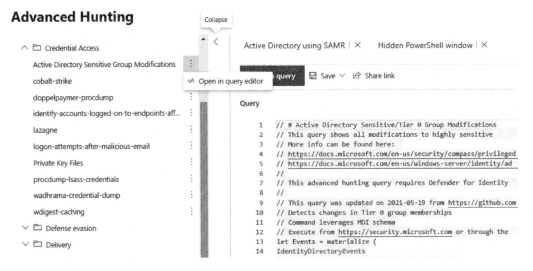

Figure 11.13 – Open in query editor

Next up is **Shared queries**. This is an area where you can save the queries you've built to make them available to other analysts in the organization. This lets you take what others are building on the team to leverage during your threat hunting. In the following screenshot, you can see that I saved the **ASR Rules** query we created earlier under **Shared queries**. Now, others on the team can take that and mold it into something better or different:

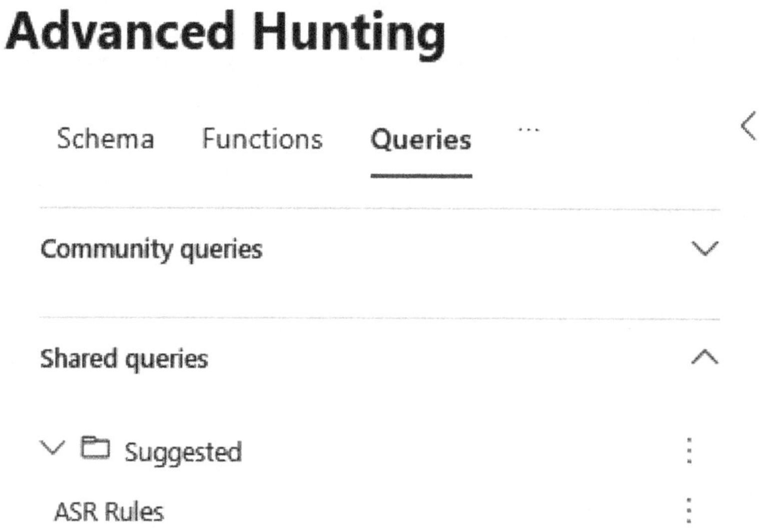

Advanced Hunting

Schema   Functions   **Queries**   ...   <

Community queries   ∨

Shared queries   ∧

∨ 🗀 Suggested   ⋮

ASR Rules   ⋮

Figure 11.14 – Shared queries

Next, we will learn about custom detections.

Custom detections

Custom detections are a fantastic way for you to create queries that are looking for specific behaviors, events, or system states. These are signs of either malicious behavior or simply just misconfigured endpoints that must trigger an alert. Not only can you trigger alerts, but response action can be taken as well.

Let's look at an example. We'll use the ASR rule query we built earlier. This time, let's target a specific type of rule that registers as `AsrOfficeProcessInjectionBlocked`. This will look as follows:

```
DeviceEvents
| where Timestamp > ago(30d)
| where ActionType  startswith
"AsrOfficeProcessInjectionBlocked"
```

Upon running it, we'll some results. Now, let's learn how to create a custom detection rule for this one. In the following screenshot, we can see **Create detection rule**, which is outlined in red:

Figure 11.15 – Create detection rule

Let's go ahead and create one for this type of detection. The custom detection window will have you fill out some generic information at first, such as the name of the detection, the frequency you want the query to run at, the alert's title, its severity, the category of the detection, its description, and then any recommended actions you may want an analyst to perform.

Next, you must fill out what entities you want to be included in the alert. This can include devices, mailboxes, or user accounts. After that, you'll get to choose from a list of actions on those entities. The following screenshot shows the actions you can take:

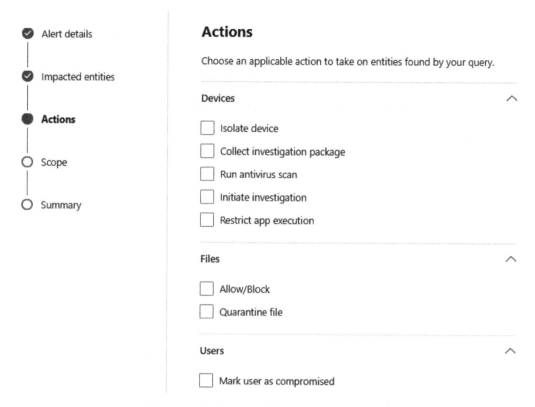

Figure 11.16 – Custom detection – entity actions

Finally, you must set the scope you want this to apply to, which will be either all devices or a particular device group.

Now that we have our custom detection in place, let's use an ASR testing tool. It's not the prettiest thing, but it tests well enough to get some alerts. The following screenshot shows the ASR testing tool we'll be using (https://demo.wd.microsoft.com/Page/ASR2):

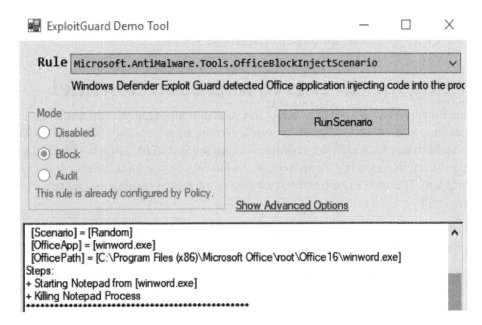

Figure 11.17 – ASR testing tool

Alright – we got an alert for our custom detection rule! As shown in the following screenshot, the detection source is **Custom detection**, and the **Impacted assets** column contains the device name that we selected in the configuration:

Alerts

ⓘ See the Microsoft 365 Compliance center for additional compliance-related functionality

↓ Export   1 Week ∨   ✎ Manage alerts

Filters: Status: New +1 ✕

Alert name	Tags	Severity	Investigation state	Status	Category	Detection source	Impacted assets
ASR IOC - Custom Indicator	Corp	▓▓▓ Medium	Running	● New	Malware	Custom detection	🖥 srv2016 ☐

Figure 11.18 – Custom detection rule alert

That sums up the custom detection rules that are available. Feel free to go through the documentation to read more about them, as well as to learn more about how to create them:

- Overview: https://docs.microsoft.com/en-us/microsoft-365/security/defender/custom-detections-overview?view=o365-worldwide

- Create and manage: https://docs.microsoft.com/en-us/microsoft-365/security/defender/custom-detection-rules?view=o365-worldwide

In this section, we learned about advanced threat hunting and M365 Defender portal. Next, let's dive into hunting for threats in Microsoft Sentinel.

Hunting for threats in Microsoft Sentinel

Hunting for threats in Microsoft Sentinel lets you hunt more holistically across your organization because you can hunt across much more than just the M365 security stack. You can add things such as Syslog, **common event format** (**CEF**), REST APIs, and a host of external third-party data sources. For a full list of the available data connectors, go to `https://docs.microsoft.com/en-us/azure/sentinel/data-connectors-reference`.

Being able to pipe in all of the data from your systems and security appliances makes it much easier to parse it into something meaningful, in one central place.

The following screenshot shows the Microsoft Sentinel **Hunting** dashboard. This should give you some sense of everything that's going on, such as the tabs for **Queries**, **Livestream**, and **Bookmarks**, which we'll touch on later in this chapter. The main section of this page lists all of your queries, both custom and built-in ones written by Microsoft security analysts. This lets you run one or many at once, with the ability to view the results for each as well:

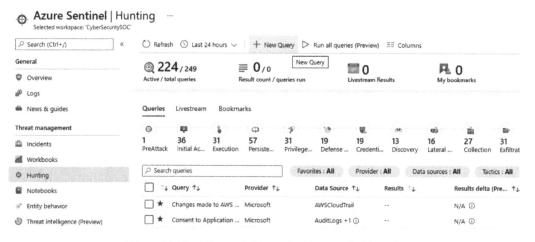

Figure 11.19 – Microsoft Sentinel – Hunting dashboard

The dashboard is a great place to figure out where you should start hunting. Something you can identify is the results counter on your queries to see which ones are hitting. Analysts can search for things such as a specific query and sort by results, tactic, or technique.

Custom hunting queries

This is where you start adding new custom queries, which is similar to advanced hunting and is similar to the custom detection rules without the run-on-schedule feature. With custom hunting queries in Sentinel, you enter the query you want to search for events with, then give it attributes such as **Entity mapping**, where you align it to an entity type, such as **File**, **Host**, **Mailbox**, or **Process**:

Figure 11.20 – Custom hunting query – entity type

With each mapping you select, you'll need to enter an identifier and value. This goes for each identifier you add:

Figure 11.21 – Custom hunting query – entity values

Then, you must assign it MITRE ATT&CK techniques and tactics, depending on where it resides in the framework:

Figure 11.22 – Custom hunting query – MITRE ATT&CK techniques and tactics

You can always go back in and edit your custom queries, as well as add them to your favorites, clone them (if they're built-in queries), delete them, add them to Livestream (which we'll cover next), and create analytics rules.

Speaking of creating an analytics rule, this is like a custom detection rule on steroids. You get a considerable amount of options to go along with your queries. They are broken down into three categories, as follows:

- Defining how events and alerts are processed
- Defining how alerts and incidents are generated
- Choosing automated threat responses for your rules

There are two ways to create one. The first is clicking the ellipses on one of the queries in the queries tab and then clicking **Create analytics rule**. The other is going right to **Analytics** under **Configuration** from the Sentinel home page, as shown in the following screenshot:

Figure 11.23 – Configuration – Analytics

Analytics rules look for events that have been defined by the query and alert you when that event is found in the environment, or when certain defined conditions are met. It can then generate an incident for your SOC to investigate, as well as kick off an automated response.

The following screenshot shows a sample of the section where you set the rule's logic. In this step, you can also add five additional entities for entity mapping to enhance the alert. On the right-hand side of that pane, there's a results simulation section, where you can test the query to see how it will return:

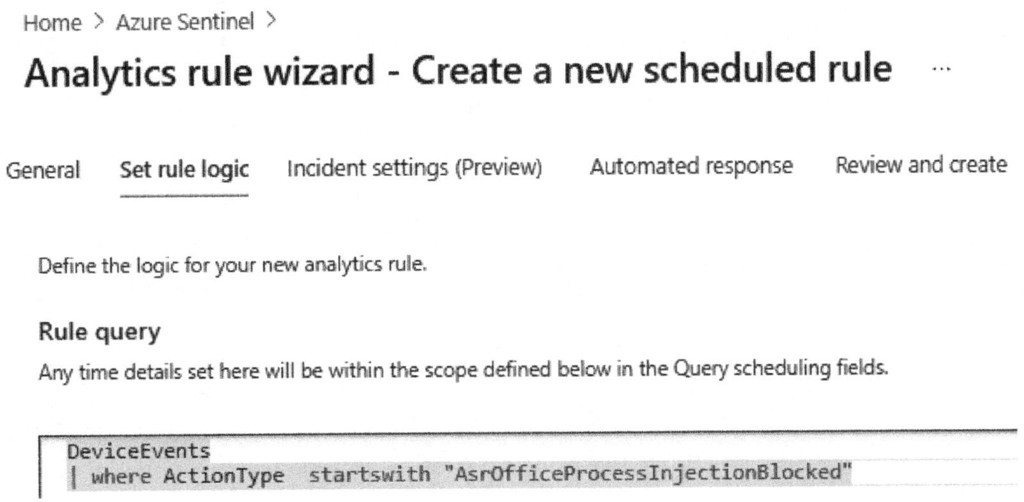

Home > Azure Sentinel >

Analytics rule wizard - Create a new scheduled rule   ...

General   **Set rule logic**   Incident settings (Preview)   Automated response   Review and create

Define the logic for your new analytics rule.

Rule query
Any time details set here will be within the scope defined below in the Query scheduling fields.

```
DeviceEvents
| where ActionType  startswith "AsrOfficeProcessInjectionBlocked"
```

Figure 11.24 – Analytics rule wizard

After putting the rule logic in place, you'll be taken to the **Incident settings (Preview)** section, as shown in the following screenshot, which is relatively new to the interface. This is where we can set how Sentinel handles the alert, taking it from an alert and creating an incident. If you leave the defaults as-is on this tab, Sentinel creates a single incident with each alert, so figure out what you're looking for with this rule to appear. Take a look at the following documentation to learn more about these settings:

Incident and Alert grouping – `https://docs.microsoft.com/en-us/azure/sentinel/detect-threats-custom#incident-settings`:

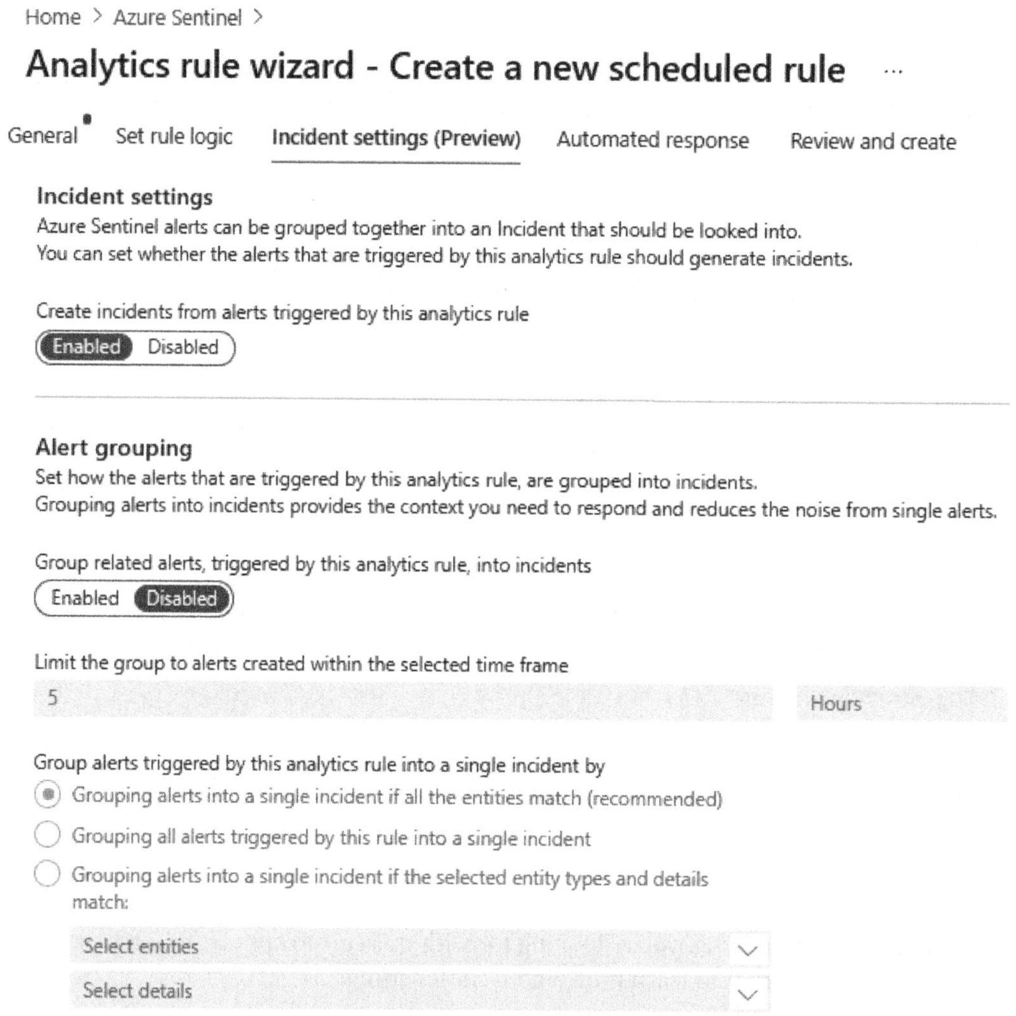

Home > Azure Sentinel >

Analytics rule wizard - Create a new scheduled rule ...

General •   Set rule logic   **Incident settings (Preview)**   Automated response   Review and create

Incident settings
Azure Sentinel alerts can be grouped together into an Incident that should be looked into.
You can set whether the alerts that are triggered by this analytics rule should generate incidents.

Create incidents from alerts triggered by this analytics rule

(**Enabled**   Disabled)

Alert grouping
Set how the alerts that are triggered by this analytics rule, are grouped into incidents.
Grouping alerts into incidents provides the context you need to respond and reduces the noise from single alerts.

Group related alerts, triggered by this analytics rule, into incidents

(Enabled   **Disabled**)

Limit the group to alerts created within the selected time frame

5	Hours

Group alerts triggered by this analytics rule into a single incident by

- (•) Grouping alerts into a single incident if all the entities match (recommended)
- ( ) Grouping all alerts triggered by this rule into a single incident
- ( ) Grouping alerts into a single incident if the selected entity types and details match:

Select entities	∨
Select details	∨

Figure 11.25 – Analytics rule wizard

Next up, we have the **Automated response** settings, where you can set any workflow automations for **Alert automation**. Alternatively, you can choose from workflow automations, automatic triaging, and closing incidents for incident automation:

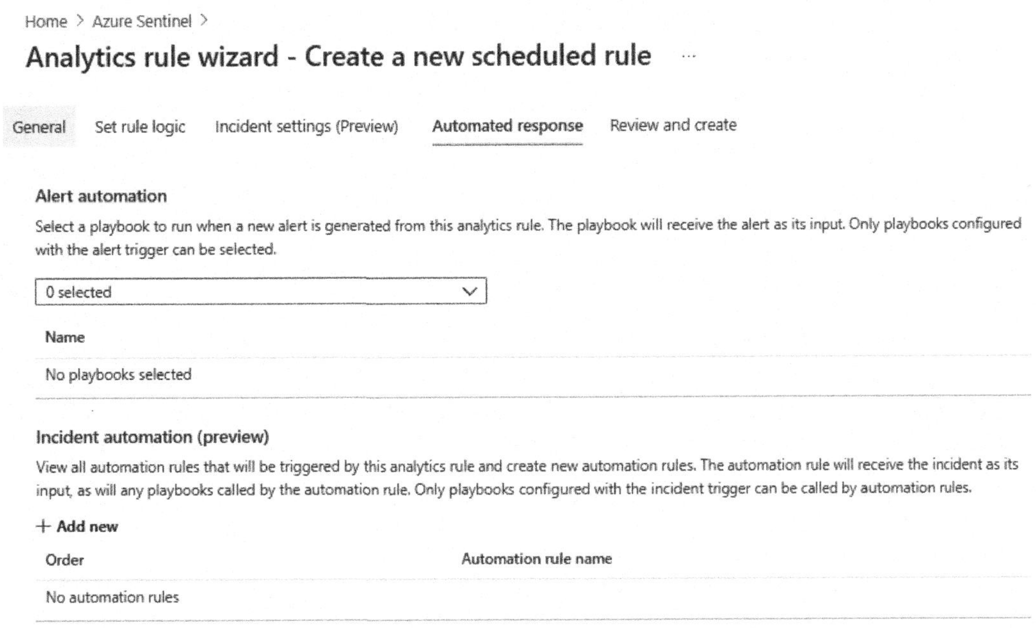

Home > Azure Sentinel >

Analytics rule wizard - Create a new scheduled rule   ⋯

General   Set rule logic   Incident settings (Preview)   **Automated response**   Review and create

Alert automation

Select a playbook to run when a new alert is generated from this analytics rule. The playbook will receive the alert as its input. Only playbooks configured
with the alert trigger can be selected.

0 selected   ∨

Name

No playbooks selected

Incident automation (preview)

View all automation rules that will be triggered by this analytics rule and create new automation rules. The automation rule will receive the incident as its
input, as will any playbooks called by the automation rule. Only playbooks configured with the incident trigger can be called by automation rules.

+ **Add new**

Order	Automation rule name
No automation rules	

Figure 11.26 – Analytics rule wizard

Once you're done there, review and create your analytics rule! From there, you can
review the rule and its output. Next, let's learn how to hunt queries with Microsoft
Sentinel Livestream.

Monitor hunting queries with Sentinel Livestream

Hunting with Sentinel Livestream lets you create an interactive session so that you can test
queries on the fly as events occur. This lets you test them out without any conflicts with
current rules that are being applied to certain events. Queries that are added to Livestream
will generate toast notifications in the Azure portal so that you can quickly return to and
launch an investigation.

You can add existing queries to livestream from the **Hunting** home page, as shown in the following screenshot:

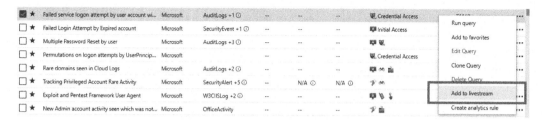

Figure 11.27 – Adding to livestream

As you add queries to livestream, you'll be redirected to the **Livestream** page to see the addition, as shown here:

Figure 11.28 – Sentinel Livestream

From there, you can open up the livestream, as shown in the following screenshot, and start watching for some results:

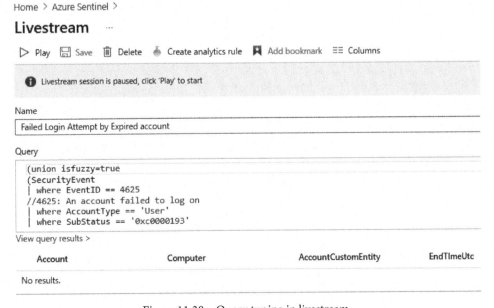

Failed Login Attempt by Expired account

| -- | ⊘ 0 | SecurityEvent |
| Last hit | Results | Data source |

Query

```
(union isfuzzy=true
(SecurityEvent
| where EventID == 4625
//4625: An account failed to log on
| where AccountType == 'User'
| where SubStatus == '0xc0000193'
```

View query results >

Pause   Open livestream

Figure 11.29 – Open livestream

In the Livestream window, you can see live results. So, here, you can either perform testing to check you're getting what you would expect or continue tuning the query. As shown in the following screenshot, I'm not getting any results, so you could either tune it further or take it as-is. Either way, when you're happy with what you see, you can create an analytics rule right from here and then add it to your bookmarks:

Home > Azure Sentinel >

Livestream ...

▷ Play   💾 Save   🗑 Delete   🍶 Create analytics rule   🔖 Add bookmark   ≣≣ Columns

ⓘ Livestream session is paused, click 'Play' to start

Name

Failed Login Attempt by Expired account

Query

```
(union isfuzzy=true
(SecurityEvent
| where EventID == 4625
//4625: An account failed to log on
| where AccountType == 'User'
| where SubStatus == '0xc0000193'
```

View query results >

| Account | Computer | AccountCustomEntity | EndTImeUtc |

No results.

Figure 11.30 – Query tuning in livestream

We have just learned about hunting with Sentinel livestream. Now, let's learn how to work with bookmarks in Microsoft Sentinel.

Working with bookmarks

Bookmarks within Microsoft Sentinel are pretty straightforward. As you're hunting and investigating, you may come across some results within a query that are helpful that you may want to save for later. This can be for something such as enriching an incident that's already open and being triaged.

In the preceding screenshot, we can see **Add bookmark**. So, let's say that, during a livestream, you get some results that you think may be useful for another incident or for something another SOC analyst is working on – bookmark it. The following screenshot shows an example of this workflow. It doesn't always have to be something malicious – it could simply be something you find interesting that you want to investigate later:

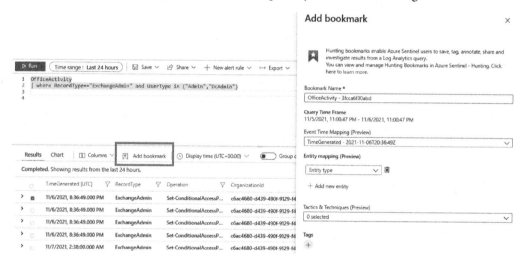

Figure 11.31 – Add bookmark

To learn more about hunting with bookmarks, I suggest reading the documentation as there is a lot of depth there: Hunting with Bookmarks – `https://docs.microsoft.com/en-us/azure/sentinel/bookmarks`.

Advanced hunting with notebooks

To wrap up this chapter, we're going to cover some additional hunting methods. For more complex hunting situations, notebooks can be used. Notebooks can provide you with a deeper analysis by including machine learning, visualizations, and data analysis. They provide you with a virtual sandbox, as well as a kernel where you can do your investigations.

Notebooks can become useful when investigations have become too large and there are lots of details to keep track of. One of the most common and popular to use are Jupyter notebooks. Some benefits of using them are as follows:

- Data persistence

- Scripting and programming

- You can have external data

- You're provided with specialized data processing and machine learning

You can read more about using notebooks in investigations at `https://docs.microsoft.com/en-us/azure/sentinel/hunting#use-notebooks-to-power-investigations`.

Some more documentation to call out is the MSTICPy project, a project that the Microsoft Threat Intelligence Center authored. This contains a library of information that you can use to hunt with Jupyter that is tailored toward making it easier to set up and use Jupyter notebooks. The MSTICPy notebook allows you to do the following:

- Create analytics rules

- Query log data from multiple sources

- Enrich your data with threat intelligence, geolocations, and Azure resource data

- Extract **Indicators of Activity (IoA)** from logs

- Provide session detection and time series decomposition

- Visualize data using interactive timelines, process trees, and multi-dimensional morph charts

- Documentation: `https://docs.microsoft.com/en-us/azure/sentinel/hunting#mstic-jupyter-and-python-security-tools`

The following screenshot shows a ProcessTree visualization that you can create within this framework:

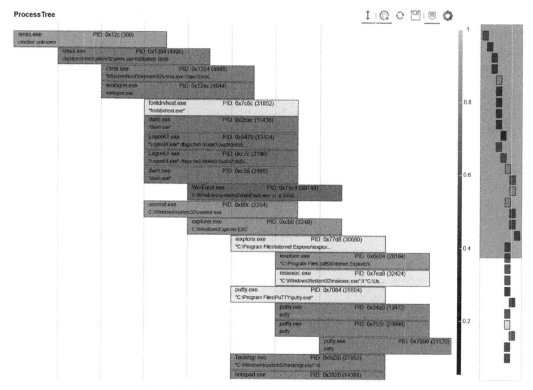

Figure 11.32 – MSTICPy process tree visualization

To wrap things up, check out the following documentation to learn a lot more about hunting in Jupyter notebooks: Hunting in Jupyter notebooks – `https://docs. microsoft.com/en-us/azure/sentinel/notebooks`.

Summary

In this chapter, we covered a lot but also seemingly didn't even touch the surface. There is so much more to each of these categories that I feel each could be a chapter on its own. We covered what Kusto queries are and some best practices to help optimize them. Then, we looked at hunting in the M365 Defender portal and working with the results that have been obtained from queries. From there, we looked at shared queries, as well as the community-provided ones. Don't forget about custom detections, as we spent some time working without ASR rule examples.

Finally, we went through some of the hunting capabilities of Microsoft Sentinel by touching on custom hunting queries, livestream, bookmarks, and hunting with notebooks.

As I said earlier, we hardly touched the services in some of these areas. The goal was to get you more familiar with what they are and how they work so that you're prepared to digest exam questions regarding what they can do and if they're viable solutions.

The next chapter contains a mock test to give you an idea of the questions and the way they're structured in the Microsoft exam.

12
Knowledge Check

We made it! 12 chapters of **Microsoft Defender for Endpoint (MDE)**, **Microsoft Defender for Identity (MDI)**, **Microsoft Defender for Cloud (MDC)**, **Microsoft Defender for Cloud Apps (MDCA)**, and **Microsoft Sentinel**, going through various deployment methods, configurations, and feature sets. Trevor and I tried to give you as much as we could within the confines of this book to help you not only with the exam but also in whatever security role you are occupying in your career. We believe that with what's in this book, you should be armed with enough information to understand and answer questions in the exam.

With that said, we're going to end this book with a quick knowledge check to give you some examples of questions you may come across. This will give you an idea of how to translate what you have learned and read in the documentation into functional solutions and answers. Just as with the actual exam you'll take, the questions will be in no particular order.

Example exam questions

1. You are hunting in the **Microsoft 365 Defender** (**M365 Defender**) portal and writing a query but need to narrow down the results. Which two lines of code should be added to give a quick sample of 10 from the last 30 days?

    a. `| where Timestamp > ago(30d)`

    b. `| join Timestamp > ago(30d)`

    c. `| limit 10 by Timestamp > ago(30d)`

    d. `| limit 10`

2. If you're hunting in Sentinel and come across results you want to use later, what would you use to save them for later?

    a. Notebook

    b. Livestream

    c. Bookmark

    d. Analytics rule

3. Which operator would you use to show only specific columns in your Kusto results?

    a. `select`

    b. `project`

    c. `take`

    d. `limit`

4. You're reading an analyst report for one of the latest campaigns in the wild. In it, you learn about some behaviors that you can hunt for. What could you use to have that searched for on a cadence to then alert you?

    a. Custom indicator

    b. Custom detection rule

    c. Shared query

    d. Function

5. Which permissions are needed to enable Sentinel, keeping **principle of least privilege** (**POLP**) in mind?

    a. Contributor on the subscription containing the Sentinel workspace

    b. Reader on the resource group containing the Sentinel workspace

c. Reader on the subscription containing the Sentinel workspace

d. Contributor on the resource group containing the Sentinel workspace

6. Which solution would you use to determine which unsanctioned **software-as-a-service (SaaS)** applications are being used in the environment?

   a. Azure Monitor

   b. Microsoft Defender for Cloud

   c. MDCA

   d. MDE

7. When creating a custom rule in Microsoft Sentinel whereby you want all alerts generated to be grouped into a single incident but by severity, which setting would you select?

   a. Grouping alerts into a single incident if all the entities match (recommended)

   b. Grouping all alerts triggered by this rule into a single incident

   c. Grouping alerts into a single incident if the selected entity types and details match

8. When deploying MDI, you need to identify what server types you can install it on. Choose the two you can install a sensor on.

   a. **Active Directory Federation Services (AD FS)**

   b. File server

   c. Domain controller

   d. Exchange server

9. Let's say you're looking to increase the **security orchestration, automation, and response (SOAR)** capabilities of your Sentinel instance by adding and ingesting information from third-party appliances or tools. What type of connector should you configure?

   a. Trigger

   b. Custom detector

   c. Data connector

   d. Repository

10. What type of policy would you create in MDA to monitor employee credentials being used in another country?

    a. Access policy

    b. Session policy

    c. Activity policy

    d. Privileged accounts

11. If you were going to add a file hash for a custom indicator in MDE to allow a specific file to run but already had a policy there for the same file with a block, what would you need to do first?

    a. Add a new policy; the allow action will take precedence.

    b. Keep both but add a different hash type.

    c. Delete the indicator with a block action and add the allow action.

    d. Delete the newly added allow action.

12. The **Human Resources (HR)** team reports that their M365 account has been compromised. Your manager wants to implement a solution that notifies them when this happens. Which solution would you recommend?

    a. Azure Lighthouse

    b. **Azure Active Directory Identity Protection (Azure AD Identity Protection)**

    c. Microsoft Defender for Cloud

    d. Sensitivity labels

13. You enable Microsoft Sentinel in your company, and your manager wants to integrate log data from M365 and non-Azure **virtual machines (VMs)**. What would you recommend?

    a. Using **data loss prevention (DLP)**

    b. Adding a workflow automation to Sentinel

    c. Creating data connectors in Sentinel

    d. Using Microsoft Graph

14. You need to implement a solution that detects the origin of data attacks and also identifies potential loss. What would you recommend?

    a. Cloud connectors in Microsoft Defender for Cloud

    b. DLP policies

    c. Sensitivity labels

    d. Analytics rules in Sentinel

15. Which tool would you recommend to monitor on-premises AD?

    a. MDI

    b. MDC

    c. AD backup

    d. Azure Firewall

16. Your manager wants to implement the Analytics Efficiency workbook in Sentinel. What must you do first?

    a. Use data connectors in Sentinel

    b. Create security incidents

    c. Use protection status in Sentinel

    d. Create security events in Sentinel

Answer key

1. A & D
2. C
3. B
4. B
5. A
6. C
7. C
8. A & C
9. C
10. C
11. C

12. B

13. C

14. D

15. A

16. B

Index

Z

Zero-hour purge (ZAP)
  about 171
  reference link 171
zero trust
  principles 20
Zscaler integration 194

Other Books You May Enjoy

If you enjoyed this book, you may be interested in these other books by Packt:

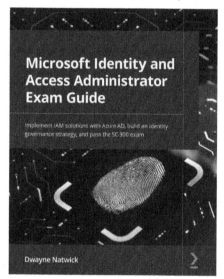

Microsoft Identity and Access Administrator Exam Guide

Dwayne Natwick

ISBN: 9781801818049

- Understand core exam objectives to pass the SC-300 exam

- Implement an identity management solution with MS Azure AD

- Manage identity with multi-factor authentication (MFA), conditional access, and identity protection

- Design, implement, and monitor the integration of enterprise apps for Single Sign-On (SSO)

- Add apps to your identity and access solution with app registration

- Design and implement identity governance for your identity solution

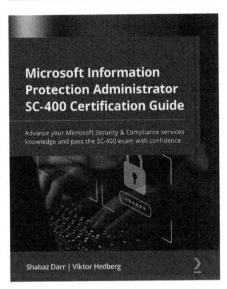

Microsoft Information Protection Administrator SC-400 Certification Guide

Shabaz Darr, Viktor Hedberg

ISBN: 9781801811491

- Understand core exam objectives to pass the SC-400 exam with ease
- Find out how to create and manage sensitive information types for different types of data
- Create and manage policies and learn how to apply these to Microsoft 365 SaaS applications
- Broaden your knowledge of data protection on M365
- Discover how to configure and manage the protection of your data in M365
- Monitor activity regarding data access in M365
- Understand and implement Data Governance in M365

Packt is searching for authors like you

If you're interested in becoming an author for Packt, please visit `authors.packtpub.com` and apply today. We have worked with thousands of developers and tech professionals, just like you, to help them share their insight with the global tech community. You can make a general application, apply for a specific hot topic that we are recruiting an author for, or submit your own idea.

Share Your Thoughts

Now you've finished *Microsoft Security Operations Analyst Exam Ref SC-200 Certification Guide*, we'd love to hear your thoughts! Scan the QR code below to go straight to the Amazon review page for this book and share your feedback or leave a review on the site that you purchased it from.

`https://packt.link/r/1-803-23189-0`

Your review is important to us and the tech community and will help us make sure we're delivering excellent quality content.

Made in the USA
Columbia, SC
26 April 2023

15791749R00161